THE LIVING WORLD
OF SHAKESPEARE

THE LIVING WORLD
OF SHAKESPEARE

A Playgoer's Guide

By John Wain

© John Wain 1964, 1978

ISBN 0 333 04303 0
    0 333 29233 2 Pbk

First published 1964 and reissued with a new preface 1978 by
MACMILLAN LONDON LIMITED
London and Basingstoke
Associated companies in Delhi, Dublin,
Hong Kong, Johannesburg, Lagos, Melbourne,
New York, Singapore and Tokyo

Published 1980 by
THE MACMILLAN PRESS LTD in Papermac

Printed in Hong Kong

WILLIAM EMPSON'S

Some passages in this book have appeared in *Encounter*, whose editors are thanked for permission to reprint.

CONTENTS

PREFACE TO THE SECOND EDITION

WHEN this book first appeared, fifteen years ago, I subtitled it
'A Playgoer's Guide' because I particularly wanted to associate it
with the experience of seeing Shakespeare's plays in the theatre. I
believed then, and believe just as strongly now, that analytical
literary and scholarly study can only be a preparation for the
experience that the plays can give us when acted. This is none the
less true while recognizing that no stage production is final, that
each leads on to the next; our experience of any great play is a
lifelong relationship, made up of all the times we have read it,
thought about it, seen it performed. Many times, both before
writing this book and since, I have seen a production of Shakespeare in the theatre and come away reflecting that I would have
been much happier with the text and my own imagination. But
even these unsatisfactory productions, some of them the merest
travesties, have given me *something*. Their very absurdities have
pointed out routes for meditation. And a good production has
a richness that no solitary reading can ever have, because it is
an experience shared and thereby rendered more deeply human.

In believing that the best way to study a Shakespearian play is
to produce it in the theatre of one's mind, to ask oneself at every
point what one would tell an actor or actress to *do*, we have the
authority of the poet himself, who in the speeches of Chorus in
Henry V tells us to use our imagination to see beyond the in-
adequacies of the theatre to what must have been the reality. This
is not an injunction to by-pass the theatre. On the contrary,

A*

physical representation is the indispensable avenue to imaginative vision.

My hope, then, was that the book would be welcomed by playgoers. I hope it does not seem boastful if I report that this object was achieved and more than achieved. Not only play-goers, but play-producers, have found it useful. More than one stage director has told me that he looks up my book before going to work; as I write, there lies before me a current theatre pro-gramme for a production of *King Lear* in which it is liberally quoted (without, I may add, the tedious formality of asking my permission). This rejoices my heart. The book is out there, doing its work in the world, and this alone would justify a new edition.

Given that new edition, and the chance to introduce it to another generation, what needs to be said that did not need to be said in 1964? Only, I think, one thing. In 1964 the Western world stood on the verge of a period of upheaval and rebelliousness. Not since the end of the eighteenth century had Europe, and the 'developed' world generally, seen such an upsurge of the re-volutionary spirit. The waves boiled to their highest point in 1968; and I, who found myself teaching Shakespeare to a class at the University of Paris a few months later, was in no danger of ignoring the fact.

In those heady years, the only writers who seemed in tune with our current *Zeitgeist* were the nihilists, the extremists, the overturners, those who questioned every premise. And one frequently met people who had no hesitation in dismissing Shake-speare from this magic circle. Had not Shakespeare supported the regime of the Tudors? Was not Shakespeare a *bourgeois*, a con-formist who cherished his newly acquired coat of arms, a man of property and a Conservative?

Now, it is true that Shakespeare was no revolutionary, had no wish to lay the axe to the root of social order. He knew that the existing order of things was often cruel and unjust, and like all good men he wanted to improve it; but he also knew that even in its unimproved state it offered *some* framework for a tranquil life, *some* protection of the weak against the strong, *some* restraining of the anarchic and predatory impulses of man. Much as he disliked injustice and the power of wealth, there was one thing he feared more: mob rule, as dramatized in that unforgettable few minutes in *Julius Caesar* when the crowd, in their ungovernable fury, lynch a harmless poet who has the same name as one of Caesar's assassins. Shakespeare's work testifies to his belief that the complex human spirit is host to many qualities. Goodness and gentleness and love and heroism are to be found there, and so are selfishness and hatred and cruelty – sometimes in one and the same person – and which qualities emerge in action may depend on circumstances: it may be a matter of which qualities are given encouragement and a framework. In Shakespeare's view, the ungoverned, unthinking, impulse-obeying human animal is more likely to be cruel and predatory than gentle and giving. To believe this is not necessarily to be a misanthrope like Timon. It is confirmed by observation. All species flourish best under the right conditions; rats in an overcrowded cage become vicious to one another, and so do people in overcrowded slums; the right condition for *homo sapiens* includes a firm structure of law and custom.

In believing, then, that almost any laws and customs are better than none, Shakespeare was out of step with the tousled revolutionary of the 1960s with his (or her) demand that all institutions should be abolished forthwith. But this does not make him a reactionary, toadying to the forces of oppression. There is abundant, indeed overwhelming, evidence throughout his work that Shakespeare tested all political systems on the pulse of the common man. This is such a self-evident truth that examples are probably unnecessary, but for the sake of concreteness let me refer to one I have already given in its proper place (p. 168). When Lear is driven out into the storm, the shock of finding that to be treated like this can happen even to him, a king, unhinges his reason, but also begins to let in a chink of light to his previously closed mind. As he moves towards madness, he moves also towards compassion and a shared humanity. The first sign of this is that he can pity the sufferings of his Fool, whom previously he has treated more or less as an animal; the second, immediately afterwards, is the prayer he utters, a prayer addressed directly to poverty, in which he asks pardon of the 'poor naked wretches' who wander shelterless in the storm, not, as he does now, as the result of some great catastrophe, but habitually.

The Shakespeare who, at a supreme moment of tragic awareness, can make the king kneel before the shrine of beggary is no reactionary. And if we acquit him of that charge, then surely we acquit him of all, for no other has ever been brought against him to blur his recognition as our supreme magician with words, the supreme comprehender, the 'gentle Shakespeare' who saw into our hearts so deeply and so compassionately, who knew us before we knew ourselves.

July 1978   JOHN WAIN

I

THE NATURE OF SHAKESPEAREAN DRAMA

WHEN Shakespeare began work, in the early 1590s, the drama he inherited had both popular and learned elements. In form, it was descended from the late mediaeval plays which had been acted in inn courtyards. In content, it had already picked up elements from the Roman theatre as well as from Renaissance Italian. The popular *commedia dell'arte*, with its stock characters and half-improvised plots, was well known to English dramatists. So were the stately and declamatory tragedies of Seneca. This blend of interests and traditions gave the Elizabethan drama one advantage that no modern theatre has. It made it a drama for the entire nation. The uninstructed groundlings flocked to it as eagerly as the lettered patrons in the covered seats. The fashionable gallant was there, but so was the eager young scholar already dreaming of fame and genius.

From the beginning, then, the Shakespearean drama has one great freedom; it does not have to channel itself to one stratum of public taste. It can be lowbrow or highbrow according to the needs of its subject-matter. But this is not its only advantage. It has, in addition, the freedom conferred by the unfettered imagination. It is not a consumer-art but an art of participation.

What I mean is this. The arts differ one from another in the extent to which they invite the co-operation of the onlooker. The novel, for instance, is largely pre-packaged. It is put into the

I

reader's hands complete with descriptions of how people looked, what they said, and what went on inside their minds; further, it is written in the language of everyday life. All the reader has to do is sit down and absorb it. Poetry, by comparison, invites participation. To read a poem is to join in a mental dance. If the rhythms, the imagery, the weight and colour of the poem are to have their effect on us, we must meet the poet's sensibility with our own. And the more we bring to it, the more we shall take away.

I

In the field of drama, we have on the one hand an art like that of the cinema, which demands only that the audience goes into a trance, and on the other the art of full participation as practised by, say, Ruth Draper. Miss Draper would walk on to a stage and proceed to act out scenes, playlets of her own composition, in which she took every part. The fascination of her performances, which was felt by people of every type and every age, arose from the fact that she invited audiences to use their imagination. And the exercise of the imagination is delightful to everyone. (Who does not enjoy telling stories to children?) Ruth Draper created, on a bare stage, the atmosphere of a court-room, a customs-house a country mansion. In one of her sketches she wanted to give the impression of a hostess standing before a great fireplace. So she raised one foot about twelve inches off the ground, as if resting it on a high fender — and kept it there during the entire act. That was enough. Every member of the audience saw the fireplace. At the other extreme, we have the cinema, which is — in Jean Cocteau's famous words — 'a dream that can be dreamt by many people at the same time'. It lulls its audience to sleep: often, no doubt, a very creative and renewing sleep, but a sleep. Whereas the art of a Ruth Draper incites and stimulates the audience to participation. They join with her in creating the entertainment.

In Shakespeare's day the theatre was an art of full participation.

Not only did it make use of poetry, which draws the hearer into a close union with the speaker. It also employed the Ruth Draper technique of making the audience supply the visual background by imagination alone. The result was a freedom never again approached until the beginning of radio drama in the 1920s. Without waiting for tardy changes of unconvincing scenery, the action can whisk from one country to another, from the deck of a ship to the streets of a city, from a ballroom to an orchard.

When I was a boy it seemed to be the general opinion that the Elizabethan stage was a crude, makeshift affair. Because it did not have backdrops, cycloramas, floats, tabs, a proscenium arch or an orchestra pit, it was presumed to be hopelessly primitive. Perhaps things are better now. Certainly the average playgoer is less parochial, more aware of different modes of drama, than he was thirty years ago. He knows that if ancient Greek drama, or Japanese Noh plays, or classical Chinese theatre, could do without stage-illusion and coloured lighting, these things cannot be so important as all that. He is even ready to accept a partial return to Elizabethan techniques of acting and staging.

Modern theatre is a consumer art. It pushes the actors back behind a proscenium arch, in a lighted picture-frame stage. The result is a convention whereby the actors talk entirely to one another and the audience overhears them. To get an idea of Elizabethan acting, the best place to go is the opera-house. When an operatic singer is engaged in recitative, he speaks directly to his interlocutor, but when he steps forward to sing some great aria, he sings to the audience. The conventions of opera do not require that the singers should ignore the presence of an audience. Old-style music-hall comics, the kind who talk rapidly at each other from opposite sides of the stage, use the same technique. They are continually pitching lines towards the audience. On the Elizabethan stage, which had no proscenium arch but moved the actors out into the midst of the audience, participation was not merely invited; it could hardly be avoided. In such a theatre, poetry seemed natural, as it seems artificial on the modern stage. Soliloquy, too, was more acceptable when the actor was in so direct a relationship with his hearers.

With this freedom at his disposal, Shakespeare wrote what literary textbooks call 'poetic drama'. The phrase has been much misunderstood. Poetic drama is not merely a kind of drama which proceeds on the same basic assumption as prose drama, except that it happens to be in verse. It is a different medium altogether. The poetic language is not an overlay. It is integral to the whole experience. Go through a prose drama and versify it, and you have nothing; go through a poetic drama and turn it into prose, and once again you have nothing.

It is important to make this matter clear, so let me come at it from another angle. Very recently — during the writing of this book — I happened to take part in a literary Brains Trust, held at a Grammar School and attended by senior pupils. The questions had been prepared in advance. One of them was, 'Should the works of Shakespeare be put into modern prose so that more people of this generation would read them?' The operative words there are 'modern' and 'prose'. They are actually two sides of the same coin. If language is modern, then naturally it is in prose, and preferably the prose of the *Daily Mirror*. These children have grown up in a world that uses language only for the most limited of purposes: to convey information. The entire imaginative side of life has been handed over to the visual media of cinema and television. Instead of reading prose narrative and supplying the pictures and sounds inside their heads, the young now have pictures and sound supplied mechanically. They have become total consumers. And language is mixed in only in tiny doses that make no demand on their powers of participation. Naturally, then, these powers begin to shrink and atrophy. The imaginative arts of language — poetry or figurative prose — become simply unintelligible. With pictures to do all our imagining for us, with sounds to echo in our ears, we need language only to supply the information that will link one picture with the next.

Hence the demand for 'modern prose'. If you must use language, then keep it crisp.

The tragedy is that these young are separated only by a thin wall from the riches that could be theirs. Living in an age where everything is expressed concretely in images, and nothing abstractly in words, they are actually very close to the world of Shakespearean drama. Because the essence of the poetic language — not only Shakespeare's, but any poetic language — is that it is concrete. It does not deal in abstractions. It proceeds by metaphor, or by simile that has the force of metaphor. It flashes image after image, without pausing to reduce these images to discourse, in the way these children have learnt to expect from film and TV. If they could only grasp the fact that the language of poetry is not an outworn way of putting things obliquely, but an immemorial way of saying them with the utmost possible directness, they would have no other adjustment to make. They could step straight into an appreciation of Shakespeare that previous generations could acquire only by study.

Any example that comes to hand will serve to illustrate this. Take Angelo's speech in *Measure for Measure*, Act II, Scene ii. He has condemned Claudio to death for fornication, and Claudio's pious and chaste sister, Isabella, already admitted to her novitiate in a convent, has come to beg for mercy on his behalf. During their conversation Angelo suddenly conceives the horrible idea of striking a bargain — her chastity against her brother's life. As a man always excessively self-controlled and prudish, he is violently disturbed at this revelation of his own lower depths, and as soon as the girl has gone he bursts out in agitation:

> What's this, what's this? Is this her fault or mine?
> The tempter or the tempted, who sins most? Ha!
> Not she; nor doth she tempt; but it is I
> That, lying by the violet in the sun,
> Do as the carrion does, not as the flow'r,
> Corrupt with virtuous season.

What violet? What carrion? Obviously, these are the images

thrown up in Angelo's mind as he recoils from knowledge of his own sin. They are introduced without explanation, and no explanation is needed. Present-day film directors are much given to this technique. After a passage in the story which introduces some strong emotion, the camera switches to an object — a lizard on a wall, a ragged shirt flapping on a line — which provides a symbolic visual equivalent. Shakespeare uses the same cinematic method. In the midst of Angelo's self-accusation, we get the image of hot sunshine, a violet growing in a hedgerow, and nearby the decomposing corpse of a dog, a rabbit, a cat — any animal will do. At once we imagine the smell of decay cutting across the sweet scent of the flower. The violet, of all flowers, has a delicacy that typifies everything pure and unspoilt; we remember Laertes' words on Ophelia: 'And from her fair and unpolluted flesh May violets spring'. But Angelo's words go further in their visual and tactile concreteness. 'Lying by the violet in the sun' suggests the act he longs to perform; the sun shines on Isabella because she is young and in the springtime of her life, and Angelo 'corrupts' with 'virtuous season' — at once the seasoning that disguises the taste of bad meat, and the fresh early season he is spoiling.

Or take another short example. In *Timon of Athens*, Act IV, Scene ii, Timon's servants gather for the last time and lament the fall of their master. Now that his wealth is gone they are unemployed — 'All broken implements of a ruin'd house', as Flavius calls them — and one of them sums it up in six lines:

> Yet do our hearts wear Timon's livery;
> That see I by our faces. We are fellows still,
> Serving alike in sorrow. Leak'd is our bark;
> And we, poor mates, stand on the dying deck,
> Hearing the surges threat. We must all part
> Into this sea of air.

From the notion of community in loyalty and suffering — of being, as the modern phrase has it, 'all in the same boat' — the imagery moves to a real boat, holed and about to sink. The men huddle on the tilting deck; behind them is a fellowship of service

6

and discipline, but at this moment their fellowship is one of fear; in a moment they must dive, separately, into the 'surges'. But in its closing words the metaphor makes another jump. What surrounds these servants is not the heaviness and strength of the sea but the emptiness of air. What the poor fellows have reason to fear is not that they will be drawn under and suffocated quickly, like drowning sailors, but that they will be left to waste away in hunger. The insubstantiality of air, rather than the thick embrace of water, is what faces them. And the metaphor, as usual in Shakespeare, links admirably with the play's larger purposes. This 'air', which surrounds the dispossessed serving-men, is that same nothingness which confronted Timon when he reached out for help from his friends. Their offence against him is negative, rather than positive; they have not molested him in any way; they were simply not there when needed. Their absence, not their presence, has driven him mad. Hence the sudden switch from the pounding and threatening of the sea to the empty stillness of 'air'.

II

We have seen that, by its nature as poetic drama, Shakespeare's theatre involves the spectator in participation. Now we must go beyond that simple statement. What it involves him in is not merely participation, but a sensitive imaginative adjustment, from minute to minute, of the nature of that participation. The timid playgoer may reassure himself; it is not necessary to be a genius. All we have to do is put ourselves in Shakespeare's hands and accept his directives, which are always quite clear. These matters do not become complicated until we excogitate them.

In a modern play, the level of realism is stated at the outset and then adhered to. If it is a straightforward prose play, the assumption is that the characters are using language exactly as they would use it in real life. And if we catch them defining their feelings with a fineness and aptness which in 'real life' would be beyond their capacity, we fault the play at once. If we want that kind of language on the stage, we go to a 'poetic' play: which also defines

7

its level at the beginning, and stays there. In Elizabethan drama, and most finely of all in Shakespeare, the level shifts continually. At one moment the characters before us are speaking as men would speak in the street or the inn. The next, they are using the full resources of poetry. It is tailored, naturally, to fit their characters, but it is not damped down to avoid clashing with the naturalistic tone of a few lines earlier. The audience is expected to make the adjustment.

There are, of course, certain easily recognized devices which Shakespeare uses to signal these changes in tone. The most obvious is the move from prose to verse and back again. As a general rule, Shakespeare uses prose for realism and verse for the more exalted and intensive writing which overtops realism. Simple examples abound. When in *Antony and Cleopatra* (Act II, Scene ii) the triumvirate Caesar, Antony and Lepidus meet and prepare their campaign against Pompey, they naturally speak in verse. The dignified conclave ended, they leave the stage to the three shrewd, tough officers, Enobarbus, Mecaenas and Agrippa. These down-to-earth fellows naturally talk conversational prose — until the moment when Enobarbus begins to describe the unearthly beauty of Cleopatra and her entourage on the river of Cydnus. The transition is made with perfect naturalness.

> ENOBARBUS. When she first met Mark Antony she purs'd up his heart, upon the river of Cydnus.
> AGRIPPA. There she appear'd indeed! Or my reporter devis'd well for her.
> ENOBARBUS. I will tell you.
> The barge she sat in, like a burnish'd throne,
> Burn'd on the water. . . .

That 'I will tell you' is like a bowler's skipping run-up to the wicket. It carries the dialogue over from prose to verse; partly by its easy rhythm, suitable for either, and partly because it enoins silence and attention on its hearers. Or take a slightly more complex example from the same play. In Act V, Scene ii, Cleopatra has decided on suicide and has done with mundane concerns. She is, naturally, speaking very high poetry.

> Now from head to foot
> I am marble-constant; now the fleeting moon
> No planet is of mine.

At this moment, the 'rural fellow' is shown in with his basket of figs, within which is the asp that will bring the death she longs for. She questions him, and he answers in homespun and even laughable prose. (Only a writer of Shakespeare's high audacity could get away with humour at such a moment. Or, for that matter, with the sudden switch from ancient Egypt to Elizabethan England. For the countryman, of course, has nothing Egyptian about him; he obeys the universal Shakespearean rule that no matter where the scene is set, the low-comedy characters are never anything but English, and preferably Warwickshire.)

The bumpkin addresses Cleopatra in prose. Her replies are short; mostly, they do not extend to ten syllables, and could therefore be either prose or verse; no incongruity is felt when she says 'Get thee hence; farewell', or 'Will it eat me?'. As for her longer replies, they are all just about the ten-syllable mark. With the sort of delicacy that makes its effect without being noticed, Shakespeare halts her lines just at the point where they would have to declare definitely for verse or for prose. 'Remember'st thou any that have died on't?' fits in perfectly with the clown's prose without deserting, or too obviously holding to, the verse of the passage before and after; so does 'Take thou no care; it shall be heeded.' The result is that Shakespeare is able to introduce a prose scene, resting our emotions for a few minutes before we begin the dizzy climb up to the play's last peak, without making Cleopatra speak prose, which in fact she never does throughout the play.

Anyone who is tempted to think that this effect is mere accident may consult a clinching example of the same thing earlier in the play (Act I, Scene ii), when Antony is talking to Enobarbus.

Antony, like Cleopatra, is a character who speaks only verse; his lofty presence expresses itself naturally in the statelier rhythm, and he lacks the complexity of a character like Hamlet who moves from prose to verse because his thoughts and feelings range over a wide spectrum. In this early scene we find him shaken into gravity by the news that Fulvia his wife is dead. He immediately forms the resolution to return to Rome, and expresses it in his usual lofty verse; he then summons Enobarbus, who comes on and speaks in *his* usual sardonic prose. Antony lets him do most of the talking, only breaking in with, 'I must with haste from hence'. 'I must be gone.' 'She is cunning past man's thought.' 'Would I had never seen her.' 'Fulvia is dead.' All these are fragments which could be either verse or prose. But as soon as Antony takes over the initiative once more, he pushes the scene back into verse with a curtly dignified speech beginning, 'No more light answers' — an opening which has the same effect as Enobarbus's own 'I will tell you'. It launches the boat into midstream. And now it is Enobarbus who answers with a mere fragment, conformable to either rhythm: 'I shall do it.'

The ease with which the mature Shakespeare enables prose and verse to run together, as exemplified by these two exchanges in which, in the lightest and least strained manner, one character talks in prose and the other in verse, reflects years of experience. It did not come quickly. The early Shakespeare often puts prose-material into verse — as in the Nurse's speeches in *Romeo and Juliet* — and, when he does write prose, tends to stick to the demotic and comical. There are times in the early historical plays when the distinction seems to be almost along social lines: the man in the street uses prose and leaves the verse to the higher-ups. But Shakespeare gradually trusts prose more and more, allowing genuine poetic feeling to flow through it, notably in the Falstaff scenes, and by the time we reach *Hamlet* we find the two instruments equally subtle, equally ready for any important task, so that Hamlet's 'Alas, poor Yorick' speech is no less poetic than 'To be or not to be'. The difference, as usual, is one of degrees of realism. The Yorick speech is uttered in the graveyard, with the gravediggers standing by; it comes into a great scene written in prose, and the fact that Hamlet does not take off into verse reflects his involvement with the scene of which he is a part. He is soliloquizing, but with full consciousness of his hearers. If Shakespeare had meant us to visualize Hamlet as stepping apart and musing strictly to himself, he would probably have put the speech into verse.

Mention of the soliloquy brings us firmly back to the shifting nature of Shakespearean realism. The term 'soliloquy' covers a very wide range. First, there is the informative speech to the audience — indulged in without self-consciousness by all dramatists till very recently, and found in Shakespeare's most mature work as often as in his crudest. (Along with this goes the simple stage device of reading aloud from letters and so forth.) Then there is the soliloquy which a character utters in the presence of others. Its function is to reveal his thoughts and feelings to us, the audience. Sometimes the speech is evidently meant to be uttered as an aside, and the other persons on the stage are meant to show no awareness of it. At other times they are brought in, without being addressed directly, and their relationship to the speaker is the same as ours. An example would be the speech of Troilus after witnessing the infidelity of Cressida, which we shall be examining later on (p. 114). The auditors onstage in this case are Ulysses, who is accompanying Troilus and giving him safe conduct, and Thersites, who is skulking nearby and eavesdropping. Troilus is oblivious of both of them until brought down to earth by Ulysses's question as to whether he really means, and will stand by, what he has just said. Ulysses, that is, voices the question that we ourselves would ask Troilus if we could intervene in the play. Thersites, meanwhile, listens and puts in his remarks, which are not heeded by either of the others and are, in fact, intended for the audience. At the conclusion of the scene it is Thersites who stays behind to utter his final comment: 'Lechery, lechery; still, wars and lechery; nothing else hath fashion.'

In short, the question 'Who is addressing whom?' is always a real and delicate one in Shakespeare, and it cannot be answered by using block terms like 'soliloquy'. The convention of the modern theatre — that the characters are addressing one another and the audience is eavesdropping — exists in Shakespeare, but it is one of a number of conventions, all healthily operative. This modern eavesdropping convention is restrictive in a number of ways. It allows, for instance, of no chorus to comment on the action and invite the audience to reflect and moralize. Yet much of the world's greatest drama would be unthinkable without such a chorus. Shakespeare has it, not rigidly distinguished as in classical Greek drama, but lightly and unselfconsciously interwoven with the action. Any character may at any time make a comment whose real function is choric.

In *The Winter's Tale*, for example, when Leontes is revealing in soliloquy the consuming jealousy that gnaws him and will presently break out into the play's action, he suddenly says, almost parenthetically,

> There have been,
> Or I am much deceiv'd, cuckolds ere now;
> And many a man there is, even at this present,
> Now, while I speak this, holds his wife by th' arm
> That little thinks she has been sluic'd in 's absence,
> And his pond fish'd by his next neighbour, by
> Sir Smile, his neighbour.

Such an interjection would come fittingly from a chorus, particularly a cynical chorus like Thersites. The insistent 'even at this present, Now, while I speak this' is a finger pointed directly at the audience, reminding each of us that we are in a theatre, among a crowd of strangers, any one of whom might conceivably represent a threat to our emotional security — just as the discussion of the actor's art in *Hamlet* turns our thoughts towards the nature of dramatic illusion even while we are under that illusion. And fittingly, because we must be guided into that state of heightened sensibility, that sense of subtle detachment *within* an involvement, that can fitly contemplate the play within a play. To watch actors watching actors, to be aware of both the illusion they feign and the non-illusion we feel, and to bring the two into a harmony, needs a cool imaginative sympathy. And to have Hamlet coach the actors, before our eyes, establishes a mood in which that sympathy comes more readily.

Twentieth-century attempts to revive the 'poetic drama' have very seldom succeeded. They have tended to start from the assumption that verse, and figurative language, will do the job by themselves. Actually the chief enemy of 'poetic drama' is not prose but the proscenium arch. Sitting in darkness, with an orchestra pit between ourselves and the stage, we feel so much cut off from the action that participation becomes impossible. We are still moved by the drama we witness, but we are not involved in its minute-to-minute shifts of tone: and poetic drama depends essentially on this involvement.

That this is so is borne out by stage history. When the theatres opened in 1660, after the Puritan interregnum, the proscenium arch was established. But not in its fully developed modern form. Restoration theatres used a small proscenium arch, with folding doors that opened to reveal painted scenery, so that the scene could be changed without lowering a curtain. And much of the action took place on the space — reduced, it is true, but still significant — in front of the arch. In other words, the contact between actor and audience was diminished but not quite abolished. And the theatre in this period still used verse a good deal, still considered the use of verse as normal, at any rate for high subjects. What kind of verse? Significantly, the rhymed heroic couplet: the rhythmically regular, end-stopped couplet that comes down heavily on its rhymes. Such verse lacks the conversational fluidity of Elizabethan blank verse just as the Restoration stage lacks the freedom and intimacy of the Elizabethan. The heroic couplet, in fact, is a public-address system. It chimes or booms at the audience, throwing its meaning well out over the footlights. That such an idiom should have developed at the same

13

time as the proscenium arch began to creep forward, shows clearly the relation between a 'poetic' drama and an audience-to-actor *rapport*.

The Restoration stage, for instance, could not have managed the multiple shifts of convention that we find in *King Lear*, Act I, Scene ii, any more than the modern stage can manage them. This scene begins with Gloucester's bastard son, Edmund, making a verse speech to the audience in which he expresses his bitterness at being illegitimate, his determination not to let it cheat him of any of the fruits of existence, and his intention to oust his legitimate elder brother by whatever means come to hand. This speech is in verse; i.e. though intensely dramatic, it is formal and not naturalistic. When Gloucester enters, Edmund makes a clumsy show of hiding the forged letter he is holding, so as to make Gloucester demand to see it. Before catching sight of Edmund, Gloucester soliloquizes, also in verse, about the fateful happenings at the court of King Lear, from which he has just returned. This short soliloquy has the double function of expressing amazement and conveying information to the audience, who now learn that the King of France has departed in a rage and that Lear has set out on his wanderings, his power abdicated and his resources 'confin'd to exhibition', i.e. to a maintenance allowance. This is conveyed in three lines, whereupon Gloucester notices Edmund, and in an exchange of naturalistic dialogue insists on seeing the letter. He reads the letter aloud, for the benefit of the audience, and immediately modulates back into naturalism for further questioning of Edmund, interspersed with ejaculations addressed to no one in particular, just as people do in everyday life. He is so amazed and distressed by the murderous intention disclosed in the letter, whose authenticity it never occurs to him to question, that he hardly knows what he is saying; he repeatedly orders Edmund to go and find Edgar, but detains him by further incoherent questions. 'Go, sirrah, seek him,' is followed some twenty lines later by 'Edmund, seek him out'. Gloucester then falls into out-and-out soliloquy as he ruminates on the perilous state of things and the portents which have preceded it. 'These late eclipses in the sun and moon portend no good to us.' After going on in this strain for some time, he catches sight of Edmund still standing beside him and listening, no doubt with a sneer on his face, and reiterates, 'Find out this villain, Edmund; it shall lose thee nothing.' The order given, he returns again to his musing on the recent scene at Lear's court, and goes off muttering, 'And the noble and true-hearted Kent banished! His offence, honesty! 'Tis strange.'

Throughout this exchange, with its constant slipping in and out of soliloquy, the tone is naturalistic or very close to naturalism. The pair speak in realistic prose, and if Gloucester talks to himself, this is common enough in people who are deeply disturbed. The only thing that stands out obviously as a stage convention is the reading aloud of the letter, and since the tone of the letter is also naturalistic we feel no bumpy transition into non-realism and out again. Now, with Gloucester gone, Edmund continues the naturalistic vein by a mocking soliloquy in which he makes savage fun of his father's gullibility and faith in astrological portent. Continues it, that is, in that he continues to speak conversational prose; but departs from it in that he is obviously making another of his speeches to the audience. With the entry of Edgar, complete naturalism takes over again and continues throughout the brother's dialogue. Edgar then makes his hurried exit, and leaves Edmund alone on the stage to round off the scene, which he does by reverting to the verse in which he was speaking when he first entered.

> A credulous father! And a brother noble,
> Whose nature is so far from doing harms
> That he suspects none; on whose foolish honesty
> My practices ride easy! I see the business.
> Let me, if not by birth, have lands by wit:
> All with me's meet that I can fashion fit.

This speech, with its concluding couplet to indicate that the scene is now over, represents a move completely away from naturalism.

It is in the vein of the cruder and simpler drama of thirty years earlier. Edmund identifies himself once again as a villain, and clarifies his position in a complex and shifting plot that might well tax the attention of any audience, by telling us plainly that he is a dirty dog and does not intend to play fair. In so doing, he completes the showcase of available attitudes to realism and stage-illusion which has been exhibited to us in the space of about three minutes. Only the Elizabethan theatre could handle material of this flexible kind. And this is the reason why, in our time, both cinema and sound radio have frequently outgone the conventional theatre in their effectiveness as vehicles for Shakespeare's imagination. They have the necessary freedom to make shifts in tone, to superimpose one convention on another, and generally to simulate 'the quick forge and working-house of thought'.

III

Shakespeare moved from the sophisticated to the unsophisticated, from the current and topical to the fundamental and symbolic. His early comedies show him joining in the chic Italianate revels that placed him at one bound far out of reach of the slower mentality of rural Warwickshire and made him a successful rival of the University Wits. His early tragic vein is equally of the moment, whether he is telling a romantic Italian love-story, with the young couple outwitting the tedious grown-ups, and giving it a tragic instead of a happy ending, or portraying in Richard III a Renaissance megalomaniac patterned after Marlowe and invoking the familiar turnip-ghost of Machiavelli. But as he matures, material begins to creep in that we can only describe as deriving from the collective imagination. His plots begin to resemble folk-tales; the characters become archetypal as well as increasingly complex; they grow outwards in psychological realism, but at the same time put down deeper and deeper tap-roots into the world of dream, fairy-tale and the collective unconscious. In *Hamlet*, folk-tale material appears in a setting derived from history and politics. In *Lear*, the entire opening situation of the play comes from the same imaginative area as Jack the Giant-killer or Cinderella and her ugly sisters. Make a short prose summary of the plot, of, say, *All's Well that Ends Well*, and you find yourself in the same world. The Duke in *Measure for Measure*, who announces that he is going away on a journey, and instead puts on disguise and moves among his people so as to see them more closely, is a pure fairy-tale figure. And in the last plays of all, the 'romances', even psychological realism shrinks and leaves the bulk of the interest centred in the mythopoeic. *The Tempest*, Shakespeare's last play, cannot be traced, as nearly all the others can, to one definite source. On the other hand, everything in the play can be paralleled from widely diffused material which crops up again and again. As Mr. Frank Kermode puts it in the Introduction to his edition of the play in the 'Arden' series:

'Ultimately the source of *The Tempest* is an ancient *motif*, of almost universal occurrence, in saga, ballad, fairy-tale and folk-tale. The existence of this story accounts for the many analogues to *The Tempest*. That both Prospero and the father of Ayrer's Sidea are irascible is, in the last analysis, explained by the fact that they descend from a bad-tempered giant-magician. [Jakob Ayrer, a German dramatist contemporary with Shakespeare, has a play called *Die Schöne Sidea* which foreshadows some features of *The Tempest*.] It is likewise a feature of the archetype that the princess, like Miranda and Sidea, should aid the captive prince in his task and frankly own her love. The log-bearing is also a very ancient feature, and appears in the story at a primitive stage when the task was to chop down the wood as a preparation for the second task, which was to plough the ground; later the prince had to reap the harvest, and all these tasks were to be accomplished in one day. The Jason story suggests itself as an early analogue, and the ramifications of the fable have been traced throughout Europe and the Orient.'

In other words, Shakespeare's art, unlike the characteristic modern writer's, does not depend on striking out brand-new material, but rather on the fusing together in a new whole of

¹ Methuen, 1954.

components that had become familiar inmates of the European consciousness. Where modern writers are like journalists, each striving to scoop an 'exclusive', Shakespeare is more like a force of nature which gathers up long-recognized material and organizes it into a new and more valuable synthesis.

This is the true nature of Shakespeare's originality. His mind did not play over the surface of things. It started from the deepest layer and moved upwards, gathering up material and transforming it as it went. This is so unfamiliar to the twentieth-century mind that young students, on approaching Shakespeare for the first time, are often surprised to learn that he did not make up his own plots. To them, a reliance on stories already to hand suggests a weakness, a failure to come up with something fresh. Much the same attitude has been expressed by people old enough to know better; by Bernard Shaw, for instance. In fact, it is to the credit of the Elizabethans that they were not interested in the kind of 'originality' that would impress a Bernard Shaw as it impresses any pulp-magazine editor. They were still rooted in the mediaeval world in which the story matters more than the man who re-counts it. To Chaucer, the poet's main task is to re-tell, freshly and effectively, the tales which have always held men's attention. He enjoys pointing out that what he is giving the reader is to be found in 'olde bokes'. He is plugging the reader in to a source of power, power which transcends any individual contribution. A writer like Malory will even claim a source where none exists; it gives dignity to the material. If we grasp this it will help us to realize that the legendary and fairy-tale element in Shakespeare's work is entirely unselfconscious. We look back at Shakespeare across two centuries of a literature predominantly realistic, during which the use of legend and folk-tale stamped a writer as either antiquarian or elvish. For a modern artist — for Grieg, say — to use material from folk-culture usually indicates some consciously worked-out programme of getting back to the roots. To Shakespeare, it was as instinctive as breathing. The world of commerce, logic and industrialism swept the folk-imagination into the nursery and kept it there. But in Shakespeare's time, as in Ovid's, this had not happened.

Ovid, Shakespeare's favourite poet, deserves a glance here. Like Shakespeare, he did not invent 'original material'. He used the myths that were familiar to everyone, and his art consisted in the imaginative skill with which he orchestrated story with story, and clothed narrative with words and images. (And this remained the chief claim of the literary artist until well after Shakespeare's day.) Ovid's principal work is the *Metamorphoses*, an immense collection of stories linked together only by the fact that in each of them, someone is changed into something. It presents a world of sharply visualized surrealist fantasy in which images of change crowd on one another so fast, and with such rapid switches of mood, that no one situation has time to stick in the reader's mind. What sticks is rather the all-pervading atmosphere of flowing and instability, an atmosphere that was not again to be captured until the coming of the *avant-garde* cinema in the 1920s. It is the world of Cocteau's *Le Sang d'un Poète*, where mirrors sprout arms, the laws of gravity are suspended, the horrible and the comic jostle with the lyrical, and the spectator is less concerned with the fate of this or that individual character than with his own experience of being drawn into this surreal world and breathing its atmosphere. The intoxicating sense of melting, changing and dissolving in the *Metamorphoses* has always fascinated artists — visual artists in particular, since the sharp selection of detail and the visual precision in Ovid's writing are a continual challenge to them. Ezra Pound, at a formative stage in his poetic career, found himself drawn to various Renaissance re-handlings of material from the *Metamorphoses*. At this time Pound was well launched into the *Cantos*, a poem on the epic scale that keeps well away from Virgil and veers towards Ovid — avoiding, that is to say, the stately, settled progression of Virgil, majestically sweeping from point to point with a grand predictability, and cultivating the Ovidian technique of discontinuity, sudden jumps of focus and switches of scene.

Shakespeare's relationship to Ovid moved from outside to inside, from surface to centre, in the same way as all his interests. In the early plays, it is mainly a matter of a young man's enjoyment of the fancifulness of Ovid's writing. When, in Henry IV, Part I (Act I, Scene iii), Hotspur is ranting in indignation, trying to convince the king that his cousin Mortimer put up a brave resistance against Glendower, he can spare breath for a typically Ovidian conceit:

> Three times they breath'd, and three times did they drink,
> Upon agreement, of swift Severn's flood;
> Who then, affrighted with their bloody looks,
> Ran fearfully among the trembling reeds
> And hid his crisp head in the hollow bank.

The conceit has no dramatic relevance, and such fanciful by-play is out of character for Hotspur. But it was Ovidian, and that was enough. And when, in maturer years, Shakespeare ceased to feel the attraction of this merely fanciful side of Ovid, his work continues to show how deeply felt is his affinity with this poet of melting, changing, flowing, other-seeming.

It could not be otherwise. Shakespeare's work is one vast metamorphosis. In every story he tells, people put on disguise, alter themselves, pretend to be what they are not. Sometimes it is a matter of deliberate guile. At other times it is self-deception. Edgar in *Lear* dresses in rustic clothes and feigns insanity, while remaining perfectly rational. Malvolio, on the other hand, dresses in clothes inappropriate to his position, and is then treated as mad by the other characters and locked in a cell. Characters exchange clothes and are taken for one another. Falstaff and Hal put on a burlesque in which each in turn speaks with the assumed voice of outraged royalty, and Hal rejects Falstaff in play before he does so in earnest. Masquerade, disguise, confusion are everywhere. Every comedy is a comedy of errors. And every tragedy is a tragedy of errors. Mistake, misassessment, illusion, start the action going in every case. Iago deceives Othello, but Othello has already made himself vulnerable to deception by deserting his own world of free heroic action and wandering into the intrigue-world of supersubtle Venice. He is the outsider, his outside-ness dramatized by the colour of his skin, who must believe anything he is told because he has no materials for judgment. Lear, who 'hath ever but slenderly known himself', is self-deceived; Hamlet wanders confused in a world of mirrors; Antony is hypnotized by sensual passion. Macbeth profits by the fact sadly acknowledged by Duncan, that 'There's no art To find the mind's construction in the face:' but Macbeth is just as deceived by the faces he trusts in as Duncan is. In the last plays, this confusion is represented in a more purely symbolic and visual way: a shipwreck drives voyagers to the island where they must face the truth about themselves: the statue of the dead queen comes to life, Art's gift to Nature.

It is this that links Shakespeare with the folk-imagination. The witches and enchanters, dwarfs and giants, Aladdin's lamp and Cinderella's coach of folk-tale are a reflection of the universal human sense that things mysteriously change, that no two people see the same things, that the world is slipping and sliding. What the ungraspable nature of reality begins, human self-deception and error can be trusted to finish. 'Realistic' literature has a short, flickering and uncertain history, appearing here and there (usually in big-city conditions) and then disappearing for centuries. Our own age is usually taken to be an age of realism, but this is merely a journalistic blunder. Actually it is an Ovidian or Shakespearean age.

Since Shakespeare's work deals so largely with transformation and the altering of perspectives, it is natural that the plays should proceed by means of riddles, masquerades, plays within plays, mistaken identities, the melting shapes of symbol and emblem. It is natural, too, that the result should come across to us with the authority and impersonality of myth. When we examine the great myths of mankind, from ancient Egypt to the heroes of Asgard, from classical Greek to Red Indian, we cannot fail to be struck by their anonymous quality. It is impossible to imagine anyone inventing them. They seem simply to exist in their own right, unalterably and immemorially *there*, like mountains. And very much the same thing is true of Shakespeare. Though a common identity runs through his work, there is no Shakespearean 'style' as there is Miltonic or Dantesque 'style'. Shakespeare cannot be imitated; he has no habits or trade-marks. The idiosyncrasies in his work seem natural accidents, like the knots in an oaken beam. No less than humanity's great myths, these works seem too large and too inevitable to have been put together by conscious artistry and contrivance. After about 1600, Shakespeare's work strikes one less and less as the 'original' work of one individual imagination, copyrighted and hallmarked — though we know in fact that it is so. Increasingly, as we get into his work, it seems to us that we are listening, not to the words of one man, but to things that come direct from the imagination of mankind itself.

II

THE SWORD AND THE CROWN

ANY methodical reading of Shakespeare will start with the English historical plays. There are nine of these, and they not only dominate the poet's achievement in the first phase of his career, before 1600, but they already state his major themes and demonstrate his major powers. Shakespeare is from first to last an intensely political writer. He knows that the happiness of the common man is very much bound up with the question of who has power at the top. 'How shall men govern themselves?' is no academic question to him. When he draws a society, he takes care to show in surprisingly full detail how that society is governed. People in authority interest him, from the fighting general to the hereditary monarch, from the rural constable to the Lord Chief Justice.

An artist does not change; he develops. Shakespeare did not pass from one preoccupation to another like a car driving along a road. He grew outwardly, like a tree adding rings of new wood. The English historical plays deal with the realities of power and authority. Their analyses of individual character, their incidental observation of life, their humour, their pathos, their tragedy, are all contained within this framework. Later, in plays like *Hamlet* and *Macbeth*, content and framework are more subtly mingled. The struggle of an individual soul to free itself from a mesh of evil and misfortune is more in the foreground, and the question of political power more in the background. But it is a background that can never be ignored. None of the mature tragedies, none even of the golden comedies, can be understood without reference to Shakespeare's constant probing into the questions of power and authority.

The bent of Shakespeare's mind was not only political but strongly empirical and historical. He did not make the mistake of trying to see political problems in the abstract. He knew that they arose to confront men in particular places at particular times. The question was not only, 'Who shall have power?' but 'Who shall have power over Englishmen? Over Romans? Over Greeks?' Whether he turned to a prehistoric, Stonehenge Britain, as in *King Lear*, or to a modern Italian city-state, as in *Othello*; whether he imagined his characters in the world of Homer, on the imaginary island of Prospero, or in the Rome of Julius Caesar, he knew that men lived rooted in place and time. If he began with an exploration of the nature of power and politics in an English setting, that was natural for an Englishman, particularly one living in an age of intense national self-consciousness.

The English scene, viewed from an Elizabethan standpoint, was dominated by one urgent need: the need for political stability, guaranteed by an undisputed monarchy. All these nine plays concern themselves with kingship. The burning question is whether the man who occupies the throne can hold the loyalty and obedience of the realm. If he can, the reward is stability at home and foreign conquest abroad. In an age of unquestioned nationalism, the one is seen as following automatically on the other. When England has a weak king, such as King John, the French send an army and conquer some of our territory. When England has a strong king, such as Henry V, we send an army and conquer some of their territory. Military aggrandisement is an automatic index of the success of a reign. These beliefs, however, were not held in a simple form by a mind as comprehensive as Shakespeare's. In politics, as in most things, people have their official beliefs, to which they give outward and visible assent, and also their underlying personal doubts and qualifications. At times of stress they rally to their official beliefs for the sake of showing a united front;

only when no immediate danger threatens, and when they are surrounded by trusted companions, do they voice their doubts and hesitations. On paper, no Communist is anything but loyal to Moscow or Peking, no democrat doubts the value of the parliamentary system, no Catholic questions the Vatican. Grievances are aired in private.

Shakespeare's official belief, in respect of English politics, was in the theory of Divine Right of Kings. This theory held that, since church and state were bound up together, and the coronation service was a sacrament, an anointed king could not be resisted except at the price of mortal sin. In part this idea descended from the Middle Ages, when the feudal system drew its ultimate sanction from the notion of a descending scale of authority, starting with God and ending with the lowest forms of life. This would mean that the king naturally drew authority from above and transmitted it to his lieutenants below, so that to challenge the king was to challenge the divinely ordained system of created life. But it had also been given a violent boost by the Tudor dynasty, who raised it to the status of an effective historical myth.

To the modern eye, the theory of Divine Right looks merely silly and pretentious. If the sixteenth-century Englishman could be taken in by this kind of propaganda, we tend to think, he deserved all he got at the hands of his rulers. It is only when we pause to get the matter in its historical context that we see the underlying practicality. In an England still largely mediaeval, physical power could not be concentrated at the centre. Warfare depended largely on the ability to wear down heavily fortified points of resistance, one after another. Communications were slow, and no one ever knew with any certainty how things were developing in remote parts of the country. Success depended on the support of individual noblemen, each of whom could put his personal army in the field in the confidence that its primary loyalty was to him and to whatever cause he chose to follow. Granted this situation, it is difficult to see how a country could be unified without the doctrine of Divine Right, or something very like it. When power is in the hands of a number of heavily armed feudal overlords, one of whom has the title of King, some very powerful sanction is needed to unite the others in subservience to him: a mere gentleman's agreement will not do. To call in the church to bless the crown, to warn that rebellion displeases God as well as man, seems only common sense, even if we divorce the idea from its metaphysical background.

Shakespeare's working life occupies the relatively short and tense period between two rebellions against the Crown. In 1570, when he was six, a big revolt broke out in the north of England. The Catholic houses of Neville and Percy rose, the Bible and Prayer Book were torn to pieces in Durham Cathedral and Mass was said once more before its altar. Shakespeare would have seen the troops marching north to stamp out this forest fire. And since John Shakespeare was an alderman, and aldermen had the responsibility for mustering the militia, he would have seen his own father hurrying to and fro, jumping up from meals, and disrupting the life of the household in the course of his urgent duties. For months, the talk of his elders must have been of rebels, armies, bloodshed and the threat to stability. The danger was averted, and did not arise again in his lifetime. But barely thirty years after his death, England was again torn by civil war, and this time the anointed head was brought to the block. Evidently, Shakespeare's English history plays were inspired by no mere fanciful or antiquarian interest in the problem of kingship.

II

There can be no doubt, then, that Shakespeare 'believed in' the Divine Right of Kings at least to the extent that a modern lawyer 'believes in' the system of law he helps to operate. I myself would go further and say that Shakespeare gave the idea a considerable emotional and imaginative allegiance. The horror with which he views, and causes us to view, the crime of Macbeth is not only horror at the murder, for gain, of a kindly old gentleman. Nor does he mean us to absorb from *King Lear* only the lesson that girls ought to be kind to their fathers. Kingship was sacred in his mind, even though human selfishness and cruelty were continually casting shadows on that sacredness. (This attitude has died out among sophisticated people in modern England, but it has continued to flourish among the populace: so there is no excuse for our not understanding it, when it is there for us to study at any time.)

Shakespeare's official belief, then, was in Divine Right. But here we run into our first complexity. No one has affirmed the doctrine in more vigorous terms than Shakespeare. But equally, no one has scorched it with a fiercer irony. His work is full of unforgettable statements of the belief in the divinity of kingship. But these statements tend to be made by men who have no right, in the sight of God or man, to be making them. Thus, Claudius faces Hamlet's excited violence with a calm

> Let him go, Gertrude; do not fear our person:
> There's such divinity doth hedge a king
> That treason can but peep to what it would,
> Acts little of his will.

And yet Claudius is a murderer and usurper, who started the whole chain of evil which will finally cost both Hamlet and himself their lives. Similarly, the doomed Richard II, in one of his fits of manic self-congratulatory optimism, says,

> For every man that Bolingbroke hath press'd
> To lift shrewd steel against our golden crown,
> God for his Richard hath in heavenly pay
> A glorious angel; then, if angels fight,
> Weak men must fall, for heaven still guards the right.

Yet it is obvious to everyone in the audience that Richard has no chance at all against the determined Bolingbroke, and indeed does not deserve to rule England. At such times, one comes very close to the suspicion that the theory of Divine Right is being ridiculed. But I believe 'ridicule' is the wrong word here. The tone is more like that of the blasphemies of Baudelaire or Joyce.

Once a believer, always a believer. Shakespeare holds that a king *ought* to be divinely guided and sanctioned, and also knows perfectly well that he is living in a world where kings commit the same cruelties and stupidities, contain within themselves the seeds of the same failures and tragedies, as other men. At once what begins as a political theory shifts to the profoundly more interesting level of art. That is, of human life itself.

Shakespeare wrote two four-part series of historical plays, with an extra one, *King John*, thrown in. The first series comprises the three parts of *Henry VI* and *Richard III*: the second, *Richard II*, the two parts of *Henry IV*, and *Henry V*. Of these two tetralogies, the first is prentice work, doubtless in part not by Shakespeare but merely worked over and re-stitched by him: the second brings him before us as a mature poet and dramatist. But from the point of view of content, they are not dissimilar. In both, the theory of Divine Right is emphatically stated. In both, it comes in for some fierce and subtle questioning.

The content of both tetralogies can be stated shortly, if crudely. The King is the Lord's anointed, and ought to prevail. But if he is a weak king, like Henry VI, he will not prevail. His power will be wrested from him, probably by a thug like Richard III. If that happens, the thug will have himself crowned and will then proclaim that God fights on his side. But it is the duty of all men to ignore this claim and sweep him from the throne.

The same content is worked over more subtly in the second series. Richard II, like Henry VI, is a weak king who cannot hold power. So we see it knocked from his grasp. But Henry IV, the usurper, is not a brute like Richard III. He is a sober and responsible, if unlikeable, man. As a king of England, he is preferable to Richard. Though harassed by continual rebellion, he manages to hold the country in one piece. His hopes are centred on his elder son, who grieves him by being irresponsible and pleasure-loving. Only when his life is coming to an end, and the moment of accession comes near, does the prince show his kingly qualities, first on the battlefield and then in court and council. He rejects his dissolute companions, notably Sir John Falstaff, and becomes the warrior-king for whom England has waited. The final play of the series, *Henry V*, is a patriotic trumpet-call which does for English literature what Virgil's *Aeneid* did for Roman, or *The Lusiads* of Camoens for Portuguese. In Henry V's prayer before the battle of Agincourt, the stain is wiped from his family.

> Not to-day, O Lord,
> O, not to-day, think not upon the fault
> My father made in compassing the crown!
> I Richard's body have interred new;
> And on it have bestow'd more contrite tears
> Than from it issued forced drops of blood:
> Five hundred poor have I in yearly pay,
> Who twice a day their withered hands hold up
> Towards heaven, to pardon blood; and I have built
> Two chantries, where the sad and solemn priests
> Sing still for Richard's soul. More will I do;
> Though all that I can do is nothing worth,
> Since that my penitence comes after all,
> Imploring pardon.

And so, with genuine contrition, plus a strong right arm and a sharp sword to win valuable territories in France, plus a handsome profile to capture the heart of the French princess and make a love-match to rivet the peace treaty, the story is wound up and the lovers can ride off into the sunset. But not until some strong and bitter truths have been digested. Not until it has been made very clear that the king who will pull England's scattered feelings together, in an age of ferocity and danger, must be a good deal more than just a decent chap. And, in some ways, a good deal less.

III

The first tetralogy — the three parts of *Henry VI* plus *Richard III* — does not hold together in such close unity as the second. Not only is there the uncertainty as to authorship (very few scholars having decided that Shakespeare was solely responsible for the *Henry VI* plays) but there is also the matter of the poet's very rapid development during these years. His genius is growing so fast that there are times when it seems to make a jump forward within the course of a single play. (The last act of *Love's Labour's Lost*, for instance, seems more mature than the first act.) From the point of view of their importance as dramatic art, the kindest thing we can say about the three parts of *Henry VI* is that they form a long, unsteady spring-board from which Shakespeare's genius was able to leap into the superb acrobatics of *Richard III*.

Their interest as showing the workings of Shakespeare's mind on politics and power is of course much greater. Several things stand out from the confused and rambling action. The first is the utter remorselessness of the world they portray. These proud and mighty noblemen rampage over the stage, butchering one another and carrying armies of lesser men to the slaughter with them. Nobody ever mentions the will of the people; there is no democracy, and if a humble man starts up and demands a share in government he is shown as a dangerous fanatic like Jack Cade. When, as happens throughout, various lords are disputing as to who shall wear the crown, the only qualification they ever bring forward is that of pedigree. So-and-so is descended from Such-and-such, who was murdered by the ancestors of Somebody-or-other. His title can be traced in the stud-book, and therefore he must be crowned forthwith. As for the mild and conciliatory Henry, he is simply a piece of meat thrown to the wolves. In the end, the crown is snatched, by the methods of pure gangsterism, by Richard, Duke of Gloucester, a man who freely admits (in soliloquy) that he has no title to the throne except the power-urge which is a natural consequence of his deformity.

These characters recognize no motives except the grab for power and the gratification of lust and revenge. Senseless personal feuds, like that between Cardinal Beaufort and Humphry of Gloucester, can flare up like straw, and the result is to set armies at each other's throats. On the surface, since all these characters concur in recognizing the principle of Divine Right, the plays speak of the sacredness of kingship. But since they can never settle whose title to the throne is the genuine one, and are at all times ready to provoke a blood-bath in support of one claim or another, the general impression is one of anarchy. What was the effect of these three plays on the minds of their original audience? Did the ordinary Londoner go away with his belief in the hierarchy strengthened? Was he, after witnessing this unrelieved pageant of mayhem, more deeply convinced than ever of his duty to obey those whom God had set above him? Or did a suspicion creep in, now and again, that power and ruthlessness were the whole of the law?

There is a good deal of confusion in the air here. Shakespeare has not yet stabilized the emotions which drive the action. On the surface, he is writing about England's glory and majesty, and how the sacredness of the crown will eventually shine out through all the blood that is splashed on it by the daggers of ambition. He leaves us in no doubt that he believes in a feudal hierarchy of power, in which the king's authority is transmitted through a broadening series of stages from the aristocracy to the village justice. Yet there are moments when a disconcerting scepticism looks out at us.

The character of Joan of Arc furnishes an important example. Joan is a witch. She derives her power from the forces of hell. This power, in the early stages, is used to humble the English army, and consequently Shakespeare's attitude to her — on the surface — is one of simple enmity. But she is also a peasant girl, with a sharp tongue and a simple, direct attitude towards the overblown nobility with whom she has to co-operate. The result is a tug of war which Shakespeare fails to arbitrate. We have to accept that Joan is evil: the alliance of political misrule with witchcraft looks forward to *Macbeth* and no doubt comes very much from the centre of Shakespeare's interests. But whenever she appears on the stage, we lean forward eagerly, anticipating a few minutes' relief from the surrounding boredom and barbarism. She has not only the mystagogue's scorn for the dreary routines of practical men, but also the peasant's dislike of fancy talk and high-flown titles. That she should turn this scorn on the English nobility is of course very regrettable. But we do not regret it. Our lungs need a sudden flow of fresh air, and perhaps Shakespeare was conscious of a similar need. At all events, when we reach the scene (Part I, Act IV, Scene vii) when Sir William Lucy comes to the French camp after a battle, to enquire about English losses and prisoners, Joan's savage banter seems curiously sympathetic.

> LUCY. But where's the great Alcides of the field,
>   Valiant Lord Talbot, Earl of Shrewsbury,
>   Created for his rare success in arms
>   Great Earl of Washford, Waterford, and Valence,
>   Lord Talbot of Goodrig and Urchinfield,
>   Lord Strange of Blackmere, Lord Verdun of Alton,
>   Lord Cromwell of Wingfield, Lord Furnival of Sheffield,
>   The thrice-victorious Lord of Falconbridge,
>   Knight of the Noble Order of St. George,
>   Worthy St. Michael and the Golden Fleece,
>   Great Marshal to Henry the Sixth
>   Of all his wars within the realm of France?
> JOAN. Here's a silly-stately style indeed!
>   The Turk, that two-and-fifty kingdoms hath,
>   Writes not so tedious a style as this.
>   Him that thou magnifi'st with all these titles,
>   Stinking and fly-blown lies here at our feet.

I do not think it is merely a twentieth-century irreverence in me that makes Lucy's speech, with its enumeration of titles, sound absurd. Shakespeare elsewhere tosses these titles about freely enough, without giving rise to such misgivings. It is hard to resist the impression that he has succumbed here to a temptation which, though momentary, is very revealing; that he is deliberately laying the good Lucy open to Joan's mockery. Talbot's simple heroism, which is certainly presented non-ironically, is disfigured rather than adorned by these trappings. 'Honour is a mere scutcheon.' A shaft of hard, mistrustful daylight has shone for a moment on the scarlet-and-gold of the action.

Joan of Arc disappears, in the direction of the stake and the faggots, before the end of Part 1. Shakespeare no doubt felt embarrassed in the presence of a character about whom he could not clarify his own feelings. (This was not the last time he would feel such embarrassment.) In any case, he could hardly hope to succeed, at this stage, with a complex character. His art was not yet ready for psychological realism, and to make Joan three-dimensional would have called for psychological realism in plenty. In these three plays, Shakespeare is still very close to the popular chronicle plays of an earlier day. The mode of these plays is the heraldic. Their characters have the stiff unreality, but also the vividness, of heraldic animals. And they speak in a verse which, in its chiming non-realism, is the perfectly appropriate language for such figures. The effect is that of a tapestry of stiff brocade. The characters are two-dimensional and immovable, but once we have accepted this we can feel them as vivid presences.

The quickest way to grasp what I mean by calling these plays 'heraldic' is to open *Henry VI, Part 3* and read one short scene, Act II, Scene v. This scene is a self-contained inset in the main action. A battle is in progress, and King Henry, who has no taste for bloodshed, enters and tells the audience that the two strong characters, his wife and Lord Clifford, have told him to keep out of the way. He sits down on a molehill, in token of his lowliness of spirit, and talks yearningly of the peace and happiness of an unnoticed life.

> O God! methinks it were a happy life
> To be no better than a homely swain;
> To sit upon a hill, as I do now,
> To carve out dials quaintly, point by point,
> Thereby to see the minutes how they run —
> How many make the hour full complete,
> How many hours bring about the day,
> How many days will finish up the year,
> How many years a mortal man may live.
> When this is known, then to divide the times —

33

So many hours must I tend my flock;
So many hours must I take my rest;
So many hours must I contemplate;
So many hours must I sport myself;
So many days my ewes have been with young;
So many weeks ere the poor fools will ean;
So many years ere I shall shear the fleece;
So minutes, hours, days, months, and years,
Pass'd over to the end they were created,
Would bring white hairs unto a quiet grave.

After a little more of this, 'Alarum. Enter a Son that hath killed his Father, with the dead body.' Happily setting down the corpse, the young man proceeds to rifle purse and pocket, till brought up short by the discovery of its identity. He laments, in the same chiming verse, the bitter chance of war that has led him to slay his father, and the watching king is ready with the comment,

O piteous spectacle! O bloody times!
Whiles lions war and battle for their dens,
Poor harmless lambs abide their enmity.

Next, 'Enter a Father that hath killed his Son, with the body in his arms.' We go through the same performance again, leading to the same chiming lamentation. Finally, the three characters, each alone on his part of the stage, speak a kind of antiphon.

SON.   How will my mother for a father's death
        Take on with me and ne'er be satisfied!
FATHER. How will my wife for slaughter of my son
        Shed seas of tears and ne'er be satisfied!
KING HENRY. How will the country for these woeful chances
        Misthink the king and not be satisfied!
SON.   Was ever son so ru'd a father's death?
FATHER. Was ever father so bemoan'd his son?
KING HENRY. Was ever king so griev'd for subjects' woe?

In view of what Shakespeare was to give us later, we are tempted to dismiss this kind of writing as amusingly inadequate to catch the emotions that are being spilt out. But it has its own validity and strength. These figures are not real people: they are heraldic emblems. They have the reality-within-unreality of early Staffordshire pottery figures. They could not be mistaken for living beings, yet a certain kind of life pulses in them. And in the hard, bright surface of the burnished verse they speak, we find an ideal marriage of words to content. This is only one rung on Shakespeare's rapid climb upward, but it is not to be despised.

Had Shakespeare stayed there, of course, he would have remained a minor dramatist among a crowd of minor dramatists, overshadowed by the bigger writers and above all by Marlowe. That he was very much aware, at this time, of the need to measure himself against the bulky presence of Marlowe we can see from the concluding play of this tetralogy, *Richard III*. Here, the heraldic colours and chiming verse of the earlier plays are left far behind in a sudden burst of new power. Psychological realism has still not fully arrived; Shakespeare knows how to make his people react credibly, but he is not interested, as he will be in a few years' time, in the intricacies of character. He is still painting in broad strokes and primary colours. But now he is painting like a master.

The plot of *Richard III* is simple and predictable. The villainous Richard has seized the throne, with the aid of his accomplice Buckingham, and all the play has to do is to show us his cruelty, his treacherous murder of every rival including his own creature Buckingham, and finally the great heave by which a suffering England casts him forth in favour of a just king with a fair title to the crown. The plot, in short, has the broad simplicity of outline which we find in Marlowe's *Dr. Faustus* or *Tamburlaine*. Using exactly the same equipment as Marlowe, Shakespeare will proceed to outgo him and establish the fact that a new master rules the English stage. This annihilation of Marlowe was a necessary step for Shakespeare. We can see the same kind of thing in the career of many an artist, for genius has its pressing psychological necessities and one of those necessities is to breathe freely. *Richard III* is not a parody of Marlowe, but it has something of the force of a parody. It is an exercise in the style of another man, undertaken out of a need to struggle free of an influence by riding it to death. One thinks of the sudden fury with which Hemingway, in the first flush of his strength, turned and rended Sherwood Anderson in *The Torrents of Spring*.

Marlowe had specialized in the Renaissance megalomaniac. In the person of hump-backed Richard, Shakespeare carried this type to new heights. Richard is no mere ranter like Tamburlaine. He is clear-sighted as well as murderous. He knows, for instance, the value of propaganda. After he and Buckingham have disposed of their opponent Hastings, he summons the Lord Mayor of London. When the mayor arrives, the pair are full of regrets that the execution was carried out a little prematurely.

> BUCKINGHAM. Yet had we not determin'd he should die
> Until your lordship came to see his end —
> Which now the loving haste of these our friends,
> Something against our meanings, have prevented —
> Because, my lord, I would have had you heard
> The traitor speak, and timorously confess
> The manner and the purpose of his treasons;
> That you might well have signified the same
> Unto the citizens, who haply may
> Misconster us in him and wail his death.
> MAYOR. But, my good lord, your Grace's word shall serve.
> As well as I had seen and heard him speak;
> And do not doubt, right noble princes both,
> But I'll acquaint your duteous citizens
> With all your just proceedings in this cause.
> GLOUCESTER. And to that end we wish'd your lordship here,
> T' avoid the censures of the carping world.

Stalin used much the same technique more than once. As a tyrant, this Richard has solid credibility. Further, his mind has depths into which we are occasionally allowed a glimpse. Just as his cruelty and megalomania spring from his resentment at the mean trick played on him by Nature, so these same forces push him into a greater and greater loneliness. In this respect, Richard is a

preliminary study for the far subtler figure of Macbeth. And not
Macbeth only, since all Shakespeare's evildoers find themselves
shut out from the human circle of love and fellowship. Richard's
agonized soliloquy in Act V, Scene iii, after the visitation of the
ghosts, is Shakespeare's first mature statement of this great theme.
It is as far above Marlowe as Marlowe was above his own pre-
decessors.

> Give me another horse. Bind up my wounds.
> Have mercy, Jesu! Soft! I did but dream.
> O coward conscience, how dost thou afflict me!
> The lights burn blue. It is now dead midnight,
> Cold fearful drops stand on my trembling flesh.
> What do I fear? Myself? There's none else by.
> Richard loves Richard; that is, I am I.
> Is there a murderer here? No — yes, I am.
> Then fly. What, from myself? Great reason why —
> Lest I revenge. What, myself upon myself!
> Alack, I love myself. Wherefore? For any good
> That I myself have done unto myself?
> O, no! Alas, I rather hate myself
> For hateful deeds committed by myself!
> I am a villain; yet I lie, I am not.
> Fool, of thyself speak well. Fool, do not flatter.
> My conscience hath a thousand several tongues,
> And every tongue brings in a several tale,
> And every tale condemns me for a villain.
> Perjury, perjury, in the high'st degree;
> Murder, stern murder, in the dir'st degree;
> All several sins, all us'd in each degree,
> Throng to the bar, crying all 'Guilty! guilty!'
> I shall despair. There is no creature loves me;
> And if I die no soul will pity me:
> And wherefore should they, since that I myself
> Find in myself no pity to myself?

The stuttering repetition of the word 'self' in this speech brings
before us a mind trapped in its own egotism, which effectively
bars every way out to a larger and saner atmosphere. The closed

circle of 'Richard loves Richard; that is, I am I' is the ultimate imprisonment. It foreshadows the silence of Iago before his accusers, or Macbeth's comparison of himself with a bear tied to a stake. The man who has turned against humanity is left finally in the freezing darkness of his solitude.

The whole of this Act V is brilliantly managed, and is worth the close attention of anyone wishing to understand the potentialities of the Elizabethan stage. The two armies, one under Richard and the other under the liberator, Richmond, are both encamped on Bosworth field, and both camps are represented onstage. Richard retires into his tent to sleep; then our attention is directed to Richmond, as he invokes God's help for his mission, and lies down to sleep in his turn. A procession of ghosts enters, and each one crosses the stage from Richard's tent to Richmond's, with a curse for the one and a blessing for the other. This cinematic freedom of effect was very difficult to obtain on the stage once it had developed the accoutrements of 'realism'. Hence the nineteenth-century distrust of Shakespeare's stagecraft. Played simply on an open stage, the scene is magnificently flexible and alive. The firm simplicity of Richmond's prayer bounds it on one side; the thick frenzy of Richard's soliloquy on the other.

At the end of this play, the houses of York and Lancaster are united in the Tudor dynasty. Shakespeare has carried his first tetralogy through to a point of repose. England has shaken free of the turmoil caused by a disputed throne and a warring nobility. And the political message has been thoroughly driven home. Bad men can seize power, even if that power is protected by a sacrament. The throne is the essential instrument of authority and peace. But the throne is an empty symbol unless it is occupied by a man with all the power of Richard and yet with the uprightness and forebearance that will keep his subjects content. It begins to look as if the business of being a king is more complicated than we thought. It does not begin and end with getting oneself born in the right bedchamber.

IV

By the time he had written the first tetralogy — plus the
out-of-series makeweight, *King John* — Shakespeare had stated
with great clarity and force his basic conviction about the
monarchy: that Divine Right, however desirable as a principle,
would not do the work by itself; that even anointed kings must
govern, or out they would go. In the second tetralogy he stated
this view over again. But this time he approached the question as
an artist. The simple heraldic comings and goings of the earlier
plays are replaced by a truly human complexity. Where Henry
VI was merely weak and amiable, Richard II is weak in a
complicated, unpredictable, but entirely credible way. Where
Richard III is a standard Renaissance megalomaniac, Henry V has
the same urge to power, but controls it under a cold statesmanship. Where the earlier plays have virtually no sub-plot, the later
ones have a richly imagined second action, presided over by Falstaff, which mirrors and qualifies the principal action at every turn.

From the opening scenes of *Richard II* we see this new richness
at work. This, the opening play of the series, must have been
peculiarly difficult to write. It could so easily have gone wrong,
and if it had, the whole tetralogy would have been misshapen.
Shakespeare had the delicate task of first showing a king who was
manifestly unfit to govern, then showing him deposed by a man
with more kingly qualities, and finally leaving us in a mood of
elegiac sadness that such things must be. One ounce too much
weight on either side, and the effect is ruined. If Richard is shown
as merely contemptible, Bolingbroke's successful revolt carries no
stain of evil. If he shines too brightly in his martyrdom — and
the dispossessed king is a powerful symbol, for deep down every
man thinks of himself as a dispossessed king — then again the play
has failed to make its essential point and the whole tetralogy is
foredoomed.

Confronted with this task, Shakespeare put forth his full
strength, and the result is there for us to see and marvel at. Not

a foot is put wrong. No matter how minutely we study the play, we cannot fault it. Richard is a subtle and appealing figure, capable of magnificence and courage, but not of self-discipline or consistency. Histrionic to the marrow, he is at all times absorbed in his own performance in whatever role he happens to be playing. His sensibility is exquisite, but it is entirely self-regarding. There is no trace of love, or pity, or admiration, for anyone else. For himself he has all three in large measure. His egotism, except that it is allied to Narcissism instead of cruelty, matches that of Richard Crookback. His patriotism, the first requisite of a king, is to him a form of self-indulgence. It surges up when the setting happens to be right. Thus, on landing from Ireland and finding himself in an England already menaced by rebellion, he kneels and in an access of perfectly genuine emotion lays his hand in blessing on the sacred soil of his country. This emotion, like all his others, is an affair of the surface. Yet it can communicate itself to other people; and, like all fascinating self-absorbed performers, Richard has no lack of friends and lovers. Indeed, by the end of the play we, the audience, have joined their number. The exquisitely cadenced laments with which he greets each new calamity, the poignant imagery and compelling rhythms which mark everything he says, work on our minds and put us under exactly the same spell as those characters in the play who give him their love and loyalty. By the last act, when Richard's erstwhile groom creeps fearfully in to see him in his dungeon, and haltingly expresses his grief at having to witness his master's downfall, we are ready to see the king's death in terms of pure pathos. And in a short concluding scene, Shakespeare turns the action unhesitatingly in the direction it is to follow for three more plays, like a masterful rider pulling round a horse's head. Exton, the rough opportunist who took it upon himself to kill Richard as a passport to the new king's favour, brings in his coffined remains and stands back cheerfully awaiting congratulation and reward. Instead, in a characteristically short, blunt statement, Bolingbroke sets the tone of what is to come.

Exton, I thank thee not; for thou hast wrought
A deed of slander with thy fatal hand
Upon my head and all this famous land.

EXTON.　　　　From your own mouth, my lord, did I this deed.

BOLINGBROKE.　They love not poison that do poison need.
Nor do I thee: though I did wish him dead,
I hate the murderer, love him murdered.
The guilt of conscience take thou for thy labour.
But neither my good word nor princely favour:
With Cain go wander through the shades of night.

A few sentences earlier, Bolingbroke has also banished the
Bishop of Carlisle, who with reckless courage had denounced his
usurpation. Mindful of the importance of keeping our respect for
Bolingbroke, Shakespeare makes this banishment a grave and
dignified act of amnesty ('as thou liv'st in peace, die free from
strife'), but the symbolic and structural importance of the double
banishment can hardly be lost on any audience. For Richard, at
the beginning of the play, also banished two men; and to look
back at the scene in which this happens is the quickest way of
seeing the distance the play has travelled. Just as Bolingbroke's
banishment of Carlisle and Exton is motivated by consciousness of
his own sin, so Richard's banishment of the two warring Dukes,
Norfolk and 'Harry of Hereford' (i.e. Bolingbroke himself) is
motivated by his own insecurity and bad conscience.

Bolingbroke has accused Mowbray, Duke of Norfolk, among
other things, of plotting the death of 'Thomas of Woodstock',
the Duke of Gloucester. This murder, as a matter of historical
fact, was supervised by Mowbray at Calais in 1397, and King
Richard was very probably implicated. The accusation, therefore,
is just, and Bolingbroke is doing his duty as a loyal subject in
bringing to justice the murderer of the king's uncle. But, since
the king is not guiltless in the matter, he is also appearing in the
classic role of the man who knows too much. Richard, acting out
different roles in turn, first tries to reconcile the combatants and
make light of the whole affair; then, standing on his dignity as a
king ('We were not born to sue, but to command'), he orders

them to settle it by single combat; on the appointed day, they appear in the lists, and the king allows the whole procedure to unfold until the very moment when they begin to fight, then suddenly halts them and announces his decision to banish them both, Bolingbroke for ten years, Norfolk for ever. On the intercession of Bolingbroke's father, John of Gaunt, he arbitrarily shortens his sentence to six years, but Norfolk remains banished for life. The whole vacillating performance, carried out with superb assurance at any given moment but with no consistency of purpose, starts the play with a clear demonstration of Richard's unfitness to govern and the contrasting firmness and uprightness of Bolingbroke. Particularly since Shakespeare could count on a knowledge, among the more informed of the audience, of Richard's involvement in the crime. Yet by the play's end, Richard is a hallowed corpse and Bolingbroke an uneasy king. A sin has been committed, albeit a sin from which in the end a healing power can be distilled. A long expiation must be acted out, and a second generation must fight the battles, and face the issues, over again. Immediately, the attention moves to the all-important character of Prince Hal, the future Henry V.

v

Shakespeare, throughout his life, had much to say about the relationship of parent and child. We have only to think of the intensity of Hamlet's feelings towards his dead father and living mother; or of the terrible symphony of *King Lear*, scored for two suffering fathers and a total of five variously reacting offspring. Fathers bereft of their daughters recur constantly throughout the plays: from Shylock, whose loss is permanent, to Leontes, who is reunited with Perdita through the generosity of a fate that goes beyond his deserving. The two parts of *Henry IV* are Shakespeare's first large-scale study of the father-and-son relationship. Since these are political plays, the relationship is seen in its political light: dying king to emerging prince. But the personal feeling between the two is indicated with a very sure hand.

Already, before the end of *Richard II*, Prince Hal has entered the drama by hearsay. Shakespeare plants him, so that we shall be ready for his flowering in the later plays, with a short and generalized description. Bolingbroke, assembled with his supporters in council, asks uneasily, 'Can no man tell me of my unthrifty son?' Apparently no man can, except that he is wandering in London and is a great frequenter of 'taverns' with 'unrestrained loose companions'.

From this, a practised playgoer of Shakespeare's day, or any other day, would be able to foresee a feast of low-life observation. What dramatist, handling so grave and lofty a theme, would miss such an opening for comic relief? Obviously the prince's tavern companions will be seen on the stage, and every drop of wild fun extracted from their rogueries. Even a dramatist with no taste for comic relief would feel obliged to bring in a little of it, since the legend of Prince Hal's wildness, attested by almost every sixteenth-century historical writer, had passed into folk-lore. The audience would feel cheated without a few scenes of tavern life and a few memorable comic characters. We can fairly say, in view of what they were given, that no audience was ever less cheated.

However, we will bracket that discussion off for a moment. Our concern just now is the relationship between Henry IV and his son. The older man is labouring under a curse that cannot be lifted except by the new generation. (This again is a Shakespearean theme, running right through the plays and finding its fullest expression in the final group of 'romances', in which the evil set in motion by the parents is healed and forgiven by the children.) As a usurper, he can never press his claim to the loyalty of his associates. He can only rely on their forbearance and their wish for a stable government; and, when this is not sufficient — as it inevitably is not — he must be strong enough to crush them by force. Hence his obsessive concern with what he calls 'opinion', or what modern political parlance would call his 'image'. When, faced with the threat of the rebellion of the northern earls, he musters his strength, Prince Hal emerges from his *demi-monde* and reports for duty. The king takes the opportunity to caution him about this same 'image', in a speech that is a masterpiece of incomprehension.

> Had I so lavish of my presence been,
> So common-hackney'd in the eyes of men,
> So stale and cheap to vulgar company,
> Opinion, that did help me to the crown,
> Had still kept loyal to possession
> And left me in reputeless banishment
> A fellow of no mark nor likelihood.
> By being seldom seen, I could not stir
> But like a comet I was wond'red at;
> That men would tell their children, 'This is he;'
> Others would say, 'Where, which is Bolingbroke?'
> And then I stole all courtesy from heaven,
> And dress'd myself in such humility
> That I did pluck allegiance from men's hearts,
> Loud shouts and salutations from their mouths,
> Even in the presence of the crowned king.
> Thus did I keep my person fresh and new,
> My presence, like a robe pontifical,
> Ne'er seen but wond'red at.

He is not exaggerating; this careful grooming for the public was apparent in him from the beginning, and was scornfully noticed by King Richard:

> Ourself and Bushy, Bagot here, and Green
> Observ'd his courtship to the common people;
> How he did seem to dive into their hearts
> With humble and familiar courtesy;
> What reverence he did throw away on slaves,
> Wooing poor craftsmen with the craft of smiles
> And patient underbearing of his fortune,
> As 'twere to banish their affects with him.
> Off goes his bonnet to an oyster-wench;
> A brace of draymen bid God speed him well,
> And had the tribute of his supple knee,
> With 'Thanks, my countrymen, my loving friends;'
> As were our England in reversion his,
> And he our subjects' next degree in hope.

Henry's fear now is that his role and Richard's will be reversed by the next generation. Harry Percy, son to the rebel Earl of Northumberland, is the Bolingbroke of the present time; people look to him as a natural leader.

> Now, by my sceptre and my soul to boot,
> He hath more worthy interest to the state
> Than thou the shadow of succession;
> For of no right, nor colour like to right,
> He doth fill fields with harness in the realm,
> Turns head against the lion's armed jaws;
> And, being no more in debt to years than thou,
> Leads ancient lords and reverend bishops on
> To bloody battles and to bruising arms.

All this is memorably said. But, like most fathers, Henry is the last person to be able to read the mind of his own son. In fact, the prince is as conscious of his public *persona* as his father could ever have been. He is merely going about things in a different way — conscious, no doubt, that to repeat a brilliant performance in the same terms is inevitably to be undervalued by the onlookers. A new achievement demands a new idiom. His father, with no hereditary title to the throne, anxiously wooed the populace with courtesy and smiles; he, armed with that hereditary title, will affect nonchalance and irresponsibility, until the moment is ripe for a spectacular reform which will make him the focus of all eyes. We do not have to deduce all this. He has said so, in the bluntest possible terms. After the first scene in which we find him with his madcap companions, when we make the acquaintance of Falstaff and hear the prince agreeing to accompany the others on a robbery, he waits onstage while the others make their exit, and then announces his motives clearly enough for the slowest member of the audience to get the idea.

> I know you all, and will awhile uphold
> The unyok'd humour of your idleness:
> Yet herein will I imitate the sun,
> Who doth permit the base contagious clouds

> To smother up his beauty from the world,
> That when he please again to be himself,
> Being wanted, he may be more wond'red at
> By breaking through the foul and ugly mists
> Of vapours that did seem to strangle him.
> If all the year were playing holidays,
> To sport would be as tedious as to work;
> But when they seldom come, they wish'd for come,
> And nothing pleaseth but rare accidents.
> So, when this loose behaviour I throw off,
> And pay the debt I never promised,
> By how much better than my word I am,
> By so much shall I falsify men's hopes;
> And like bright metal on a sullen ground,
> My reformation, glitt'ring o'er my fault,
> Shall show more goodly and attract more eyes
> Than that which hath no foil to set it off.
> I'll so offend to make offence a skill,
> Redeeming time when men think least I will.

Anyone who misunderstands after *that* statement must have his own very strong motives for doing so. The whole thing is staged with an eye on the propaganda value of a volte-face. 'I'll so offend, to make offence a skill.' In fact, he makes it not only a skill but a cool business transaction. Small wonder that in his first interview with his father, Hal explains himself in commercial terms. He will allow Harry Percy to heap up honours, and then at one swoop transfer them to himself. It is like allowing a rival business to build itself up to a maximum before coming in with your take-over bid.

> Percy is but my factor, good my lord,
> To engross up glorious deeds on my behalf;
> And I will call him to so strict account
> That he shall render every glory up,
> Yea, even the slightest worship of his time,
> Or I will tear the reckoning from his heart.

At this, King Henry is reassured, the two are reconciled, and Hal duly goes to the battlefield and despatches Hotspur. Once this is done, however, he reverts to his former ways. The kingdom is no longer in immediate danger; his father, though feeble, is alive; and therefore the time is not ripe for his complete regeneration, that scrubbing and polishing of the outer surface that must be carefully timed.

His father, as usual, fails to see beyond the surface, and as soon as he enquires for Hal's whereabouts and is told that he is dining in London with his old gang of 'followers', he bursts out,

> The blood weeps from my heart when I do shape,
> In forms imaginary, th' unguided days
> And rotten times that you shall look upon
> When I am sleeping with my ancestors.
> For when his headstrong riot hath no curb,
> When rage and hot blood are his counsellors,
> When means and lavish manners meet together,
> O, with what wings shall his affections fly
> Towards fronting peril and oppos'd decay!

Other people can already see the prince's strategy; Warwick, to whom this outburst is addressed, replies soothingly that the young man 'but studies his companions Like a strange tongue' and will ultimately 'turn past evils to advantages'. But Henry is not convinced. And the suspicion in his heart is not stilled until that strange and tempestuous death-bed scene, when father and son at last confess to the love they bear one another.

And even then, lying back in exhaustion with no more than a few minutes of life left to him, Henry IV still has a piece of cool Machiavellian counsel to offer his son. He has spoken continually of undertaking a Crusade in the Holy Land, as an act of piety and expiation. Now, he calmly tells his son that the real motive was to provide employment for hotheads who might otherwise grow restive and turn their aggressiveness against the throne. So don't forget, my boy—plenty of military expeditions on foreign soil.

> Therefore, my Harry,
> Be it thy course to busy giddy minds
> With foreign quarrels, that action, hence borne out,
> May waste the memory of the former days.

The advice is not lost on the prince. But then he had probably made up his mind on these lines well in advance.

A few minutes later we have a beautifully contrived scene in which the new king meets his old adversary, the Lord Chief Justice. This upright man, a watchful enemy of Falstaff and his crew, has always striven to discipline the prince into good behaviour, and on one occasion even committed him to prison. Now, he expects to pay for his boldness with his life. He faces the prospect bravely, though he cannot conceal his dismay. In the event, Harry publicly congratulates him; the reconciliation between them is the first act of his reign. There follows a conversation during which Harry utters the strange and significant words,

> My father is gone wild into his grave,
> For in his tomb lie my affections;
> And with his spirits sadly I survive.

On the surface, the meaning of these lines is the same as that of Canterbury's words in the first scene of *Henry V*:

> The breath no sooner left his father's body,
> But that his wildness, mortified in him,
> Seem'd to die too; yea, at that very moment,
> Consideration like an angel came
> And whipp'd th' offending Adam out of him.

Henry IV has 'gone wild into his grave' because he has taken with him the wildness of Henry V. By dying, he has released his son from the necessity of upholding 'the unyoked humour' of Falstaff and the rest. Harry is free to welcome the gravity of a king's life, whereas for reasons of policy he had rejected the staidness of a model prince. (That unlovely role is left to the 'sober-blooded boy', his brother John.)

But there are other meanings hanging about the new king's words, and we cannot quite dispel them even if we are wholeheartedly behind his calculated statesmanship. 'Affections' did, in Elizabethan English, mean 'disposition to wildness'. It also meant warm impulses of the kind that are associated with being 'affectionate' in the modern sense. Thus Ophelia says to her father, speaking of Hamlet,

> He hath, my lord, of late made many tenders
> Of his affection to me.

To 'affect' something was to have a violent fondness for it; the nearest modern expression would be 'a craze'. It is interesting that the word has survived into our time in two such widely separated fragments as 'affectionate' and 'affected', meaning something one falsely pretends to. The same uncertainty dogged the term, evidently, in the sixteenth century; it is not a matter of linguistics so much as of ordinary human instability; no one is quite sure what he loves or needs. But for our immediate purposes it will suffice to notice that Harry declares his 'affections' dead and buried in his father's grave. And in terms of the action of the play, this means the sacrifice of Falstaff. Because Falstaff arouses the whole range of feelings that come under the term 'affection', now or in the sixteenth century. To be fond of such a man is disreputable, since it means condoning lechery, drunkenness and deceit. It is also creditable, since gaiety, wit and imperturbable good humour are great human virtues. If Falstaff is Hal's 'affection', he is also ours.

VI

It is obvious that Shakespeare, like any working dramatist, would make his first rough sketch of Falstaff in terms of the necessities of the play. If he was to allow the relationship between King Henry and Prince Hal to develop at its natural pace, which would mean spreading it over two plays instead of bundling it into one, there would be a need for comic relief on an unprecedented scale. And this in turn would provide a welcome glimpse of English common life. So far, the historical plays have neglected the English people almost entirely. Characters below the rank of knight come into the plays chiefly as paid murderers or rioting insurgents. Occasionally one of them appears in the role of *vox populi*, like the gardener in *Richard II*. But such figures have no tang of the soil. They are as impersonal as the Greek chorus whose function they partly inherit.

The sub-plot which Shakespeare planned to run through the two parts of *Henry IV* was doubtless planned at the beginning to change all that. From the council chamber and the battlefield, these scenes were going to take us out into the lanes and hedgerows, the alleys and taprooms. And all this is faithfully carried out. This underplot is Shakespeare's most elaborate portrait of the common life of his time. He had already given us Bottom the Weaver, Quince, Snout, Flute, and the rest in *A Midsummer Night's Dream*. But these rustics are designed to appear in a play which also contains fairies. Accordingly, they are fantasticated and lit by moonlight. They are half Warwickshire rustics and half gnomes. But Justice Shallow and his neighbour Silence, his servant Davy, and his tenants Mouldy, Wart and Bullcalf are pure Cotswold types. Francis the drawer is a London apprentice, Mrs. Quickly a garrulous hostess, Poins the reckless younger son of a good family, Nym and Bardolph common sneak-thieves and ruffians. As for Pistol, he is some half-crazed swaggerer who once acted for a season with a group of strolling players and has his head full of high-sounding lines, half-remembered from Marlowe, in consequence. (It is evident that the long struggle to get free of Marlowe's influence was still one of Shakespeare's problems at this time.) And Falstaff is the presiding Lord of Misrule. As a knight with a taste for low company, he can move easily in all areas of the plot, consorting with noblemen in one scene and tapsters in another. Beyond that, we cannot pin him down. He is real with a largeness that swamps ordinary realism. Unflagging, light-hearted, never at a loss for a joke, he is the apotheosis of the English public-house companion. He is the man we are always hoping to meet in the bar.

There, if Shakespeare had been an ordinarily good dramatist, the matter would have ended. Falstaff and his companions would have furnished an amusing series of scenes, taking us out and about and bringing us into contact with everyday scenes and people; then, when the long-heralded reform came to pass, they would have been swept, still laughable amid their grumbling and discomfiture, into the limbo that awaits comic characters when there is no more comic action to be played out.

What Shakespeare gives us, as usual, is something far richer than we could have thought of without him. To begin with, he shapes the first and second parts of *Henry IV* into two quite separate plays, each with its own atmosphere, and each self-sufficient and containing a completed action. Falstaff is equally important in each play, but in different ways. In Part 1, his main function is to embody a certain attitude towards the play's main subject, which is honour. In Part 2, his role is sacrificial and verges on the tragic.

Let us take these two in order. *Henry IV*, Part 1, is a play about honour. Three conceptions of honour are presented; they are thrown into conflict, and the one that comes out uppermost is the one England needs most. First, there is Harry Hotspur with his mediaeval notion of honour as something bound up entirely with a man's self-esteem. He puts honour before everything else; freely admitting, for instance, that he comes to the conference-table not with any idea of making a reasonable agreement, but solely to defend his honour. He is ready to fight with Owen Glendower over a fancied inequality in their share of the intended conquest, but as soon as Glendower generously yields his claim, Hotspur at once declares that he does not want the land at all, only the 'honour' of not being overruled.

> I do not care: I'll give thrice so much land
> To any well-deserving friend:
> But in the way of bargain, mark ye me,
> I'll cavil on the ninth part of a hair.

This is the conception of 'honour' which makes him boast in joyous arrogance,

By heaven, methinks it were an easy leap
To pluck bright honour from the pale-faced moon,
Or dive into the bottom of the deep,
Where fathom-line could never touch the ground,
And pluck up drowned honour by the roots.

Hotspur's main function in the play is to serve as a foil to Prince Hal. His flaring personal notion of honour helps to bring out by contrast the inconspicuous merits of the prince's notion. His is the code of the mediaeval knight — that his personal reputation must never for one instant be under a cloud, nor must he be expected to give way in any dispute. Hal, by contrast, can make a friend of the justice who had him locked up with common criminals. His notion of honour is a corporate, impersonal one. Honour is what is good for the state. The best kind of honour for a king to have is the kind that will help him to rule effectively. Where Hotspur flies into a rage at the first suspicion that someone is trying to cross him, Hal remains imperturbable under the most scathing rebukes, except when they come from his father.

Both Hotspur and Hal are still very much with us. Contemporary history is always throwing up figures who remind us strongly of one or the other. There is the kind of politician whose first thought is for his own reputation, his own impact, the careful fostering of his own 'legend'. Such a man will often do heroic work for a cause, and then, at the bidding of his personal ambition or some shift in his opinions, turn and betray it. But always there is a counterbalancing supply of the type represented by Hal: those who sink their identity in that of the larger unit — the team, the organization, the country.

There remains a third attitude to honour. Both Hal and Hotspur are natural leaders, men to whom it comes easily to make sacrifices in the pursuit of an end. Hal's end is less selfish than Hotspur's, but on the other hand Hotspur is self-forgetful in his own fashion. He scorns to consider his own safety or comfort where honour is at stake. If the action concerned itself only with a simple opposition of these two, it would be open to a puncturing irony. The voice of *l'homme moyen sensuel* has to be heard at some point. It is an old discovery that high-flown sentiments can be voiced in literature so long as the belly also has its voice. 'But to the girdle do the gods inherit.' The passionate idealism of Romeo and Juliet would be deflated by cynical comment from the cheap seats, were it not that this comment is supplied in the play itself, by Mercutio with his young man's bawdry and the Nurse with her old woman's earthiness. Between them they make the love story invulnerable to irony.

Similarly with Falstaff. Like Hotspur, he is primarily a creature of the plot. The rival conceptions of honour would suffer from our ironic contemplation if he were not there to provide an irony we could never rise to. He says it all for us, and so much more that we could never have said for ourselves.

PRINCE. Say thy prayers, and farewell.
FALSTAFF. I would 'twere bed-time, Hal, and all well.
PRINCE. Why, thou owest God a death.
FALSTAFF. 'Tis not due yet: I would be loath to pay him before his day. What need I be so forward with him that calls not on me? Well, 'tis no matter; honour pricks me on. Yea, but how if honour prick me off when I come on? how then? Can honour set to a leg? No. Or an arm? No. Or take away the grief of a wound? No. Honour hath no skill in surgery then? No. What is honour? a word. What is in that word, honour? Air. A trim reckoning! Who hath it? he that died o' Wednesday. Doth he feel it? No. Doth he hear it? No. 'Tis insensible, then? Yea, to the dead. But will it not live with the living? No. Why? Detraction will not suffer it. Therefore I'll none of it. Honour is a mere scutcheon. And so ends my catechism.

With this, the range of human notions of honour is complete. Falstaff speaks for the common man, content with no more than a common share of honour. The common Englishman is capable of heroism, but not of heroic speeches. He can lay down his life for an ideal, but he cannot talk about laying down his life for an ideal. Nor can he bear to listen, for long, to anyone else talking about it. When the resounding oratory begins, he feels he is being cheated by someone. The leaders who can best rally and inspire him are those who confine themselves, as Churchill did, mainly to the expression of defiance.

That, roughly, is Falstaff's role in Part 1 of *Henry IV*. He provides the worm's eye view of honour, thus making a debate out of what would otherwise be a simple juxtaposition. And he provides fun — incomparable, glorious fun, never approached anywhere else in English literature. Even Chaucer, even Dickens, never come near the Falstaff scenes. If I forbear to comment on them, that is merely because there is nothing to be said from outside. With the exception of the mock-trial scene, of which we shall speak in a moment, they are pure gaiety and high spirits, without undertow or afterthought.

In Part 2, however, a change comes over the Falstaff scenes. As everyone has always noticed, the untroubled gaiety of Part 1 has gone. Falstaff is still magnificently himself — he bears no relation to the travesty Shakespeare was obliged to cook up in *The Merry Wives of Windsor* — but the landscape in which he gambols is a sadder one, its foliage nipped by a touch of frost. His role is now a sacrificial one. The Prince, his reputation already almost redeemed and his responsibilities almost upon him, returns briefly to the *demi-monde*, but with less than his old zest. He knows, and we know, that the party is nearly over. Time, the chief enemy of Falstaff's brand of irresponsible gaiety, is on everyone's mind. Even Falstaff himself has become conscious of his age. In the first Part, there were plenty of farcical references to it ('How long is't ago, Jack, since thou sawest thine own knee?', etc., etc.) but they were easily swept aside as part of the fun. Now, suddenly, the fact of his age is inescapable. When, in the first act, he offers the Lord Chief Justice the calm impertinence of, 'You that are old consider not the capacities of us that are young,' he gets a stern answer. 'Have you not a moist eye? a dry hand? a yellow cheek? a white beard? a decreasing leg? an increasing belly? is not your voice broken? your wind short? your chin double? your wit single? and every part about you blasted with antiquity?' To this formidable catalogue, Falstaff makes a flippant reply; but the charge is proven. He is old, and his age acts as a kind of super-fault which makes all his other faults inexcusable. Though in Part 1 there are plenty of joking references to whoring, in this part we actually see him with his whore, Doll Tearsheet. And suddenly the pathos of an old man's dependence on the affection of a bought girl is there, inescapably, before us.

> FALSTAFF. Thou dost give me flattering busses.
> DOLL. By my troth, I kiss thee with a most constant heart.
> FALSTAFF. I am old, I am old.
> DOLL. I love thee better than I love e'er a scurvy young boy of them all.
> FALSTAFF. What stuff wilt have a kirtle of? I shall receive money a Thursday. Shalt have a cap to-morrow. A merry song, come. 'A grows late; we'll to bed. Thou't forget me when I am gone.

We do not doubt that she loves him. But this only underscores the pathos. The Falstaff of Part 1 does not need to seek for love. He is the spirit of gaiety; all created life loves him. In Part 2, he is an old man who craves to stay in the sunshine a little longer.

It is not that Falstaff's character changes. It is rather that, as with Satan in *Paradise Lost*, we are shown progressively sadder and darker sides of the same character. The world of Part 2 is a drabber world, more realistically drawn. The scene, for instance, where Mrs. Quickly and Doll Tearsheet are arrested by the beadles, on what would nowadays be called 'a morals charge', is lurid enough to foreshadow the world of Mistress Overdone in *Measure for Measure*, or the hideous brothel in *Pericles*. Cursing and spitting, the two women are hauled away by leather-faced officials. To Doll's claim that she is pregnant, and Mrs. Quickly's vengeful cry of 'I pray God the fruit of her womb miscarry' — so that they can lodge a complaint of ill-treatment — the stolid beadle replies, 'If it do, you shall have a dozen of cushions again; you have but eleven now'. This is realism worthy of Zola, the cobweb-scrubbing realism of the post-Romantic novel.

We see the same disenchantment in the scene where Falstaff is

misusing his commission as an officer by accepting bribes to release conscripted men. This was glanced at in Part 1, where
Falstaff gives a joking account of having 'misus'd the king's press
damnably'. But, as with the whoring, to hear about it is one
thing, to watch him engaged in it quite another. When Shallow's
tenants present themselves to answer the call to arms, a whisper
from Bardolph ('I have three pound to free Mouldy and Bullcalf') is sufficient to get these two stalwart men waved aside with,
'for you, Mouldy, stay at home till you are past service: — and
or your part, Bullcalf, grow till you come into it: — I will none
of you'.

It is worth noticing here that Shakespeare's realism is not of the
muck-raking kind that never admits to recognizing good qualities
in human beings. The cowardice of Mouldy and Bullcalf is all
too credible and understandable. So is the greedy opportunism
of Falstaff, rejecting the two fittest men because they can afford
to bribe him, and filling his muster with the least promising. But
even in this *milieu* there is a flash of courage and manliness, such
as everyday life generally provides. Francis Feeble, 'a woman's
tailor', is good for a laugh, especially since the word 'tailor' was
some sort of coarse joke in Elizabethan English; it meant, I understand, the sexual organ; hence Falstaff's reply to 'Shall I prick
him?' with 'if he had been a man's tailor, he'd ha' pricked you.'
But Feeble, with his comic name and his comic occupation, is a
brave man.

> By my troth, I care not; a man can die but once; we owe God a
> death. I'll ne'er bear a base mind. An't be my destiny, so; an't be
> not, so. No man's too good to serve's prince; and let it go which way
> it will, he that dies this year is quit for the next.

Falstaff's image is badly tarnished by the time we have sat
through these scenes. It was all very well for comfortable Vic-
torian men of letters to smile indulgently at Falstaff's misuse of the
press. But Shakespeare's audience included many who had
suffered, or might suffer in the future, from this kind of injustice.

Falstaff's swindling of Justice Shallow is another matter; he is implicated in the general grab for money and advantage; he is servile to Falstaff because he thinks Falstaff will be a royal favourite. He lends him a thousand pounds because he has grasped that 'a friend at court is better than a penny in purse'. The England we are visiting here is no picture-postcard island of sturdy yeomen and pretty thatched roofs. It is a place where money talks, where poor men are ill-treated and the law abused.

Falstaff, in his turn, sees Shallow not only as a source of revenue but as excellent copy. 'I will devise matter enough out of this Shallow to keep Prince Harry in continual laughter the wearing-out of six fashions.' He follows this with a remark that is one of the keys to the play.

'O, it is much that a lie with a slight oath, and a jest with a sad brow, will do with a fellow that never had the ache in his shoulders.'

In those words, Falstaff's life lies open to the cruel daylight. His joking description to Doll Tearsheet of Hal as 'a good shallow young fellow' was, it seems, no joke. If he is using Shallow, he is also using Hal. Shallow is vulnerable because he is provincial, senile and foolish. Hal is vulnerable because he knows nothing of life. He 'never had the ache in his shoulders', never knew the heaviness and weariness of everyday existence. And so to tickle him with a jest is to manipulate him.

Falstaff is wrong, and from the start we have known him to be wrong. But now, increasingly, his wrongness matters. He is fixed on a collision course which will smash him against Hal's granite royalty. He makes self-destructive error after error. His calculation is suddenly revealed as shoddy and superficial. On the news of the king's death, he rides day and night to be at Hal's coronation, arriving travel-stained and ungroomed, as a piece of deliberate staging. ('It shows my earnestness of affection.') With horrified fascination, we watch him offer himself up for sacrifice. But when the axe falls, it is enough to make one turn away one's eyes.

FALSTAFF.   My king! My Jove! I speak to thee, my heart!
KING HENRY V. I know thee not, old man. Fall to thy prayers.
                How ill white hairs become a fool and jester!
                I have long dreamt of such a kind of man,
                So surfeit-swell'd, so old, and so profane;
                But, being awak'd, I do despise my dream.

Once again it is Falstaff's age that counts most against him. In five
lines, it is thrown in his teeth three times. In the first line he is
'old', in the second he has 'white hairs', in the fourth he is 'old'
again. The new king passes on, and Falstaff is left standing in the
street, with Shallow at his side demanding his thousand pounds
back on the spot. A few minutes later, by what seems a deliberate
piece of cruelty (for, as Dr. Johnson pointed out, he has committed no new offence), he is arrested and carried off to the Fleet
prison. He has paid for Hal's wild oats; the score is settled, and it
is Falstaff who has settled it.

On that dreadful occasion, Falstaff makes no plea for himself.
He is given no chance to do so. But, perhaps unable to be as un-
fair to him as Hal must inevitably be, Shakespeare has already
given him a chance to speak up in his own defence. Back in Part
I (Act II, Scene iv), Hal and Falstaff act out a little comedy for
the amusement of their tavern companions. They take it in turns
to guy King Henry reproving his son. When Hal acts the part of
his father, he utters a special warning against associating with
'that swoll'n parcel of dropsies, that huge bombard of sack, that
stuff'd cloakbag of guts'. Falstaff, impersonating Hal, makes a
moving plea, in the course of which he soars upward from his
familiar prose to conclude with three lines of stately verse — a
sure sign, in Shakespeare, that lofty matter is at hand.

That he is old — the more the pity — his white hairs do witness
it; but that he is — saving your reverence — a whoremaster, that I
utterly deny. If sack and sugar be a fault, God help the wicked!
If to be old and merry be a sin, then many an old host that I know
is damn'd: if to be fat be to be hated, then Pharaoh's lean kine are
to be loved. No, my good lord: banish Peto, banish Bardolph,

banish Poins; but, for sweet Jack Falstaff, kind Jack Falstaff, true Jack Falstaff, valiant Jack Falstaff — and therefore more valiant, being, as he is, old Jack Falstaff — banish not him thy Harry's company, banish not him thy Harry's company. Banish plump Jack, and banish all the world.

PRINCE. I do, I will.

Immediately after Hal's quietly menacing words, we have the stage-direction 'A knocking heard'. We know that knocking. It is the hand of the cold reality which tells us we must search our pockets and pay up. It is the knocking on the gate in *Macbeth*. Or the knocking of Aeneas on the chamber door of Troilus and Cressida, when he comes to bear the news that Cressida must leave. 'Banish plump Jack, and banish all the world' is exactly the challenge Hal must take up. And when, finally, he says of his father 'in his tomb lie my affections,' the fullness of his meaning is precisely that this has been accomplished.

VII

With the right king at last on the throne, only one task remained: to show his heroic example bearing fruit. *Henry V*, the crown and apex of all the historical plays, is also the one that must have given Shakespeare the worst misgiving. Nothing is harder than to depict success and make it interesting. A perfect king is far less compelling on the stage than a fiendish king. But it had to be done: the series could not be left to peter out on a promise of future greatness. So Shakespeare did the only thing open to him. He got out his loudest horn and sounded a sustained blast of patriotism.

The result is very successful. The play holds the stage well — till the fifth act, at any rate — and it expresses a sense of triumphant national solidarity that only a fool would snigger at. Probably the last time the English felt really unified was in 1945: and there is no better way to recapture that feeling than to watch Olivier's film version of *Henry V*, tidied and trimmed here and there for the needs of a large and simple-minded audience, but very true to the central impulse of the play. And if, as a vehicle for patriotic emotion, the play was still doing effective duty in 1945, we need not wonder that it went down well during those years of a glowing, new-found national unity that followed the wreck of the Armada in 1588.

We can go further and say that, if *Henry V* did not exist, there would be a considerable hole in English literature. It is, as we remarked earlier (p. 29) our nearest equivalent to a national patriotic epic. When we think of epic poetry in English, we naturally think first of *Paradise Lost*, which is pretty well our only successful attempt at the classical epic, modelled after Homer and Virgil, with a large and serious subject, an exalted tone, an air of magnificent stateliness. There have been other attempts, but they are mostly unreadable and their names are known only to students of literary history. There is, however, strong evidence that Shakespeare, had circumstances turned his gifts in that direction, could have written a narrative poem in the exalted epic manner. Whenever he has an opportunity, he produces specimens of narrative verse that are magnificent. The player king's speech in *Hamlet*, for instance, is a superb piece of formal epic narrative. It is, however, strongly stylized, to make it stand out from the verse of the surrounding passages, so we need not imagine that if Shakespeare had written a long epic poem he would have pitched it consistently in such a high-flown manner. Probably a much better guide to his practice in a long poem is to be found in the speeches of the Prologue in *Henry V*. This character stands outside the dramatic action and contributes five prologues and an epilogue. His speeches have a twofold function. They supply information, and they build up the lofty patriotic atmosphere. Of these, the second function is far the more important, since other plays whose action is just as complex, indeed much more so, get along without this kind of plot-feeding commentary. The speeches of 'Prologue' also serve a third purpose. They apologize for the fact that the stage sometimes falls below the grandeur and dignity required by the action. At such moments, a curious uncertainty of tone creeps into the speeches and makes them rather poor. In a few lines 'Prologue' can drop from the heights of

> Now all the youth of England are on fire,
> And silken dalliance in the wardrobe lies;
> Now thrive the armourers, and honour's thought
> Reigns solely in the breast of every man:
> They sell the pasture now to buy the horse,
> Following the mirror of all Christian kings
> With winged heels as English Mercuries.
> For now sits Expectation in the air,
> And hides a sword from hilts unto the point
> With crowns imperial, crowns, and coronets,
> Promis'd to Harry and his followers.
> The French, advis'd by good intelligence
> Of this most dreadful preparation,
> Shake in their fear and with pale policy
> Seek to divert the English purposes.
> O England! model to thy inward greatness,
> Like little body with a mighty heart,
> What mightst thou do that honour would thee do,
> Were all thy children kind and natural!

to the apologetic banality of

>   the scene
> Is now transported, gentles, to Southampton:
> There is the play-house now, there must you sit,
> And thence to France shall we convey you safe
> And bring you back, charming the narrow seas
> To give you gentle pass; for, if we may,
> We'll not offend one stomach with our play.

Even the apologetic speeches add something valuable. They set the action in an epic framework. And they indicate a kind of reaching-out towards the stateliness of epic narrative, free from the necessities of crape hair and stage armies, that gives a valuable clue to Shakespeare's state of mind. He would really like to be writing an epic. The continual references by 'Prologue' to the irksome limitations of stagecraft, wherein the theatre becomes a 'wooden O', the stage soldiers 'four or five most vile and ragged foils, Right ill-dispos'd in brawl ridiculous,' show a very real impatience, for the moment, with dramatic poetry. If this is to be the English *Aeneid*, Shakespeare wishes — at least for the time being — that he could go the whole distance and be an unfettered epic poet. Even within the play, the style is always pulling towards epic, like a hound on the leash. Take, for instance, the little inset (Act IV, Scene vi) where Exeter describes to the king the heroic deaths of Suffolk and York.

EXETER.   The Duke of York commends him to your majesty.
KING HENRY. Lives he, good uncle? Thrice within this hour.
                  I saw him down; thrice up again, and fighting;
                  From helmet to the spur all blood he was.
EXETER.   In which array, brave soldier, doth he lie
                  Larding the plain; and by his bloody side,
                  Yoke-fellow to his honour-owing wounds,
                  The noble Earl of Suffolk also lies.
                  Suffolk first died; and York, all haggled over,
                  Comes to him, where in gore he lay insteeped,
                  And takes him by the beard, kisses the gashes
                  That bloodily did yawn upon his face,
                  He cries aloud 'Tarry, my cousin Suffolk.
                  My soul shall thine keep company to heaven;
                  Tarry, sweet soul, for mine, then fly abreast;
                  As in this glorious and well-foughten field
                  We kept together in our chivalry'.
                  Upon these words I came and cheer'd him up:
                  He smil'd me in the face, raught me his hand
                  And, with a feeble grip, says 'Dear my lord,
                  Commend my service to my sovereign'.
                  So did he turn, and over Suffolk's neck
                  He threw his wounded arm and kiss'd his lips;
                  And so, espous'd to death, with blood he seal'd
                  A testament of noble-ending love.
                  The pretty and sweet manner of it forc'd
                  Those waters from me which I would have stopp'd;
                  But I had not so much of man in me,
                  And all my mother came into mine eyes
                  And gave me up to tears.

This is not dramatic verse. It is epic. We may safely assume that if Shakespeare had written a poem of the length of *Paradise Lost*, on a patriotic theme, this would have been the manner of it.

I do not mean to suggest, however, that because *Henry V* is strongly flavoured with epic it is therefore weak as drama. Shakespeare was already too experienced in the theatre to write anything undramatic. He was merely giving a demonstration of his skill by writing a play that had the qualities of that epic poem he had to miss the chance of writing. We see this nowhere more clearly than in the scenes that concern ordinary life — the soldiers in the camp, the various humiliations of Pistol, and so forth. There is comedy here, but it is kept within strict bounds and is given a military flavour, as when Fluellen makes Pistol eat the leek. As in the preceding plays, we are kept in touch with ordinary men, but these are ordinary men in a grave mood, their powers gathered together to meet a great occasion. Even the funny men are touched with an epic seriousness. Without deserting the comic-realistic idiom of the Falstaff episodes, Shakespeare eases out the purely farcical element and brings in notes of a pure elegiac sadness. Mrs. Quickly's account of the death of Falstaff is a miraculous piece of writing. The good hostess is just as voluble as ever, just as prone to incorrect usages and slips of the tongue, but she achieves an epitaph far beyond the range of any words we could find for ourselves.

> BARDOLPH. Would I were with him, wheresome'er he is, either in.
> heaven or in hell!
> HOSTESS. Nay, sure, he's not in hell: he's in Arthur's bosom, if ever
> man went to Arthur's bosom. 'A made a finer end, and went away
> an it had been any christom child; 'a parted ev'n just between
> twelve and one, ev'n at the turning o' th' tide; for after I saw him
> fumble with the sheets, and play with flowers, and smile upon his
> fingers' end, I knew there was but one way; for his nose was as
> sharp as a pen, and 'a babbl'd of green fields. 'How now, Sir
> John!' quoth I 'What, man, be o' good cheer.' So 'a cried out
> 'God, God, God!' three or four times. Now I, to comfort him,
> bid him 'a should not think of God; I hop'd there was no need

to trouble himself with any such thoughts yet. So 'a bade me lay more clothes on his feet; I put my hand into the bed and felt them, and they were as cold as any stone; then I felt to his knees, and so upward and upward, and all was as cold as any stone.

The Falstaffian music is fleetingly heard once more, but in a key that makes it melancholy and dignified. There is no finer achievement in all Shakespeare. The death of Falstaff takes on the same kind of lofty pathos as the death of Dido in the *Aeneid*. It can fittingly take its place in the epic world of an English Aeneas. And this is what Henry V has become. He has shed his ordinary humanity and become the embodiment of a nation's ideals.

VIII

In one of his Sonnets — the ninety-fourth — Shakespeare draws a rapid but masterly picture of the kind of person on whom power and authority sit naturally.

> They that have power to hurt, and will do none,
> That do not do the thing they most do show,
> Who, moving others, are themselves as stone,
> Unmoved, cold, and to temptation slow:
>
> They rightly do inherit heaven's graces,
> And husband nature's riches from expense;
> They are the lords and owners of their faces,
> Others, but stewards of their excellence. . . .

If we take this line by line, we see that it is a perfect portrait of Henry V. *They that have power to hurt, and will do none*, are not exactly the merciful and forgiving; a truly merciful man, gentle of heart and sensitive to the sufferings of others, does not have *power to hurt*; he may think himself obliged to inflict suffering, but he will recoil from the task before much damage is done. The kind of person the line refers to is the man of iron, perfectly able to inflict agonies without flinching, who does not do so because he knows that cruelty does not pay. And this is Henry exactly. Think, for instance, of his blood-curdling threats to the citizens of Harfleur, when he and his army, newly landed in France, are halted by this fortified town.

> If I begin the batt'ry once again,
> I will not leave the half-achieved Harfleur
> Till in her ashes she lie buried,
> The gates of mercy shall be all shut up. . . .
>
> . . . Therefore, you men of Harfleur,
> Take pity of your town and of your people
> Whiles yet my soldiers are in my command,
> While yet the cool temperate wind of grace
> O'erblows the filthy and contagious clouds
> Of heady murder, spoil, and villainy.
> If not — why, in a moment look to see
> The blind and bloody soldier with foul hand
> Defile the locks of your shrill-shrieking daughters;
> Your fathers taken by the silver beards,
> And their most reverend heads dash'd to the walls;
> Your naked infants spitted upon pikes,
> Whiles the mad mothers with their howls confus'd
> Do break the clouds, as did the wives of Jewry
> At Herod's bloody-hunting slaughtermen.
> What say you? Will you yield, and this avoid?
> Or, guilty in defence, be thus destroy'd?

The phrase 'guilty in defence' is a good piece of character observation. If the French are so wicked as to resist Harry the Fifth of England, who fights with God's full approval (two learned bishops have given him a certificate to this effect), then of course they must be punished by rape, pillage and indiscriminate slaughter — meted out, we note, by the same English soldiers who will be held up, later on, as a gallant band of outnumbered heroes. This is not inconsistency. It is realism. Common soldiers *are* heroic in a desperate situation; they are also cruel and licentious. By the time the battle of Agincourt is joined, Shakespeare has taken care to give Henry and his army every attribute that will win our sympathy; but he is too honest, even so, to gloss over the hardness that a military king must have. During a lull in the fighting, some French soldiers enter the English camp, which is guarded only by boys; they kill the boys and commit various acts of theft and destruction; 'wherefore', says Gower, discussing the incident with Fluellen, 'the king most worthily hath caused every soldier to cut his prisoner's throat. O, 'tis a gallant king!' But the word 'wherefore' is misleading. We, the audience, were present at the preceding scene, and we know that at the moment when Henry gave this order, he knew nothing about the attack on the camp; only that the French, having been beaten off, were returning to the attack.

> But, hark! what new alarum is this same?
> The French have reinforc'd their scatter'd men:
> Then every soldier kill his prisoners!
> Give the word through.

Shakespeare has sown various examples of a wise clemency throughout the play, so that we cannot think of Henry merely as a murderous ruffian; but the fact that he has *power to hurt* is made sufficiently plain.

Line 2, *That do not do the thing they most do show*, applies obviously enough to the prince we have seen in the two preceding plays, upholding the unyok'd humour of his companions' idleness. But for good measure we are given a first-rate demonstration of it in *Henry V*, Act II, when the king, choosing his time effectively, unmasks the conspirators Cambridge, Scroop and Grey. With complete outward calm he accepts their protestations of loyalty and good wishes for his French expedition, and even engages in an argument with them as to whether he should, or should not, pardon a man who has been imprisoned for offering him a personal insult. Then, when the cat-and-mouse game has gone far enough, he hands each man a scroll, purporting to be his royal commission for authority in the king's absence; actually they are indictments for treason. As the three open their papers and stand guilty and stunned, Henry treats the assembled nobility to a resounding speech on loyalty. His father, watching from the shades, could not demand a more polished performance.

> *Who, moving others, are themselves as stone,*
> *Unmoved, cold, and to temptation slow.*

All this is true of Henry V, but the phrase that is especially illustrated in this play is, of course, *moving others*. Henry is a magnificent orator. Shakespeare, who loved to write public speeches for his characters, has lavished on the hero of Agincourt some of his finest examples. The passage beginning 'This day is called the feast of Crispian' (Act IV, Scene iii) is the most celebrated patriotic speech in the English language; we have all heard it quoted, out of context, so many times that it is not easy to set it back in its dramatic place and consider the motivation behind it. Yet that motivation is complex enough to be interesting. Clearly, Henry is perfectly 'sincere' in the sense that he is prepared to fight bravely and wants his men to be no less brave than he is. Wandering through the camp, in the early hours of the morning, he talked *incognito* to the three soldiers Bates, Court and Williams; and what he heard there was the same bitter truth that any commander would hear, if he went among his troops before a battle.

KING HENRY. I myself heard the king say he would not be ransomed.
WILLIAMS. Ay, he said so, to make us fight cheerfully; but when our throats are cut, he may be ransomed, and we ne'er the wiser.
KING HENRY. If I live to see it, I will never trust his word after.
WILLIAMS. You pay him then! That's a perilous shot out of an elder-gun, that a poor and private displeasure can do against a monarch. You may as well go about to turn the sun to ice with fanning in his face with a peacock's feather. You'll never trust his word after! Come, 'tis a foolish saying.

'A perilous shot out of an elder-gun' means 'Very big deal. You'll shoot him with your pop-gun.' Toy guns for Elizabethan children were made by removing the pith from elder-wood; Williams is expressing the ordinary man's unshakeable conviction that the higher-ups will make use of him for their own purposes, to the accompaniment of fine words and uplift, and leave him in the mud when these purposes are answered. Henry fobs him off, first with a side-issue about a personal quarrel, and then with a piece of hearty banter. But the barb has stuck, and when he makes his great speech he emphasizes national solidarity above everything else. Anyone who fights beside the king shall be the king's brother; in addition, he will be certain of lifelong respect from the population in general; the 'gentlemen in England now abed' will permanently acknowledge an Agincourt veteran as a better man than themselves. I am not saying, of course, that the speech is delivered in a mood of cynicism; merely that Henry chooses, as he always must, exactly the right thing to say to his particular audience. He even borrows Hotspur's idiom for a few lines. 'The fewer men, the greater share of honour' is in Hotspur's character, not his own. So, for that matter, is his courtship of the French princess in the last act. The young man who has lived so many merry years does not need to say gruffly, 'If thou would have such a one, take me; and take me, take a soldier; take a soldier, take a king'. It is merely that he has selected the Hotspur *persona* as the one likely to make the best impression. *Moving others*, while yourself being *as stone*, involves this kind of projection, and he is a master of it. It is, in fact, quite impossible to tell whether Henry has any genuine feeling for Katharine. He has to marry her, partly because it is what such a man would naturally do, to underpin the peace treaty with a marriage, and partly because it is what the historical Henry V did, so that the audience would be expecting it. But I think an actor would be justified in giving these scenes any interpretation that squared with the words on the page — a Henry in love, or a Henry going through the necessary motions with gusto and good humour; or even a Henry in cynical mood, loading his performance with irony: *unmoved, cold, and to temptation slow*.

Such a character may seem to us merely distasteful, but it is evidently Shakespeare's earnest intention to show him as the man we need for the English throne. *They rightly do inherit heaven's graces;* including the grace of kingship. The *riches of nature* which such men *husband from expense* are enjoyed by all of us; a true king keeps society in order, sees that people do their jobs, and stops things from going to rack and ruin. Men like Henry are the *owners of their faces* — in complete command of their outward behaviour — while other people, whom they induce to serve their ends, are *stewards of their excellence,* called upon to administer it but not in a position to use it for their own profit — a thought that leads us straight back to the prince's description of Hotspur as his 'factor', running up a credit balance of honour for his, Hal's, benefit.

Shakespeare thought England was only safe when a man like Henry V was on the throne. This did not mean that he had to like Henry V. But he admired him, and he took a great deal of trouble to endow him with all the sympathetic qualities that such a man can have. Thus, he is wise enough to refrain from cruelty except when it is essential to terrify an enemy; he is free of the false pride of aristocracy that makes the high-born despise the common man; he sees and rewards merit. In his fooling with Fluellen and Williams, there is a kingly echo of his wild princeling days. Yet none of this is enough to rouse any real affection for him. He is no nearer to our hearts than Aeneas.

However, the play is more likeable than its hero. Because Shakespeare was honest and clear-sighted about the qualities that make a successful king, there is no need to talk about him as if he were some debunking writer of the 1920s. There is no sneer at courage or patriotism. The age of Jingoism, of the senseless nationalism of cheap newspapers, was still to come. And if we shiver at the lack of warmth in Henry we can find plenty of it in the people he governs. The characters of Gower, Fluellen, Macmorris and Jamy are all brilliantly sketched and all delightful. The scenes in which they figure are the ancestor of all stories that begin, 'There was an Englishman, an Irishman and a Scotsman . . .' My own favourite (and perhaps Shakespeare's, since of all these officers he has the largest part in the play) is Fluellen, the spelling of whose name indicates that the English tongue, then as now, balked at the Welsh double 'l'.

There are only three Welshmen in Shakespeare's plays: Sir Hugh Evans in *The Merry Wives of Windsor*, Owen Glendower in *Henry IV*, and Fluellen. Of these, Sir Hugh is an amusing sketch of a pedantic country schoolmaster; Glendower a powerful but generalized portrait of a half-legendary chieftain with mystical fervour and the reputation of a wizard; but Fluellen is a perfect miniature of the Welsh character — volatile, boastful, quixotic and so passionately literate that he questions everything that is not done according to the book; he knows 'the disciplines of war', and is fertile in parallels between things now happening and the episodes of the heroic past. His endearingly funny comparison of Henry V to Alexander the Great (Act IV, Scene vii) shows his ingrained bookishness. As any student of the Renaissance art of rhetoric can demonstrate, it is done in accordance with the accepted form of the 'comparison', beginning with a mention of the birthplaces of the two heroes, and going on via a description of the natural features of the places ('there is salmons in both') to a comparison of their two characters. In the course of this delicious foolery (on Shakespeare's part, that is: to Fluellen it is deadly serious) we suddenly get one of those small dramatic shocks that abound in Shakespeare. Fluellen unexpectedly throws in a reference to the rejection of Falstaff.

> If you mark Alexander's life well, Harry of Monmouth's life is come after it indifferent well; for there is figures in all things. Alexander — God knows, and you know — in his rages, and his furies, and his wraths, and his cholers, and his moods, and his displeasures, and his indignations, and also being a little intoxicates in his prains, did, in his ales and his angers, look you, kill his best friend, Cleitus.
>
> GOWER. Our king is not like him in that: he never kill'd any of his friends.
>
> FLUELLEN. It is not well done, mark you now, to take the tales out of my mouth ere it is made and finished. I speak but in the figures

and comparisons of it; as Alexander kill'd his friend Cleitus, being in his ales and his cups, so also Harry Monmouth, being in his right wits and his good judgments, turn'd away the fat knight with the great belly doublet.

Fluellen, at least, has no doubt of the rightness of Henry's decision: where the pagan Alexander killed his general Cleitus in a fit of temper at a banquet, the Christian Henry turned Falstaff away 'in his right wits and his good judgments'. There is seriousness everywhere in this play. Its dignified epic atmosphere permits of lighter passages, but never of simple knockabout.

With *Henry V*, the long and splendid series of Shakespeare's English historical plays is over. A national patriotic epic? Yes, but also a sober and realistic discussion of the realities of honour and kingship: and, in the low-life scenes, a disenchanted view of what life was likely to be for the common man. It is noteworthy that the comic rapscallions of Falstaff's crew do not share the immunity to physical harm that most writers give their comic characters; in *Henry V*, we learn that Nym and Bardolph have been hanged, and that Mrs. Quickly and Doll Tearsheet are dead, the latter from venereal disease. No one could feel that Shakespeare, however patriotic his mood, was out to whitewash English life or the English people.

On the other side, we may legitimately set the great power of the patriotic idea as it burns through these plays. From the great arias in praise of England — Falconbridge in *King John*, Gaunt in *Richard II*, King Henry before the field of Agincourt — to the essential good humour and sanity of the common people as they make their fleeting appearances, we can feel Shakespeare's pride of nationality, his urgent wish that Englishmen should stand together and defend their country and their way of life. That way of life included a great deal that was treacherous, venal and brutal. But at bottom it was sound and admirable. So Shakespeare felt, and so he makes us feel when we see or read these plays. The voice from the bottom of the heap, the voice of the underdog, the private soldier, the man who carries the weight of the whole set-up on his back, is neither a whine nor a snarl. It is the voice of little Feeble, the woman's tailor, marching off to the wars from which his well-fed neighbours have bought themselves out. 'By my troth, I care not; a man can die but once; we owe God a death: I'll ne'er bear a base mind: an't be my destiny, so; an't be not, so: no man's too good to serve 's prince.'

III

LAUGHTER AND JUDGMENT

SHAKESPEARE's comedies handle themes not unlike those of his tragedies. They face the problems of human wrong-doing and suffering, and the struggle of man to organize himself into a social order without doing violence to his fundamental nature — which involves, first of all, making up one's mind what that nature is. To read these plays attentively is, as well as a delightful amusement, a good preparation for the more challenging experience of the tragedies.

Like most people, when I speak of Shakespeare's 'comedies' I mean the group of straight comedies he wrote between *The Comedy of Errors* (*c.* 1594) and *Twelfth Night* (*c.* 1601). The title of 'comedy' has also been given to the final group of four plays with happy endings, but it is more helpful to follow the convention of grouping these apart under the name 'romances'. There are, besides, two plays with a bitter, questioning tone but no tragic ending, *Measure for Measure* and *All's Well that Ends Well*, both of which date from well inside the period in which Shakespeare's mind was working mainly on tragic material; but these again are usually put into a separate category, one that also includes the savagely mordant *Troilus and Cressida*. We shall discuss these plays in their turn, but first we must deal with the so-called 'golden comedies', those in which Shakespeare is content to work as a pure practitioner of his own kind of comic drama.

What is this kind? Nevill Coghill, in his essay, 'The Basis of Shakespearean Comedy', indicates a helpful starting-point.

73

The distinction between satiric and romantic comedy he finds to be an old-established one. It was laid down by fourth-century Latin grammarians, who separated the realism and harshness of satire, concerning itself with the vices and follies of people in a middle station of life, from the gentler glow of romantic comedy with its emphasis on young love and on the resolving of difficulties. Moving forward *via* Boethius, Mr. Coghill finds a classic definition in the work of a thirteenth-century writer, Vincent de Beauvais: *a kind of poem which transforms a sad beginning into a happy ending.* These two hints, joined together, give us a provenance for Shakespearean comedy. It is not satiric; it does not observe realistically; it move. from shadow into sunshine.

From there, we can carry on by ourselves. Anyone can see the main characteristics of Shakespeare's comedies. They deal with the question of how to live, and particularly of how to treat other people in our varying relationships with them, from business to courtship. They tell of love and harmony, initially disturbed, finally restored. They contain low-life comedy, which always has an English flavour no matter in what country the main action is sited. Beyond this, they are firmly separated from the more familiar comic convention which runs through Plautus, Jonson, Molière and Wilde. In the work of those writers, the setting is familiar and the observed details are those of our everyday experience: the action, on the other hand, is amusingly noncredible, so that to follow it is to escape from reality; Wilde's characters eat real cucumber-sandwiches while conducting impossible conversations. In Shakespearean comedy the setting is fantastic, but the characters are credible. Realism is completely banished from the locations of the plays, and almost as completely from their sudden *dénouements*: it presides triumphantly, however, over their characterization.

I

All Shakespearean comedy seeks to absorb violence and suffering into its healing and regenerating wholeness. *The Comedy of*

Errors, at the very beginning of the series, opens with a grey-haired man being led away to execution. Exile, dispossession and the threat of death are the common background of the plays. The foreground, of course, is generally occupied by one or more pairs of young lovers. The only activity which is taken with complete seriousness is courtship, ending in marriage. The multiple wedding is as habitual to the comedies as the multiple death to the tragedies.

Courtship, though frequently conducted in a light-hearted atmosphere, is an important part of the business of life. It makes a magnet strong enough to draw our attention consistently to itself and thus provides a centre which keeps these plays, with their many heterogeneous elements, from falling to pieces. Especially since Shakespeare takes us, in all his comedies, to the deep heart of courtship — which is, of course, self-knowledge. The reason why young people so frequently select the wrong partner is because they hold mistaken views about their own characters. The first essential for a lasting love of someone else is a sound assessment of one's own identity. Only when we see clearly what we have to give, and what we need from others, can we begin to be happy *à deux*.

The familiar Shakespearean theme of appearance versus reality thus finds in the comedies a special application. The poet's mind always dwelt with particular interest on the question of identity; Prince Hal seems a wastrel but is really shrewd and determined, Hamlet covers his inner conflict with a *façade* of madness. But in the comedies this march and countermarch of self and *persona* is geared to the essential purposes of self-discovery and mating. When Prince Hal and Falstaff act out a mock interview between king and heir-apparent, its motive on the prince's part seems to be half a grim jest and half an oblique warning to Falstaff; but when the same basic situation crops up again between Orlando and Rosalind, its purpose is wholly constructive. The girl, in boy's disguise, uses the immunity of that disguise to instruct her lover in how she wishes to be approached. It is an elaborate sexual game, as solemn and intricate as the courting-dances of birds and insects.

This pattern is most fully worked out in *Twelfth Night*, in which Duke Orsino and Countess Olivia typify the false emotion that comes with blurred vision, she hugging the memory of a dead brother, he absorbed in a masochistic pursuit of her that grows more fascinating with each rebuff. Enter Viola disguised as a boy; she loves the Duke, he employs her as an emissary to the Countess who at once falls in love with her, and the tangle is finally straightened out by the appearance of her twin brother Sebastian, who pairs off with a grateful Olivia, leaving Viola free to marry her Orsino, the true passion in each case driving out the artificial one. The story is as simple and as contrived as a quadrille, but its monotony is no longer visible when Shakespeare has clothed it in light, gay colours, thrown in a tuneful song or two, and diversified it with the robust comic sub-plot of Sir Toby Belch, Sir Andrew Aguecheek, Maria and Malvolio: and, in addition to all this, has sent Feste to wander in and out of the action, spinning his web of poetry and melancholy. With their aid, the debate on self-knowledge becomes multiple, ironic, supple; the simple conventions of girl-in-boy's-clothes and ship-wreck-separated-identical-twins give place to something far more organic, not reducible to a formula.

Even if Shakespeare had tried to work to a formula, he would have found it very difficult to keep within it. His mind is always running ahead of the task it has begun. This is true of all his work, but particularly of the comedies, where the enclosing form is frailest. There is nothing in the tragedies that is not made of the stuff of tragedy, and nothing in the histories that does not bear in one way or another on the problems of authority and kingship, but in the comedies we are constantly running into material that threatens to tear the delicate envelope of comedy. Evidently this envelope never entirely satisfied Shakespeare. Time after time he set out hopefully in the cockleshell boat of romantic comedy, only to see it sink under the load of actuality he tried to pack into it. The sub-plot of *The Merchant of Venice*, about Portia's suitors and the caskets of various metals, is a good example. Shakespeare must originally have hoped that it would somehow stand up by the side of the story of the wicked Jew; which can only have meant that he did not, at the beginning, foresee just how much emotional power he was going to send pumping through the story of Shylock. And when he did, of course, it was too late to scrap the play and start again with a better choice of sub-plot. The actors were waiting. Shakespeare was the opposite of that kind of artist who brings his work slowly to perfection, watching and waiting, simmering and stirring, making a fresh start and sacrificing years of work if necessary. He worked for a theatre that used up material at a killing pace; further, he himself set a killing pace, always striding ahead to the next problem, and the next after that, while he was still grappling with the problem of the moment. Hence the high proportion of his plays that show some flaw, some imperfect stitching or unfortunate juxtaposition that would be rejected by a more fastidious artist.

It is important not to be misunderstood here. I am not saying that Shakespeare lacked an artistic conscience. He was simply one of those artists who prefer to start a new work rather than go back over a flawed one. Such artists do not revise; they learn their lesson and incorporate it in the next work. Shakespeare, in the course of a working life lasting less than twenty years, left us at least fifteen plays that are perfectly achieved, plays in which the most scrupulous craftsman would not change a word. We need not wonder that he left us as many again that show the marks of an uneven pace, a too rapid development of one power at the expense of another. The comedies show this casualty-rate at its highest. Every one of them, except the two masterpieces, *As You Like It* and *Twelfth Night*, calls for our indulgence in one way or another: an indulgence we give very readily, in view of the superb material in which even the poorest of his comedies abound.

The chief cause of imbalance in these comedies is, of course, the uncertain mating of plot and sub-plot. *Much Ado About Nothing*, for instance, starts out with two plots very widely removed from each other in tone and idiom — the grand-opera plot of Hero and Claudio, and the comic story of Dogberry and his fellow-townsmen of the Watch. These two plots, which are directly geared to one another, inasmuch as the rustic constables unmask the villains' plot and engineer the happy ending, would have fitted together perfectly well; they are insulated against jarring impact, and both have about the same amount of reality. Unfortunately — but even as I write that word I know that it is a hypocrisy, and that I don't really think it a misfortune at all — Shakespeare has thrown in a third plot, dealing with the courtship of Beatrice and Benedick, which has a beautiful observed reality, a poise and maturity, a refreshing humour and candour, that make the operatic main-plot seem absurdly unreal, and thus makes the Dogberry plot curve away into its own isolation. The play falls into three pieces. The youthful Charles I wrote into his copy of the play the alternative title 'Benedick and Beatrice', and it is a fact that every reader and spectator of the play, from that day to this, has come away with a stronger memory of the sub-plot than of the plot. In fairness to Shakespeare we should note that he makes, in the course of the action, one mighty effort to right this balance. Having got his nuptial pair to the altar, and having to get through the preposterous business of Claudio's denunciation of Hero, he puts his best foot forward and writes a scene (Act IV, Scene i) which, in purely dramatic terms, is utterly dazzling. There are eight characters on the stage, and anyone who has ever wrestled with the problems of dramatic writing can only bow down and admire the unswerving skill with which Shakespeare has given each one something to say or do, in unflagging succession, whipping the scene along at a pace fast enough to mask its unreality and yet not so fast as to blur its narrative outlines.

If the harmonizing of these two stories had been less of an impossibly difficult task, Shakespeare might not have troubled to throw his whole skill into this crucial scene, and we should have lacked a show-case example of his dramatic technique which, by itself, would be enough to justify the play. Formal perfection is well sacrificed for a reward like this. And very much the same is true of *The Merchant of Venice*. That play seems to have come unstuck so early that Shakespeare more or less gave up trying to press it into a whole. He seems, even, to be contriving additional complications, to keep himself (and us?) from being bored with the ill-assorted box of tricks he has to work with. The relationship between Antonio and Bassanio, for instance, suddenly blossoms under his touch into a lightly-sketched but subtle relationship between a rich, gifted and melancholy homosexual and a brisk, shallow adventurer with a handsome profile. The play begins with Antonio's sadness, which he is being quizzed by two minor characters to explain. In fact, there is no mystery about it; he loves Bassanio and must shortly lose him to a woman. The only reason he does not explain all this to the puppet-figures Salerio and Salanio is because they have no right to know the inner secrets of his heart. In the trial scene, when the chips are down and it looks as if Antonio's generosity to Bassanio will cost him his life, the relationship between them suddenly jumps into life. Bassanio makes a more or less routine protestation:

> Good cheer Antonio? What, man, courage yet!
> The Jew shall have my flesh, blood, bones and all,
> Ere thou shalt lose for me one drop of blood.

As Nevill Coghill trenchantly remarks, this is 'A manifest lie, for were it true, he had only there and then to run a rapier through Shylock and save his friend at the cost of being hanged for murder.' Antonio, in his reply, does not even bother to take the declaration seriously; his thoughts are already turning towards death and sacrifice.

> I am a tainted wether of the flock,
> Meetest for death; the weakest kind of fruit
> Drops earliest to the ground, and so let me.

The 'taint' he speaks of is the homosexual cast of his emotions; not, of course, that he need be presented on stage as a thorough-going, practising homosexual. But neither, on the other hand, need the point be masked behind a hedge of footnotes about how high a theme was 'amity' in Elizabethan literature, etc., etc. Of course it was, but it happens sometimes that a friendship between two people of the same sex will grow towards passion, and, as everyone knows, this happened to Shakespeare himself at one period of his life. Part of the interest of Antonio's character is that he seems, from this point of view, to take on some of Shakespeare's own features: not a full self-portrait, but a few brush-strokes towards one.

Twelfth Night is in all probability the latest of the golden comedies; the traditional Christmas merrymaking lasted twelve days, and the title of the play perhaps indicates that these 'revels now are ended'. In a general discussion of Shakespearean comedy, however, one instinctively goes to *Twelfth Night* first. It is the finest development, the distillation, of Shakespeare's romantic comedy; what the others in various ways point to, this play *is*. Its predecessor and nearest rival, *As You Like It*, is an equally successful play, but less well adapted to be the starting-point for a survey, inasmuch as it has certain special features which make it untypical. The most important of these features, of course, is that it belongs to the *genre* of 'pastoral'. But perhaps 'belongs to' is too blunt, too rough-and-ready, a phrase here. What *As You Like It* does is to play with the pastoral form; now entering fully into its conventions, now mocking them, and in a third mood subjecting them to a grave, meditative examination. The result is a uniquely delicate blend: on the one hand a romantic comedy of love and adventure, on the other a debate, almost Shavian in its wit and irreverence, on an important social and artistic question.

II

Pastoral is an urban form. It is written by civilized and learned poets who see a poignant contrast between the artificiality of their own way of life and the natural simplicity of the countryman's. They do not, of course, wish to change places with the countryman and undertake his rude toil, or exchange their own refinement for his simplicity: but they are aware of the serious considerations involved in the comparison. The shepherd, who appears to the townsman's eye to enjoy an idyllic life, meditating and playing on his pipe, has always typified rustic simplicity and wisdom; Christian tradition pays the shepherd the supreme compliment of making him the first mortal man to hear the news of Christ's birth, and a similar episode occurs independently in the Greek poet Hesiod.

At the very beginning of the history of pastoral as a literary form, the urban poets who practised it are thought to have picked up some of their themes from genuinely rustic songs, written by actual shepherds. Many of these songs reflected the countryman's resentment at being patronized by the visiting city man. They took the form of debates in which the courtier was put down by the peasant. The seriousness and range of Shakespeare's exploration of pastoral attitudes, in *As You Like It*, is shown by the fact that when he came to twine together the various traditions of pastoral he did not forget this one: the conversation-piece between Touchstone and the aged Corin (Act III, Scene ii) is a perfect little example of it.

Pastoral was a form much enjoyed by the Elizabethans, and Shakespeare would have pleased his audience if he had adopted its conventions without criticism or reservation, as Lodge had done in *Rosalynde*, the novel which gave him his basic story. In fact, of course, he gave them something more complex: an entertainment which at the same time revelled in pastoral and quizzed it. The Forest of Arden (Ardennes, in the original French story) is as lovely and haunted as the 'Wood near Athens' of *A*

Midsummer Night's Dream. To the banished Duke Senior, it represents both refuge and consolation: overthrown and banished by his brother, he makes his way to the forest, and there lives a life which is specifically compared with that of Robin Hood, that lost hero of England's mythical state of innocence, mourned in Shakespeare's day as he is mourned in ours. And Charles the wrestler, who supplies this parallel, adds, 'they say many young gentlemen flock to him every day, and fleet the time carelessly, as they did in the golden world'. This 'golden world', which Shakespeare would early have read about in the first book of Ovid's *Metamorphoses*, is the classical equivalent of the Old Testament's Garden of Eden. Here is the full pastoral faith, resoundingly professed by the Duke in his famous speech on 'the uses of adversity' (Act II, Scene i). This forest (like the wooded Arden region which lay near Shakespeare's birthplace and from which his mother presumably derived her maiden name) evidently abuts on sheep-farming country, for it is inhabited by the typical Dresden figures of pastoral: Phoebe and Silvius, proud shepherdess and sad amorous shepherd, and old Corin the weathered philosopher.

So much for the affirmation of pastoral values. It is wholehearted and full of imaginative joy and tenderness, for the poet cherishes it as we cherish a dream that brings happiness. And when Rosalind is banished in her turn, and Celia elects to go along with her, what could be more natural than that their steps should turn to this same Arden? But as soon as they arrive there a note of disenchanted realism is struck. Celia has brought with her, for comfort and protection, the 'roynish clown', Touchstone. 'Roynish' means coarse or rude, and the first words we hear Touchstone utter are peevish enough. To Rosalind's cry 'O Jupiter, how weary are my spirits!' he answers sullenly, 'I care not for my spirits, if my legs were not weary'. Celia, sinking down, pleads 'I pray you, bear with me'. 'I would rather bear with you than bear you', is his reply. And when Rosalind, trying to strike a cheerful note, says 'Well, this is the forest of Arden',

Touchstone comes back sourly, 'Ay, now am I in Arden; the more fool I; when I was at home I was in a better place: but travellers must be content'. Wearied out, she can only reply, 'Ay, be so, good Touchstone'.

The two girls belong, of course, to the pastoral world, as firmly as the Duke and his merry men. But they bring their awkward lump of reality, their intrusion from the workaday world, with them in the person of Touchstone. And the Duke has his corresponding deflator in Jaques, the melancholy man, who excels in pointing out the darker side, refusing to be pleased, casting a shadow of cynicism in the soft radiance of pleasing illusion. It is Jaques who maintains that just as the Duke's authority has been usurped by his brother Frederick, so the Duke himself is now a usurper, thrusting into the territory that rightly belongs to the wild creatures, and slaughtering the deer 'in their assign'd and native dwelling-place'. Like Touchstone, Jaques is regarded by his companions chiefly as a source of amusement; on hearing that he is in one of his melancholy moods, the Duke proposes that they seek him out: 'I love to cope him in these sullen fits, For then he's full of matter.' Matter for sport, one supposes, rather than for reflection. His function is similar to Touchstone's in that they both have to convey their home truths in a glancing fashion; they may get in a shrewd hit now and then, but they are not respected as oracles Indeed, when Jaques shows signs of taking himself too seriously, the Duke disciplines him with a stern reprimand.

JAQUES.   give me leave
> To speak my mind, and I will through and through
> Cleanse the foul body of th' infected world,
> If they will patiently receive my medicine.

DUKE.   Fie on thee! I can tell what thou wouldst do.

JAQUES. What, for a counter, would I do but good?

DUKE.   Most mischievous foul sin, in chiding sin:
> For thou thyself hast been a libertine,
> As sensual as the brutish sting itself;
> And all th' embossed sores and headed evils

That thou with licence of free foot hast caught
Wouldst thou disgorge into the general world.

Neither Touchstone nor Jaques plays any part in the story, as such; their contribution is to the play's atmosphere, and it is no surprise to turn to the source and find them both missing; they are purely Shakespearean additions. Jaques is brought in to make savage fun of the lovely pastoral song, 'Under the greenwood tree', and to utter the speech (Act II, Scene vii) which compares human life to the artificial actions of players on a stage. This speech, largely owing to the needs of elocution classes, has become one of the most familiar of Shakespearean set-pieces, and is often quoted as if it were a gem of its author's maturest wisdom. In fact, it is as superficial as the rest of Jaques's moralizing. His cynical conclusion, that when a man's life is over there is nothing to point to but an oversized baby,

Sans teeth, 'sans eyes, sans taste, sans everything,

is revealing, for to Shakespeare the word 'sans' was an affectation which betrayed insincerity. When Berowne, in *Love's Labour's Lost*, is vowing to cast off his youthful attitudinizing and expresses himself henceforth in plain, manly terms, he says to Rosaline:

> And to begin, wench — so God help me, law! —
> My love to thee is sound, sans crack or flaw.
> ROSALINE. Sans 'sans', I pray you.
> BEROWNE.   Yet I have a trick
> Of the old rage; bear with me, I am sick;
> I'll leave it by degrees.

If he is to express himself as an honest man should, the girl tells him, he will have to drop fashionable Gallicisms like 'sans'. So much for Jaques as a purveyor of Shakespeare's wisdom. The chief function of his celebrated speech, as a matter of fact, is dramaturgical. Orlando has come upon them, his sword drawn, as they sit down to dinner; their courteous reception disarms him and they invite him to feed, but he says that he must first go and fetch the fainting Adam. This presents an awkward small problem: the action has to halt for long enough to convince us that Orlando is really bringing Adam from some little distance, and the resulting gap can best be plugged by having someone make a speech that will hold the audience's attention.

Having created both Jaques and Touchstone, Shakespeare allows himself the luxury (a dangerous luxury, it would have been to a lesser playwright) of bringing them on the stage together and letting them see who can patronize most effectively. Jaques, interrupting the improvised marriage ceremony which Touchstone has arranged for himself and Audrey, doubtless intends to carry on the condescending tone of their first encounter offstage; but Touchstone, not to be put down before his bride, patronizes Jaques first. 'Good even, good Master What-ye-call 't: how do you, sir? You are very well met: God 'ild you for your last company: I am very glad to see you: even a toy in hand here, sir: nay, pray be cover'd.'

It is in keeping with the play's warm and positive tone that Touchstone should not be bested by Jaques, for of the two he is the more sympathetic character. His place mid-way between the two worlds entitles him to condescend to the shepherds of Arden — or try to, though he makes no impression on the simple dignity of Corin — but he willingly enough takes a mate from among them. The basic recognition underlying Shakespeare's golden comedies is that love, however romantic, exists to make bedfellows and fill cradles; the multiple marriage at the end, bringing the courtly characters to their destined pairing-off and also propelling the Dresden figures of Phoebe and Silvius into a human relationship at last, is completed by the earthy coupling of Audrey and Touchstone, and Jaques is wrong as usual when he predicts that their 'loving voyage Is but for two months victuall'd'.

The plot of *As You Like It*, like that of *Twelfth Night*, contains absurdities which, under the influence of the warmth and gaiety of the play, we swallow light-heartedly enough. The double conversion of the two villainous characters, Duke Frederick and Orlando's brother Oliver, is sketched in with a perfunctoriness that saves the play, perhaps, from ridicule; if Shakespeare had not shown us so plainly that he did not care whether we believed in the story or not, if he had made it even a shade more credible, we might have tried to believe in it. And this could only have led to disappointment. We must take the action as a mere charade, and let Shakespeare guide our serious interest into areas where it has something to feed on.

Frederick's change of heart, like Oliver's, can simply be accepted as a *donnée*. But what of the haste with which Duke Senior and his co-mates abandon the forest and go back to their life at court? That, certainly, is part of the play's comment on the values of pastoral. The only character who freely elects to stay in retirement is Oliver, who in a spirit of contrition and gratitude says to Orlando, 'My father's house and all the revenue that was old Sir Rowland's will I estate upon you, and here live and die a shepherd.' What are we to understand from this? That it is the reformed offender, conscious of the need to remake his life, who is most fit for simplicity? Certainly Jaques, who belongs to this category, has chosen to go off and share Duke Frederick's monastic repentance rather than come back to court with the others.

Perhaps. But the pastoral setting of sheep-cote and forest glade is not to be undervalued merely because the good characters leave it when their difficulties are resolved. For it is, like the wood in *A Midsummer Night's Dream*, a healing place. Truth and recognition are to be found there. Like Prospero on his island, which he also leaves as soon as his old life beckons again, the Duke and his companions have spent a fertile period of meditation and renewal. They have been in contact, for a time, with an older and simpler scheme of things. There are no supernatural beings in this forest (for the descent of Hymen at the marriage-feast is a mere masque-interlude), but there are immemorial customs and rituals, such as the ceremony of dressing up the successful hunter in the horns and skin of the animal and bringing him so attired into the presence of the Duke — obviously a memory, on Shakespeare's part, of some immemorial folk-custom, living on in Warwickshire minds alongside the deeds of bold Robin Hood. A world where these things can still be met with, he seems to be saying, is no bad place for the powerful and the clever to revisit for a time. Certainly the Duke's *aperçu*, that the icy wind has a useful lesson for him, so that

> when it bites and blows upon my body,
> Even till I shrink with cold, I smile and say
> 'This is no flattery; these are counsellors
> That feelingly persuade me what I am,'

commonplace as it is, looks forward to Lear's self-discovery amid the tempest on the heath, and beyond that to the unforgettable question hurled at Timon by Apemantus,

> What, think'st
> That the bleak air, thy boisterous chamberlain,
> Will put thy shirt on warm?

III

About 1599 a new actor joined the company for which Shakespeare worked. He was Robert Armin, a talented man who specialized in comic roles and approached them in the spirit of a connoisseur. Armin could sing, a fact which Shakespeare did not at first realize, if we are to judge by the fact that none of the songs in *As You Like It* are given to Touchstone; and he was a clever man, who wrote three books about his craft of foolery: *Fool Upon Fool*, *A Nest of Ninnies* and *Quips Upon Questions*.

Before Armin, the company's principal funny man had been Will Kempe, who seems to have been a knockabout comedian, excellent at portraying simple laughable fellows like Dogberry and Bottom the Weaver, but less able to cope with a part that called for quickness of wit and subtleties of light and shade.

Armin's appointment was an excellent thing for English literature; without him we should probably have had no Feste, no
Touchstone, and no Fool in *King Lear*.

In showing his wealthy and high-born characters as con-
noisseurs of 'fooling', Shakespeare was reflecting contemporary
life. The court jester was an ancient institution. His lineage was
complex: on the one hand his ancestors were idiots and freaks of
nature, on the other they were quick-witted professional
entertainers.

To take the first strain first, we need only note that the custom
of keeping imbeciles or dwarfs as pets was already well-estab-
lished in Roman times. A strangely deformed human being,
whether in body or mind, was sought after by the rich and curious
as a collector's item. In ancient Rome, idiots were bought by
public auction at a market specially held for the purpose. During
the Christian era, the practice continued to spread. Not only
kings and nobles but rich and powerful priests would keep their
simpletons for the sake of the fun they provided. Revolting?
Perhaps. But the idiots themselves, if allowed a choice, would be
quite likely to prefer such a life to the modern practice of tidying
them away into 'institutions'. There are people in England today
who have been in lunatic asylums for fifty and sixty years; if
I were an imbecile I think I would rather spend my life at a
sixteenth-century court. Especially since, while modern people
regard an idiot as a piece of obscene *débris*, to be swept under the
carpet and left there, the Middle Ages had a certain reverence —
superstitious, if you will, but a reverence — for the 'natural'
who might at any time utter a piece of inspired wisdom; the
tradition of the holy madman was well grounded in Scripture
and elsewhere. Thus the half-wit wandered unchecked through
the great mediaeval and renaissance households, uttering sublime
impertinences which would have cost a sane man his life.

The professional funny man, whose wits were very much about
him, tended to merge into this background. He was, of course,
related to the minstrel and that other and more grotesque figure,

the *joculator*, who roamed Europe after the dying-out of the Roman stage and became the French *jongleur* and the English *juggler*. Unlike the minstrel, the *joculator* went in for antics and satiric aggressiveness. Originally a travelling entertainer, the *joculator*, juggler or jester early began to attach himself to a court or great household that would offer him shelter and protection. Finding the natural half-wit already established there, he tended to adopt the same role. So that the 'fool by nature' and the 'fool by art' were both contained within the ample tradition which Shakespeare inherited.

The custom of keeping a Fool was in full force during Shakespeare's lifetime and did not die out till more than a hundred years after his death (the last recorded one died in 1728); we must not, therefore, think of the motley-clothed, 'all-licensed' figure as a piece of fantastic imagination but as sober observation and realism. Comedy is more intellectual than tragedy, which no doubt explains why Touchstone and Feste are sharp fellows who live on their wits while the Fool in *King Lear* is more of a 'natural'.

Both Touchstone and Feste are skilled entertainers whose employers judge their performances critically. Feste, when we first meet him, is threatened with dismissal or even (if Malvolio is to be believed) with hanging, for disobedience and failure to please. Olivia's first words to him are 'Go to, y' are a dry fool; I'll no more of you'. 'Wit, an't be thy will,' he breathes, 'put me into good fooling!' And then proceeds to enchant her. Touchstone is never in danger of being turned away; there is a bond of genuine love between him and Celia, and when we see them together we remember Yorick, so beloved by the child Hamlet ('he hath borne me on his back a thousand times . . . here hung those lips that I have kiss'd I know not how oft'). But Touchstone, too, is put on his mettle; when Jaques brings him before the Duke and his court, it is with the pride of a man introducing a discovery. Touchstone obliges by rattling off a long set-piece, obviously polished through the years, about 'a quarrel on the seventh cause', the Retort Courteous, the Quip Modest, the Reply Churlish, the Reproof Valiant, the Countercheck Quarrelsome, the Lie Circumstantial and the Lie Direct: a cascade of professionally-contrived nonsense. Jaques breaks into spontaneous applause with 'Is not this a rare fellow, my lord?' and the Duke smilingly agrees, 'He uses his folly as a stalking-horse, and under the presentation of that he shoots his wit'.

The characters of Touchstone and Feste, in fact, are adapted, with a beautiful inventive delicacy, to the plays in which they figure. *As You Like It*, for all its sharp-witted atmosphere of debate, is very much a play of the heart, warm and generous. It administers rebuke and correction, but very lightly and gently. It contains nothing like the humiliation of Malvolio or even the harsh dismissal of Sir Andrew Aguecheek, whose relationship with Sir Toby is precisely the same that Roderigo will soon have with Iago. *Twelfth Night*, though its lyrical quality makes it magical, is really the end of the line. Twelfth Night is here, and soon we shall be unpinning the decorations and facing bleak reality. Already there is a sharp nipping air blowing from the tragedies: not merely in the harsh nature of some of the action — for this, as we have seen, has been a feature of Shakespearean comedy from the beginning — but in the disenchanted note that sounds, somewhere, in its most Mozartian harmonies. Feste acts as the vehicle of this disenchantment. He is not only cleverer than the other characters but also — it is not quite the same thing — more 'intellectual'. Touchstone uses his wit as a stalking-horse, no doubt, but Feste uses his as the weapon with which he defends himself and carves out a place in a world basically hostile. In that indefinable Shakespearean way in which we are made to sense a biography behind every character, we feel that Feste has needs and problems that Touchstone would never have to face. Touchstone, loved and protected like a child, can afford to make up in warmth what he lacks in wit; he can even grumble and be a nuisance; he will always be kept on, because life would not be the same without him. He doesn't, it is evident, need money, whereas Feste is twice shown using his foolery to wheedle coin out of people he talks to, and the relationship is one of wit-pedlar to customer — if his nonsense amuses them enough they pay up. With Duke Orsino (Act V, Scene i) he keeps it up so determinedly that, having been paid twice and still coming back for more, he is dismissed — rather curtly, I fancy — with 'You can fool no more money out of me at this throw'.

Feste would have been out of place in *As You Like It*; he fits perfectly in *Twelfth Night* because his cold eye sees through all pretence, and the play turns on pretences, conscious and un-conscious. The chastisement of Orsino and Olivia is gentle, because they are noble characters and all that is necessary is to awake them to love. Malvolio, whose delusion springs from egotism ('You are sick of self-love,' Olivia tells him in their first scene together), is corrected harshly, even cruelly; unlike the unsympathetic characters in *As You Like It*, he is not allowed to see the light at the end of the play; he goes off snarling about revenge. Feste, naturally, plays no part in the love-story, but he sees exactly what kind of mistake his mistress is making, and even exercises his privilege of telling her the truth to her face in Act I, Scene v. ('The more fool, madonna, to mourn for your brother's soul being in heaven.') He does the same thing for Orsino in Act II, Scene iv; asked for 'the song we had last night', he obliges with 'Come away, come away, death', which with its slight elegance and its exaggerated mournfulness hits off exactly the tinsel nature of Orsino's emotions. In their dialogue afterwards he even hints at the forthcoming switch in these emotions ('the tailor make thy doublet of changeable taffeta, for thy mind is a very opal'). Nothing is hidden from him, the onlooker who sees more of the game than the players.

Twelfth Night, predictably, ends on a less exuberant note than *As You Like It*. There is the standard multiple marriage, but joy and benevolence do not gather in the entire roll-call of char-acters. Sir Andrew, and of course Malvolio, are outside the happy circle. So is Feste. He has no Audrey to lead into the nuptial dance — it is impossible to imagine him with one — and his bitterness at Malvolio, justified as it is, strikes a jarring note; it is his baiting that finally sends Malvolio striding off, tight-lipped and furious. 'Pursue him,' says Orsino, 'and entreat him to a peace.' But Feste, who has so often carried messages in the play, does not carry this one. He stays behind and sings the song which comes back later, at the storm-centre of tragedy, to the half-crazed mind of Lear's 'poor fool and knave'. This, like his other songs, uses an empty-sounding form of words to hint at a perception of reality. When I was a little tiny boy, a foolish thing was to be laughed at and enjoyed; but the same attitude, carried over into adult life, caused me to be herded together with the knaves and thieves against whom all gates are shut. 'When I became a man, I put away childish things,' and with my innocence went my happiness. Women are a trouble in this adult life, and drink is an unsatisfactory escape, and perhaps the only facts we know for certain are that 'a great while ago the world begun' and 'the rain it raineth every day'. The figure of this sad, clear-sighted man, as aware of his difference as Hamlet, as helpless before his destiny as Othello, stands at the exit of this garden of Shakespearean comedy. And as he sings he bows us out and closes the gate behind us.

IV

It remains to consider the two 'problem comedies', *Measure for Measure* and *All's Well that Ends Well*. Of these, *Measure for Measure* is by far the more interesting. It contains some of Shakespeare's finest scenes; if all his other works were lost and we had only this play to go on, we should know that he was the greatest playwright and in some ways the greatest poet England had ever known. But this is as far as one can go in unqualified praise. The play is no doubt Shakespeare's most interesting failure, but a failure, all things considered, it is.

Perhaps the most convenient way of getting a grip on *Measure for Measure* is to start from the story as Shakespeare found it in his sources. There were several of these, but the principal one was Giraldi's *Hecatommithi* (1565), a collection of prose tales from which Shakespeare had already taken the story of Othello. There was also an English play on the subject, George Whetstone's *Promos and Cassandra*, which added a few details but kept to the main outlines. In this basic story the wicked deputy sentences a man to death for rape, is approached by his sister who begs for his life, and agrees to spare him in exchange for the sister's virtue; he also hints that he will afterwards marry her. The condemned man begs his sister to agree to this, especially in view of the possible marriage; she does so, but once the deputy has had his way the brother is executed nevertheless. She states her case to the Emperor, who is about to have the deputy executed in his turn when she pleads for his life; her plea successful, she marries him and they live happily ever after.

This plot, rather like the Othello–story, must have struck Shakespeare as crude but promising. Obviously it wouldn't have done as it stood; the girl's intercession for the life of the man who wronged her would seem insufficiently disinterested if her motive for wanting him spared was matrimonial, and in any case if she was prepared to be his wife it would argue that his original proposition to her was not so distasteful after all. On the other hand, simply to remove this from the plot would mean softening the deputy's character by removing one of his crimes, the broken promise of marriage. Shakespeare solved the problem by having Isabella refuse Angelo's offer, and inventing the character of Mariana, a woman whom he had once been pledged to marry, but had rejected when her dowry did not come up to his expectations. Whetstone had already softened the brutality of the original story by having the prison officer, indignant at the deputy's callousness, substitute another and more deserving victim, whose head was then duly sent to the girl so that she mistook it for her brother's. Shakespeare kept this detail, softening it still further by having yet another inmate of the prison die of a fever at the opportune moment, so that his head can be provided and no one need go to the block at all, not even a minor character. He then topped it off by making the condemned man's sister a novice in a convent, so that her recoil from sexual indulgence would seem reasonably motivated even when weighed against a brother's death.

Altogether Shakespeare's reworking of the Giraldi–Whetstone plot is beautifully designed to engineer what he wanted: a play about forgiveness. This, the only play with a title from the gospels, is on the subject of forgiving them that trespass against us. 'With what measure ye mete it shall be meted to you again.' Therefore 'Judge not, that ye be not judged'. Claudio, at the beginning of the play, is condemned to death because he has got with child a girl who is, as he protests 'fast my wife, Save that we do the denunciation lack Of outward order'; they have put off getting married in case it should prejudice some arrangement or other concerning money. (Shakespeare leaves the details vague; something to do with 'the propagation of a dower'.) By making Angelo sleep with Mariana by mistake for Isabella in the dark (the conventions of Elizabethan drama do not allow tactile recognition of women), Shakespeare has him commit the very same offence for which he has condemned Claudio to death. In his own mind, of course, Angelo thinks he is committing an even worse one, and it is a subtle touch to soften his crime and bring it exactly into line with Claudio's.

As rehandled by Shakespeare, the story now has a beautiful dramatic line. Claudio and Juliet have a chance to get married, but for prudential motives they refuse. Angelo condemns Claudio to death and is asked several times to pardon him, but refuses. Isabella then approaches him and begs for his life, and he again refuses. He then makes his offer; she indignantly tells Claudio about it, and he begs her to accept for the sake of saving his life, but she refuses. Meanwhile the busily scheming Duke has dug up Mariana, whom Angelo had once offered to marry and then refused. Angelo enjoys Isabella, as he thinks, and then refuses to keep his bargain. Finally, when the Duke sheds his disguise and reappears to distribute reward and punishment, he orders Angelo to be married to Mariana and then at once passes sentence of death on him. Mariana begs for his pardon, and the Duke refuses. It is at this point that Isabella goes down on her knees. After this long string of No's, a large resounding Yes — that is the pattern of the play.

This summary makes *Measure for Measure* sound a great success, but of course one of the difficulties of literary criticism is that it is fatally easy to flatter any long work, such as a novel or play, out of recognition, by boiling down the story and bringing its most significant features into focus. It is the moment-by-moment, page-by-page experience that dictates our final estimate. In this respect, *Measure for Measure* disappoints, if only because it goes off so disastrously after the first two superb acts. If the whole play had been on the level of these acts, it would have been one of Shakespeare's greatest. Act III, indeed, begins with a scene on the same high level — the interview between the terrified Claudio and the unbending Isabella — but immediately, in fact in the latter half of that very scene, the Duke button-holes Isabella and begins a long, rambling narrative, couched for some reason in an over-written prose which seems unendurable after the swift and pantherine verse of the preceding few minutes; and in the course of it he tells her the story of Angelo's desertion of Mariana, not as something he has just discovered but as a known, long-established fact. This affects, retrospectively, the opening scenes of the play. If the Duke already knew that Angelo had committed an act of mean selfishness, his motive for entrusting the authority to him during his feigned 'absence' could hardly have been what honest Escalus thinks it is — that Angelo is the fittest man for the job. It must be that he is observing and testing Angelo along with everyone else, and indeed he had said, 'we shall see If power change purpose, what our seemers be'. All this is acceptable enough, but we wish we had known of it earlier; the third act is rather late in the play to introduce important evidence about the characters. It has the effect of making the Duke seem more tedious and paltering than ever; he is already a boring and un-sympathetic character, one of Shakespeare's real, unequivocal failures. He is, of course, one of those characters who have one foot in folk-lore; to leave the throne and mingle with the people disguised as a friar is the kind of thing good kings do in fairy-stories. And on the level of symbolism he is evidently meant to be something like a divinity, a kind of puppet-figure of God. The trouble is not in the conception but in the execution. Shakespeare does not seem to have felt able to whip up any real interest in such a contriving, sermonizing waxwork; the dramatic tension drops whenever he comes onstage. Except once: the friar-duke is given a fine speech at one point, when he comes to the con-demned cell to bring spiritual comfort to Claudio in Act III, Scene i, just before the fatal visit of Isabella which throws the youth back into turmoil. But even here, when he is for once allowed some fine poetry, the Duke contrives to miss an obvious opening; he is supposed to be a Christian friar, and in this play on an overtly Christian theme he might be expected to bring com-fort by speaking of heaven and the forgiveness of God the Father. Instead, he brings out a pure piece of 'high antique morality', derived point by point from the Roman stoicism of Seneca, and talks throughout the whole speech like a man who has never heard of Christianity. If Shakespeare meant him to embody virtues of a Christian prince, this is an odd way of going about it. The only explanation is that the figure of ruler-turned-priest simply failed to engage Shakespeare's full interest. He found it impossible, in writing speeches for him, to keep his mind fully on what he was doing. Anyone who has ever sat down to write a work of fiction will know that the characters who bore the author, who owe their presence in the story solely to its schematic requirements, usually show this kind of loss of grip.

At all events, it is hard to agree with the view taken by Mr. Wilson Knight and critics under his influence, who tend to try to get the Duke taken at his full face-value and treated with a quasi-religious reverence. This view ignores his self-importance (he is furious with the comic-relief character, Lucio, for saying unkind things about him in the belief that he is talking to someone else); and also his cowardice (he specifically tells Friar Lawrence in Act I, Scene iii, that his reason for leaving his authority temporarily in Angelo's hands is that he wants the old laws about chastity enforced, but does not care to do so because of the unpopularity that would result). This argument doesn't seem to be wholly truthful, but it leaves a bad taste nevertheless, and is certainly not Christ-like. Altogether, I think William Empson is right when he says, in that fine chapter on the play in his *Structure of Complex Words*, 'when the Duke buzzes from Claudio to Isabella, all agog, and busily telling lies to both, I do not see how the author can be banking on the simple-minded respect of the audience for great persons. . . . What makes the Duke ridiculous on the stage is the fuss he makes about the back-biting of Lucio, that is, precisely what makes Mr. Knight think him high and pure.'

Isabella is the other problem. By making her a novice, Shakespeare ensured her a respectful hearing; surely a nun, if anyone, is entitled to say 'More than our brother is our chastity', because a nun would think that anyone's chastity was better than anyone's brother. Having got this far, however, he seems to have experienced a failure of sympathy. He is continually giving Isabella lines to speak that show a cold, self-regarding righteousness rather than a generous holiness. In the interview with Claudio, for instance, the story demands that he should break down and beg her to save his life even in this forbidden way, and that she should refuse him. But surely, within this framework, it would have been easy enough to make her refusal a gentle and pitying one. Grieved that her brother's fear was stronger than his religion, more grieved still that the sacrifice demanded of her was not one that she could make, she might have talked to him in accents of love and sympathy. What Shakespeare actually gives her to say is,

> O you beast!
> O faithless coward! O dishonest wretch!
> Wilt thou be made a man out of my vice?
> Is't not a kind of incest to take life
> From thine own sister's shame? What should I think?
> Heaven shield my mother play'd my father fair!
> For such a warped slip of wilderness
> Ne'er issu'd from his blood. Take my defiance;
> Die; perish.

This is not holiness. It is affronted vanity. So, I am afraid, is her remark to the Duke, 'I would rather my brother die by the law than my son should be unlawfully born.' There is a horrible egotism in the words. Then there is that blood-chilling remark in the very speech in which she begs for Angelo's pardon:

> I partly think
> A due sincerity govern'd his deeds
> Till he did look on me.

Mr. Empson, writing as usual with great subtlety, has produced the only possible justification of this repulsive remark: it is 'pathetic that the intended nun should say [such a thing]. Her new sensual vanity seems meant to imply a partial awakening of her senses after the battering she has gone through; and her decision to marry the Duke is perhaps not so grossly out of character as critics have supposed.'

The chief drawback about both Isabella and the Duke is that we don't believe in their goodness; it doesn't come over to us with sufficient imaginative impact. As the wise and benevolent ruler, who, like the Christian God, puts his subjects on their mettle by leaving them to cope with their problems under his unseen but unwavering eye, the Duke simply will not do; he is too fussy, too self-important, and too clumsy in his incessant scheming. As the wronged, innocent girl who finally reverses the series of negatives with a grandly generous affirmative, Isabella likewise will not do. Generous people simply do not say things like 'I would rather my brother die by the law than my son should be unlawfully born'. The parts of the play in which we have to identify with these characters are non-credible and unmemorable. What we do find blazingly credible, and entirely memorable, are the scenes that concern human behaviour under the stress of temptation: Angelo's feverish interviews with Isabella, Claudio's agonized plea to be spared, even Lucio with his philosophical joking about venereal disease. Those parts of the play which manipulate the material of folk-lore, and reach out for symbolic effects beyond that material, do not succeed; those parts which concern themselves with psychological realism succeed perfectly. Once again, Shakespeare has tried to clap together two different kinds of material, and they have fallen apart. The symbolic manipulation of romance had to wait for its perfect development until the last plays; the unflinching contemplation of human conflict and suffering was what occupied Shakespeare's mind at this time, and the inner authority of his genius would permit of no straying from that furrow.

Very much the same is true of *All's Well that Ends Well*. The fairy-story of a girl who cures the king of a fatal illness, after his physicians have given him up, and, being allowed to choose her own recompense, asks for the husband of her choice — this might, in Shakespeare's last period, have been carried off with the right blend of mythical authority and symbolic distance. It is no more artificial than the story of *The Winter's Tale*, and no more repulsive than that of *Cymbeline*. But, once again, it is the folk-tale element that fails to convince. What does convince is the realistic analysis of the characters' motives. It is as if Shakespeare had said to himself, 'Given that this preposterous situation could have arisen among human beings, how would they — real, flesh and blood people — have reacted?' Accordingly, we have the utterly convincing reaction of Bertram: browbeaten by the king into marrying a girl he does not want, he slips away from the court and goes off soldiering, vowing never to return while his wife lives; once clear of the king's authority, he devotes himself to the uproarious enjoyments of a dissolute young officer, laying siege to the first pretty girl he encounters, and making a close companion of Parolles, whom everyone but Bertram can recognize for a cad and a coward. Parolles fits in perfectly with the psychology of these scenes; young men in Bertram's position, asking for nothing but to forget their troubles and indulge their appetites, nearly always take up with worthless but accommodating pseudo-friends who have no genuine qualities; they are not ready for genuineness; it is the emptiness and casualness of such a relationship that appeal to them.

Bertram's behaviour is perfectly observed and credible; so, for that matter, is Helena's. In a fairy-tale, Helena's motives would not be examined; of course the goose-girl wants to marry the young prince, and of course we are all glad to see her do it — as long as the action is confined to the world of fairy-tale. Shakespeare, having set himself the problem of transferring it to the world of realism, gives her at the beginning of the play a speech that reminds us of Prince Hal's soliloquy beginning 'I know you all, and will a while uphold.' It has the same rather unattractive briskness in owning up to a self-seeking motive. After her first despairing soliloquy ('Twere all one That I should love a bright particular star And think to wed it, he is so far above me,') Helena enjoys an exhilarating exchange of dirty jokes with Parolles; then, evidently heartened, she declares her resolve to seek, in the King's illness and her father's love, some way of getting Bertram for her own.

> Who ever strove
> To show her merit that did miss her love?
> The King's disease — my project may deceive me,
> But my intents are fix'd, and will not leave me.

When her medicine works, and the King's health is restored, she claims her reward in the teeth of Bertram's obvious horrified recoil from her. This is realism; the kind of girl who engineers a marriage for herself is not the kind to worry about whether her bridegroom loves her or not; once the ring is on her finger, she feels, there will be plenty of time to bring him round to her point of view. Helena has an egotism that matches Isabella's, just as Bertram parallels Claudio; both are young men of weak character, put into an awkward position by the demands of the plot and finally extricated by stronger characters who do not trouble to consult them. The feebleness of the ending, too, reminds us of *Measure for Measure*; we have gone so far into psychological realism that it is impossible to beat a path back to the safety of folk-tale and romance; the hasty, perfunctory writing merits Dr. Johnson's blistering comment:

'Shakespeare is now hastening to the end of the play, finds his matter sufficient to fill up his remaining scenes, and therefore . . . contracts his dialogue and precipitates his action. Decency required that Bertram's double crime of cruelty and disobedience joined likewise with some hypocrisy, should raise more resentment; and that though his mother might easily forgive him, his king should more pertinaciously vindicate his own authority and Helen's merit: of all this Shakespeare could not be ignorant, but Shakespeare wanted to conclude his play.'

The couplet in which Bertram enters on his new life of married felicity is a good example of the kind of thing Shakespeare sank to when his pen was racing over the paper in an effort to finish something whose interest for him was exhausted:

> If she, my liege, can make me know this clearly,
> I'll love her dearly, ever, ever dearly.

In both these two plays, what succeeds is the portrayal of humanity under the lash of the instincts. Angelo, who proudly denied his animal nature; Isabella, who turned her sexual vanity into the destructive channel of a self-centred holiness; Claudio, who first took the easy way by mitigating the rigour of a strategically long engagement, and then tried to take the easy way again; Lucio, who accepts that his instincts will drive him to be one of Mistress Overdone's clients, and have hideous diseases in consequence — all these characters, driven on by their instincts, are paralleled by others similarly driven in *All's Well*:

Bertram, the young male seeking freedom and adventure; Helena, hungry for the man she loves and ready to use any means to get him: Lavache the clown, who desires his mistress's permission to marry because he is 'driven on by the flesh'; Parolles, his cowardice revealed by a pitiless practical joke, clinging desperately to mere animal existence. Parolles is humiliated by his blind drive towards self-preservation as thoroughly as Angelo by his blind drive towards sexual fulfilment. After his cruel exposure, when his former companions have contemptuously left him to his shame, Parolles gathers up the fragments of his life. What they add up to is mere bedrock survival: breathing, digesting food, moving about. His first words, when left to himself, are the final soliloquy of the 'poor, bare, forked animal'.

> Yet am I thankful. If my heart were great,
> 'Twould burst at this. Captain I'll be no more;
> But I will eat, and drink, and sleep as soft
> As captain shall. Simply the thing I am
> Shall make me live.

His begging for life is like Claudio's; both are inspired by that instinct that keeps human beings and animals alive in any degree of misery. 'Simply the thing I am Shall make me live' is the affirmation of a bitter strength that is left when all other strength is drained away.

The blind fight for life; the 'brutish sting' of sex; this is the subject-matter of these two strange comedies. And here, perhaps, we can find the justification of the tedious and artificial plot device of the bed-trick, which features in both. 'The story of *Bertram* and *Diana*,' wrote Johnson severely, 'had been told before of *Mariana* and *Angelo*, and, to confess the truth, scarcely merited to be heard a second time.' But if it must be heard at all, surely these plays provide the right setting: the mindless drive of lust, like the animal rush for survival, does not pause to recognize its object. As Helena muses,

> O, strange men,
> That can such sweet use make of what they hate,
> When saucy trusting of the cozen'd thoughts
> Defiles the pitchy night. So lust doth play
> With what it loathes, for that which is away.

Love feeds on recognition and knowledge of the loved person; lust, by contrast, is blind; its patterns are laid down in advance and it feeds on whatever approximates to those patterns. Thus, while we know that in 'real life' Angelo and Bertram would soon have recognized the girls they were lying beside, nevertheless the episodes have their own kind of reality. Love enters into communion with people; lust uses them.

I have been assuming here, as Johnson did, that *All's Well* was written later than *Measure for Measure*; in practice, it makes no difference which came first. All that matters is to note that both of them, plus *Troilus and Cressida*, were written during the early years of the seventeenth century. Shakespeare has already written *Hamlet*; his 'tragic period' has begun. The conventions of the 'golden' comedies, which at the best of times worked in an uncertain manner, will now no longer work at all. Later, after the cosmic explorations of the tragic years, the poet will win through to a new set of conventions, where the free imagination of myth and legend will be orchestrated with the searching truth of symbolic vision in a fresh series of masterpieces. But meanwhile, in these three *comédies noires*, the comic spirit is struggling for survival in the harsher climate of a world of tragedy. And that struggle is unsuccessful. What we remember from these plays is not comedy, not the vision of a harmony coaxed out of discord, but the unflinching analysis of discord itself.

IV

LOVERS APART

ANY artist works by means of metaphor. For the abstract and generalized appreciation of a truth, he substitutes its concrete enactment. This makes it natural for him to have certain images, certain situations, certain embodiments, that are peculiarly important to him and recur throughout his life's work. In Shakespeare's case there are several that come to mind; the father seeking his lost daughter, for instance, or the clear-sighted man who adopts a disguise and utters his judgments in code. But the strongest of these images, occupying the foreground in no fewer than four major plays, is that of a man and woman who love each other, and whose love is trampled down by the blind purposes of the world.

Sexual love is the supreme emblem of our personal relationships. It is both primitive and sophisticated. Like the bond uniting parent and child, it is rooted in our biological nature. But unlike that bond, it is an affair of choice and will. We cannot decide to have one set of parents rather than another, but we can decide to have one lover rather than another. Hence the inexhaustible richness of interest. It is a wise instinct that makes almost everyone prefer a love-story to any other kind. But 'The course of true love never did run smooth,' or it would be a simple affair of biology. And the truer the love, the more agony is generated by the things that frustrate it. When a love that is total, uncompromising, all-giving, meets an obstacle too strong to be pushed aside, the tragic nature of human life is illuminated right down to its depths.

Shakespeare returned to this theme so many times that we may suspect that he felt no one treatment could explore more than a corner of its interest. Certainly the four plays he based on it are entirely different from each other. Not only the nature of the impediment, but the relationship of the lovers, changes completely each time. To glance briefly at these four plays is to begin to appreciate the range of his tragic artistry.

In *Romeo and Juliet* the situation is stated in its simplest terms. Two young people, citizens of the same town, under the same law, coming from the same caste, fall in love and their love is brought to tragedy by a senseless vendetta between their families. There is no reason, other than sheer stupidity and bloody-minded pride, why the Montagues and Capulets should be at each other's throats. That they are so, and have long been so, is simply accepted by everyone as a fact of nature, like the weather. That is, the roots of the tragic situation are not explored. It is simply a case of bad luck. When Romeo and Juliet have succeeded in outwitting their families, when they have come within sight of making their escape and starting a new life somewhere else, bad luck intervenes again. A letter fails to arrive in time, a plan collapses, and their love finds its end in the double suicide in the tomb.

Shakespeare's mature conception of tragedy had not, at this time, taken shape. He was still working to the mediaeval idea of tragedy as a cautionary tale, illustrating that man is never out of range of the side-swipes of fate. This is the view we find in Chaucer. 'Tragedie is to seyn a dite of a prosperitie for a time, that endeth in wretchednesse.' High-born persons were the natural protagonists of tragedy, because tragic misfortune strikes at people who are conspicuously getting away with it, and thus open to the temptations of pride and forgetfulness of God's power. Mediaeval tragedy did not site the tragic element within man's nature, except in so far as that nature was corrupted by the Fall.

It was content to point out the inescapable presence of calamity. The lesson it taught was one of piety and resignation; man was to look for mercies from the hand of God and nowhere else.

Romeo and Juliet is a mediaeval fate-tragedy. As such it can have no deep psychological interest. The impression it makes is one of pure pathos. 'Never was a story of more woe Than this of Juliet and her Romeo.' And since everyone is responsive to pathos, it has always been a favourite on the stage. Shakespeare is still growing; he will do far greater things soon. But within its limitations, *Romeo and Juliet* is as perfectly achieved as anything in his work. It is a flawless little jewel of a play. It has the clear, bright colours, the blend of freshness and formality, of an illuminated manuscript. The eagerness and innocence of the young lovers is captured in words that are uncomplicated and memorable, and verse that chimes with a fresh, springy rhythm.

Not that this play is without indications of the more intricate richness that is to come. In the figure of the Nurse, we are already entering the area of mature Shakespearean realism. She is a sketch for Falstaff; Romeo is a sketch for Hamlet. There is a morbid, self-wounding streak in the young man's nature that marks the dawn of Shakespeare's interest in characters of this type. After his impulsive killing of Tybalt, Romeo gives way to suicidal despair and tries to stab himself in the presence of Friar Laurence. This hot rashness recalls Hamlet's stabbing of Polonius, or his leaping into the grave with Laertes. And the Friar restrains him with a vehement rebuke that foreshadows some of Hamlet's reproaches against himself.

> Hold thy desperate hand.
> Art thou a man? Thy form cries out thou art:
> Thy tears are womanish; thy wild acts denote
> The unreasonable fury of a beast.
> Unseemly woman in a seeming man!
> And ill-beseeming beast in seeming both!
> Thou hast amaz'd me. By my holy order,
> I thought thy disposition better temper'd.

Hast thou slain Tybalt? Wilt thou slay thyself?
And slay thy lady that in thy life lives,
By doing damned hate upon thyself?

But where *Hamlet* takes us — albeit stumblingly — into purely
tragic territory, the psychological premises of *Romeo and Juliet*
are those of the early comedies. Characteristically, those comedies
concern themselves with the inborn, unargued stupidity of older
people and the life-affirming gaiety and resourcefulness of young
ones. The lovers thread their way through obstacles set up by
middle-aged vanity and impercipience. Parents are stupid and do
not know what is best for their children or themselves: that is a
donnée and does not have to be justified. *Romeo and Juliet* is in
essence a comedy that turns out tragically. That is, it begins with
the materials for a comedy — the stupid parental generation, the
instant attraction of the young lovers, the quick surface life of
street fights, masked balls and comic servants. But this material
is blighted. Its gaiety and good fortune are drained away by the
fact — also a *donnée* — that the lovers are 'star-crossed'. It is, to
that extent, arbitrarily shaped. It is a tragedy because Shakespeare decided to sit down and write a tragedy. It does not build
with inherently tragic materials. Where the comedies celebrate
order by moving from disharmony to harmony, this play moves
from surface disharmony to an almost achieved surface harmony
before being dashed by a blow from its author's fist into fundamental, irremediable disaster.

To put it another way, the form of *Romeo and Juliet* is that of a
shattered minuet. The two lovers first come together in a dance
(Act I, Scene v), and it is noteworthy that the first words they
address to each other are in the form of a sonnet. A dance; a
sonnet; these are symbols of a formal, contained wholeness.
This wholeness is already threatened. Tybalt has recognized
Romeo; and, though his demand for instant combat has been re-
strained by his host (a rare case of the older generation's being
wiser than the younger), he is glowering and planning revenge.
The worm is already in the fruit. But the nature of the worm is

not explored. The characters move in a certain pattern because the author has decided on that pattern. Romeo and Juliet are all ardour and constancy, their families are all hatred and pride; no one's motives are mixed, and there are no question marks. After the tragedy the survivors are shocked into dropping their vendetta, and Montague and Capulet are united in grief. Once again, there are no question marks. Nothing made them enemies except the clash of their own wills, and nothing is needed to make them brothers except a change of heart.

A good many years went by before Shakespeare again handled this theme of lovers pushed apart by the world. When he did, he was deep in his tragic period, and had long since left behind the simpler notion that suffering is caused solely by the willed actions of human beings. If it were, people would only have to stop behaving tiresomely and paradise would arrive at once.

Romeo and Juliet, wishing to escape from the feud-ridden city of Verona, had planned to make their escape to another city, Padua, and start life anew. The blood-feud that darkened their happiness is seen as an infection as local as a pimple. By travelling a few miles, they can set up in a place where Montague and Capulet cannot reach them. For Troilus and Cressida, this is impossible. The warring camps of Greece and Troy make up their whole world. No one in the play seems to have any consciousness of a wider scene beyond this quarrel. In that respect it is a true Iron-Curtain drama. The unhealed breach divides the world.

II

Troilus and Cressida is the first work of literature by an Englishman which really captures the atmosphere of a world split by one hideous quarrel. Not until the mid-twentieth century was this note to sound again, and then with nothing like the same deadly authority. It is a play drenched in cynicism and disillusion, demonstrating the sombre truth that an infected world is infected from top to bottom: that if a whole society bases itself on hatred and dishonesty, then personal relationships within that society are doomed to the same taint. Troilus and Cressida feel a mutual attraction just as strong as that of Romeo and Juliet. In a healthy world, such an attraction could easily be the firm basis of a lifetime's happiness. As it is, they are breathing the corrupted atmosphere of the besieged city of Troy, which knows no other way of life than an endlessly protracted struggle to keep out the Greeks who are demanding the return of Helen.

Here, even more violently than in the Elsinore of Hamlet, the time is out of joint. Everyone's values are distorted, The only men of clear vision are Ulysses among the Greeks and Hector among the Trojans. Ulysses makes his great speech on 'degree' (Act I, Scene iii), pleading memorably for a sane structure within which men can work together; Hector, acknowledged the most heroic man of war in all Troy, confesses himself weary of the senseless quarrel and counsels that Helen be sent back. Even in Shakespeare's most drab and disillusioned play, the picture is not all dark. The wisdom of Ulysses, the generosity and courage of Hector, cannot be snuffed out even by this foul atmosphere.

The happiness of the lovers, however, is snuffed out. It has no chance to begin sanely, or to go on sanely, in such a time and place. Even if the relationship could have been free of the greasy finger-marks of Pandarus, even if no cruel chance had ordered Cressida's removal to the Grecian camp, this love would have ended in tears. The evil situation — two nations locked in an endless, pointless battle — spreads a blight over everything. From that blight, nothing escapes, Neither the private virtues of love, nor the public virtues of war. Neither the political stability of government, nor the personal relationships which should be growing up within that stability.

The sexual relation is twined closely in with the military and political situations. Helen's fickleness has caused the war, and Cressida's fickleness is a consequence of it. What glimpses we get of Helen and Paris do nothing to convince us that their love is any more likely to produce happiness than that of Troilus and Cressida. The prevailing sexual gaminess is very deftly suggested in the scene (Act III, Scene i) where Pandarus visits the pair with a request that they cover up for Troilus should King Priam send for him that evening; and incidentally conveys by leering hints that Troilus will be spending the night with Cressida. His message delivered, the three exchange banter of an unsavoury nature, and then Pandarus offers to sing them a song.

HELEN. Let thy song be love. This love will undo us all. O Cupid, Cupid, Cupid!

PANDARUS. Love! Ay, that it shall, i'faith.

PARIS. Ay, good now, love, love, nothing but love.

PANDARUS. In good troth, it begins so. (Sings)
> Love, love, nothing but love, still love, still more!
> For, oh, love's bow
> Shoots buck and doe;
> The shaft confounds
> Not that it wounds,
> But tickles still the sore.
> These lovers cry, O ho, they die!
> Yet that which seems the wound to kill
> Doth turn O ho! to ha! ha! he!
> So dying love lives still.
> O ho! a while, but ha! ha! ha!
> O ho! groans out for ha! ha! ha! — hey ho!

HELEN. In love, i'faith, to the very tip of the nose.

PARIS. He eats nothing but doves, love; and that breeds hot blood, and hot blood begets hot thoughts, and hot thoughts beget hot deeds, and hot deeds is love.

PANDARUS. Is this the generation of love: hot blood, hot thoughts, and hot deeds? Why, they are vipers. Is love a generation of vipers?

'This love will undo us all.' It breeds vipers, whose poisonous fangs are in everything. Not least in the language of the play itself, which is dense, murky and shot through with images of violence.

The hot blood of love begets hot thoughts, and hot thoughts beget hot deeds, not only in the bedroom, but on the battle-field. The heroism which has treachery and wrong-headedness for its

basis cannot be true to itself. And this is driven home by the
shocking episode of the murder of Hector on the battlefield.

Throughout the action, each side has been treating the war
after the chivalric fashion, as an exercise in personal courage and
prowess. The leading warriors are not under any discipline, but
take the field on days when they feel so disposed. The fighting
goes on until nightfall, after which they troop back to their
respective bases to relax and feast. Shakespeare's attitude here
seems tinctured with a grim sarcasm. War undertaken as a sport
is likely to end as bitterly as love undertaken as a pastime. However, most of the characters are willing to abide by the code; the
fighting is an indiscriminate series of personal encounters, and
there are generally observed rules about not attacking an opponent
unless he is armed and ready to fight back. Hector himself is a
notable exponent of this sporting theory of war, as we see from
his conversation with Troilus in Act V, Scene iii.

TROILUS. Brother, you have a vice of mercy in you
      Which better fits a lion than a man.
HECTOR. What vice is that, good Troilus? Chide me for it.
TROILUS. When many times the captive Grecian falls,
      Even in the fan and wind of your fair sword,
      You bid them rise and live.
HECTOR.   O, 'tis fair play!
TROILUS. Fool's play, by heaven, Hector.
HECTOR. How now! how now!
TROILUS. For th' love of all the gods,
      Let's leave the hermit Pity with our mother:
      And when we have our armours buckled on,
      The venom'd vengeance ride upon our swords,
      Spur them to ruthful work, rein them from ruth!
HECTOR. Fie, savage, fie!
TROILUS. Hector, then 'tis wars.

Then comes the supreme betrayal. Achilles, enraged by the
fact that Hector has killed his catamite Patroclus — once again a
poisoned love lies behind a wicked act — instructs his gang of

Myrmidons to surround Hector and cut him down. He has already met Hector face to face, but, afraid to oppose him singly, has passed by with an empty taunt about not feeling in the mood for a fight and therefore allowing Hector a lucky escape.

> Be happy that my arms are out of use:
> My rest and negligence befriend thee now.

Hector, true to the rules of the game, allows Achilles to pass unharmed. He comes back with the Myrmidons, who cluster round Hector.

ACHILLES. Look, Hector, how the sun begins to set;
    How ugly night comes breathing at his heels;
    Even with the vail and dark'ning of the sun,
    To close the day up, Hector's life is done.
HECTOR. I am unarm'd; forego this vantage, Greek.
ACHILLES. Strike, fellows, strike; this is the man I seek.
                        (Hector falls)
    So, Ilion, fall thou next! Come, Troy, sink down;
    Here lies thy heart, thy sinews, and thy bone.

He then completes the horrible business by dragging Hector's body at his horse's tail.

The double betrayal is thus acted out; for Troilus has already had to watch Cressida yielding to Diomedes. Of all the plays which Shakespeare devoted to this theme of love knocked awry by the jolting of the world, this is the only one in which the lovers are left alive at the end. All the others are allowed the dignity and repose of death. They are not condemned to go on living with their loss. Troilus and Cressida are not so fortunate: theirs is the inward death of disintegration and despair.

That fate is not traced in detail. To do so would require another play, beginning where this leaves off. (And that idea had been partly anticipated, a century before Shakespeare's birth, by the Scots poet Henryson with his grisly *Testament of Cresseid*.) Shakespeare shows us the beginning of the disintegration that will overtake the mind and heart of Troilus as well as Cressida. Their fate, in which they are united though apart, is, in the simple common phrase, to 'go to pieces'. The separate strands in their characters will no longer cohere. They will lose their identity and become objects rather than persons.

The demonstration is brilliantly carried out in Act V, Scene ii, when Shakespeare brings Troilus onstage to watch Diomed's seduction of Cressida. It is a wonderfully managed piece of theatrical writing; Cressida's inward struggles and hesitations, Diomed's insolent consciousness of his sexual power, and the agony of Troilus, are all shown in a few lines with never a word going to waste. And beside Troilus stand two other characters of importance to the play; Ulysses, who is giving him safe conduct, and Thersites, acting as usual as a cynical chorus.

Ulysses, here as throughout the play, is the representative of wisdom and balance. Responsible as he is for the safety of Troilus behind the Greek lines, he has to use all his authority to restrain him from breaking out and causing a disturbance in which he would inevitably be cut down. Troilus, though feverish, is mindful of what he owes to Ulysses, and after each start he vows to keep quiet and control himself. The price of this control is, as he realizes, a temporary withdrawal from his own nature. He must not be Troilus if he is not to run mad at witnessing the defection of Cressida.

> Fear not me, my lord;
> I will not be myself, nor have cognition
> Of what I feel.

When the scene between Diomedes and Cressida is acted out, and Troilus is left alone with his unheeded companions, he makes a speech in which the warring and disintegrating state of his mind is perfectly conveyed. It begins from incredulity. His mind cannot admit the thought that the woman he has just been watching is Cressida.

> Let it not be believ'd for womanhood.
> Think, we had mothers; do not give advantage

To stubborn critics, apt, without a theme,
For depravation, to square the general sex
By Cressid's rule. Rather think this not Cressid.

He seems to be arguing desperately against an invisible opponent.
And indeed he is: against fate. But Ulysses, feeling that his words
call for some answer, puts in sensibly,

What hath she done, Prince, that can soil our mothers?

The question has something fatuous about it, but Troilus answers
in a courteous, though still stunned, manner.

Nothing at all, unless that this were she.
THERSITES. Will 'a swagger himself out on 's own eyes?
TROILUS. This she? No, this is Diomed's Cressida.
If beauty have a soul, this is not she;
If souls guide vows, if vows be sanctimonies,
If sanctimony be the gods' delight,
If there be rule in unity itself,
This was not she. O madness of discourse,
That cause sets up with and against itself!
Bifold authority! where reason can revolt
Without perdition, and loss assume all reason
Without revolt: this is, and is not, Cressid.
Within my soul there doth conduce a fight
Of this strange nature, that a thing inseparate
Divides more wider than the sky and earth;
And yet the spacious breadth of this division
Admits no orifex for a point as subtle
As Ariachne's broken woof to enter.[1]

[1] No such person as *Ariachne* is known to mythology; it was *Arachne* who
had a 'broken woof', when Athena, in jealousy of her prowess at weaving,
destroyed her loom and then changed her to a spider (Ovid, *Metamorphoses*,
Book 6). But if the intrusive 'i' is Shakespeare's slip and not the printer's, it
is an interesting 'Freudian error': *Ariadne* was first rescued by Theseus and
then abandoned by him on Naxos; Troilus, who feels abandoned by the
person who formerly rescued him from unhappiness, might very naturally
run the two together; it could be an effect contrived by Shakespeare, or the
fusion could have occurred at a pre-conscious level. Ariadne used a thread to
guide Theseus through the labyrinth and thus win his love; but her thread,
like Arachne's, proved of no lasting avail. 'Though this be madness, yet there
is method in 't.'

> Instance, O instance! strong as Pluto's gates:
> Cressid is mine, tied with the bonds of heaven.
> Instance, O instance! strong as heaven itself:
> The bonds of heaven are slipp'd, dissolv'd, and loos'd;
> And with another knot, five-finger-tied,
> The fractions of her faith, orts of her love,
> The fragments, scraps, the bits, and greasy relics
> Of her o'er-eaten faith, are bound to Diomed.

Beginning fairly intelligibly, this speech becomes more clotted as we move closer to the centre of Troilus's confusion and pain. It starts with a piece of conventional declamation, such as any Elizabethan dramatist might have managed. Cressida has changed her nature; if beauty have a soul, this is not she — though she was the soul of beauty when she was true to her own self and to Troilus. But with the line about 'rule in unity itself' we begin to move into more troubled language. If there is any singleness, if anything in the universe is unequivocal and unambiguous, this was not Cressida. Except that we know that it was. 'O madness of discourse' means partly 'I'm talking nonsense' (*discourse* meaning talk, conversation, narrative) and partly 'reason itself is mad, the nature of things is mad' (*discourse* here meaning reason or thought, which as a noun is its chief Shakespearean sense). Discourse argues, as in a court of law, but on both sides, *with and against itself*, producing *bifold authority*, the split that disintegrates a human being. Under this bifold authority, *reason can revolt without perdition*. Troilus here begins to speak very obscurely, but in dramatic terms this is an advantage: it is right that as he moves further into isolation, the outlines of his character beginning to blur, he should utter a line or two whose sense is too clotted for the audience in a theatre to catch. Even in slow motion his words are not exactly clear. *Perdition* in Shakespeare means what it means to us — eternal damnation or utter loss. (When Fluellen says, 'the perdition of the enemy hath been very great', he is merely showing what a comically bookish fellow he is. Othello's 'Perdition catch my soul But I do love thee!' illustrates the general use of the word.) This lets in a strongly Christian

undertone, since the obvious occasion when reason revolted and
led to perdition was the fall of the angels; the anachronism need
disturb no one, since a few moments earlier Troilus has spoken of
the devil. In the meaningless world into which Cressida's betrayal
has plunged him, Troilus cannot conceive of any further fall;
even a revolt of reason — a mad challenge to the created order of
things — would not lead to any worse perdition, since everything
is lost already. Alternatively, it could be reason itself that deserves
perdition, but unaccountably escapes it: why is reason still
evidently in control, still not dethroned in favour of raving
madness, when it utters such wild contradictions? *Loss* at the
same time *assumes all reason*, is perfectly credible, lays claim to full
reasonableness, *without revolt*; all nature does not, even Troilus
himself does not, rise up and fight against this tragedy. The up-
shot is that a contradiction can exist, two opposites can be true
at the same time: *this is, and is not, Cressid.*

No wonder that Troilus then begins to pile up monstrous
hyperboles on this basis of paradox. It is impossible to straighten
out the grammar of the three lines:

> Within my soul there doth conduce a fight
> Of this strange nature, that a thing inseparate
> Divides more wider than the sky and earth.

Divides could be transitive or intransitive; this· *thing inseparate*
(i.e. indivisible) could divide Troilus's soul or it could divide
itself. In either case, the shockingly irreconcilable truths are
clashed violently together with a noise of confused (and, it must
be added, very clumsy) rhetoric. *Instance* meant, as it does now,
definite example or proof. He knows, because he saw it, that
Cressida accepted the advances of Diomedes; he knows, with the
inner certainty that passion brings, that the bond between
Cressida and himself is unbreakable. The only way out for his
overburdened consciousness is to simplify itself and disintegrate
in the process.

Accordingly, at the end of the play we take our leave of a

Troilus whose nature has narrowed itself down to hatred and the will to revenge. He has become less than human, just as Cressida will. The cruel intervention of the world has driven the lovers not only from each other's arms but 'out of their minds' in the most literal sense.

III

The jump from *Romeo and Juliet* to *Troilus and Cressida* is as wide as any in Shakespeare. From a tragedy written during the years when Shakespeare was mainly working on comedy, we pass to a *comédie noire* written on the threshold of his tragic period. It is as if, as he entered the world of tragedy in which he was to live for five sombre years, Shakespeare suddenly remembered this early theme, handled in such bright primary colours, bathed in such fresh light, with only a dark splash of blood in the last act. Now, his vision of the world grown altogether darker and more complex, he took it up again. And not once only. *Troilus and Cressida* was written by 1603, in which year it was registered with the Stationers' Company. *Othello*, in which he next handled this basic theme of estrangement, was acted at Court on 1 November 1604. No more than a year or two separates the plays.

In the angle of approach to the story, of course, *Othello* represents a completely new start. Here, the force that pushes the lovers apart is not military and political. It is anthropological. While bringing in a villain to do some of the mechanical work of the plot, Shakespeare is actually basing his tragedy on the realization that human beings differ in crucial ways according to their background of race, of beliefs, of tradition. If they differed so widely as to ignore one another's existence, all might still be well. But in fact they are still capable of being strongly drawn to each other, across these barriers. Othello and Desdemona can still fall in love. And when they do, it is the differences between them, the uncharted gulf they have to cross in order to communicate, that brings them to destruction.

Years before, Shakespeare had turned his attention to the

theme of irreconcilable worlds existing side by side on this earth. In *The Merchant of Venice* he had achieved the first full-length picture in English literature of the Jew, who lives according to the laws of whatever country he finds himself in, but retains always his inner allegiances. That early play is not a success; the frail shell of comedy is far too thin to support the heavy, intractable subject-matter which seems to have welled up from Shakespeare's inner mind once composition was fairly started. No doubt he originally intended to make Shylock a stage-villain like Marlowe's Jew of Malta ('Sometimes I go about and poison wells', etc., etc.). But once he began, the true predicament of the man shaped itself under his fingers. The result is a play whose essential interest has evaporated by the end of the fourth act.

This does not greatly matter. Every fast-working, prolific writer knows the embarrassment of having a major theme creep up on him unheralded during the act of composition, so that the nature of the work changes as it goes on. In such a case the usual answer is to attack the theme more methodically later on. So the interest of *The Merchant of Venice* is largely anticipatory. In the figure of Shylock, it gives us a magnificently credible portrait of the interior alien. Living among the gay and civilized Venetians, Shylock retains the gloomy grandeur and implacability of the Old Testament. When Antonio makes it a reproach to him that he lends out money at interest, he replies with an anecdote about sanctified sharp-practice from the Book of Genesis. Though ironically subservient to the laws of Venice, and fiercely insistent on the letter of that law in upholding his 'bond' as an instrument of vengeance, he is proud of not being essentially a part of the civilization he inhabits. 'I will buy with you,' he says, 'sell with you, talk with you, walk with you, and so following; but I will not eat with you, drink with you, nor pray with you.' He relates himself to the other characters in the play by trade only; the ferocious revenge he plans to take on Antonio is merely a ghastly parody of business and mercantile legality. They retaliate by theft, both of his daughter and his ducats, and then by outwitting him in the manipulation of law. The final humiliation of Shylock, though it is horrible to a modern audience, has a certain crude appropriateness. Shylock, in his grief and pain, has invoked the humanity he shares with them. 'Hath not a Jew eyes? hath not a Jew hands, organs, dimensions, senses, affections, passions?', etc., etc. Now, having him finally in their power, they insist that he should be baptized as a Christian. To us, it looks like the final insult, robbing Shylock of his identity as a Jew. But the suggestion comes from the wronged but forgiving Antonio, who is certainly meant as a sympathetic character; and, since Shylock has claimed membership of the human race, a literal belief in Christianity would dictate that he be saved from the eternal perdition which, as an unbaptized Jew, would otherwise await him.

The disagreement between Shylock and the Venetians is deeper than trade, deeper than politics. It is religious and anthropological, an irreconcilable severance of life-styles. But the same play also contains another alien. This time the character is a mere sketch, but one that reveals how Shakespeare's imagination was busy with the theme. Into the trivial and fanciful sub-plot about Portia and her suitors, the fairy-tale business with the caskets, there strides the magnificent dusky figure of the Prince of Morocco. Valiant and dignified, this character introduces himself with two of the most majestic lines in all Shakespeare's work up to that point.

> Mislike me not for my complexion,
> The shadow'd livery of the burnish'd sun.

In fact, such is his magnificence that we feel relieved when his part in the action is over. To expect so stately a figure to tread for long on the eggshells of the basket sub-plot is asking for one of those sudden collapses into incongruity to which the earlier Shakespeare was liable. Shylock is already out of hand, the play is hopelessly lopsided, and a more rounded sketch of this Moorish prince would wreck what remains of the comedy. Shakespeare,

with evident nervousness, hurries Morocco through, giving him
a total of about ten minutes on the stage, and allowing Portia to
trim off the episode with the perfunctory couplet,

> A gentle riddance. Draw the curtains: go.
> Let all of his complexion choose me so.

But this proud Moor, with his kingly presence and the swelling
music of his speech, stays in our minds when the clockwork
action has chimed to its close. What would have happened if the
story had suddenly become real? If Portia had fallen in love with
Morocco and married him? How would the Venetians have
reacted to him, and he to them?

Othello is precisely that story, except that Desdemona is not a
self-reliant heiress but a shy, gentle daughter whose natural instinct is to obey. Her gentleness and Othello's magnificence have
one thing in common: their terrible helplessness. Both of them,
in entirely different ways, are too high-minded to see through
ordinary lying. Othello is like some huge man-of-war, aground
in a creek, an easy prey to a boarding-party in a rowing boat.
Desdemona has a natural guilelessness which, owing to her over-
protective father, has never been brought into contact with the
roughness and duplicity of the world. As a result the play
combines two kinds of tragic suffering. And this, no doubt, is
the reason for its brutal, almost sickening impact.

The painfulness of *Othello* is dreadful. Samuel Johnson con-
fessed that he found the scene of Cordelia's death in *King Lear*
so agonizing that, after his first encounter with the play in boy-
hood, he never again read that scene until he had to work over
it as an editor. Personally I find even that scene easier to bear
than the one in which Othello strikes Desdemona (Act IV, Scene i)
or the following scene in which he affects to take her for a
prostitute — to say nothing of the terribly distressing murder
scene. It is as if, in *Hamlet*, we had to watch Ophelia drown. And
the horrible agony of such scenes arises not merely from the
pathos of Desdemona's fate. We feel pity, though of a different

kind, for Othello also. It is like watching a noble building defaced and smeared with filth.

Most tragedy comes into one of two categories: either the tragedy of greatness, or the tragedy of innocence. The appalled pity with which we follow the action arises either from watching a mighty spirit battling against difficulties so huge that in the end even he goes down in defeat; or from watching some innocent and helpless being crushed, all too easily, by the casual cruelty of life. *Othello* offers both. When we are not aghast at the one, we are weeping over the other.

As we shall see later, there are no large-scale villains in Shakespeare's plays. The tragic suffering is unleashed by mistakes rather than malignities. I don't, of course, mean that Macbeth murders Duncan without realizing that he is doing so, or that Lear curses Cordelia absent-mindedly. But nevertheless, neither Macbeth nor Lear is a 'villain' in the usual theatrical sense. Shakespeare left villains behind with his Marlovian phase. His last full-scale bad man was Richard III. In the mature tragedies, the evil is either done by essentially noble characters under the influence of some temporary passion, or, if it is really cool, open-eyed wrongdoing, it is perpetrated by little people.

Iago is no exception. He is a sharper with a dirty mind. He moves nimbly through the action, keeping barely one jump ahead of the retribution that overtakes him at the end. A good many studies of Iago's character have been written to prove that he was a superhuman figure, a fiend incarnate, a superb artist in evil against whom neither Othello nor anyone else could have stood a chance. Most of these essays, one suspects, have been written by well-fed and well-warmed literary gentlemen, writing in pleasant book-lined studies, and drawing on a comfortable lack of experience of ordinary human life. In fact, anybody who has been in the army, or worked in a factory, or even just knocked about with his eyes open, has met Iago. He is the sadistic sergeant who makes the men's lives miserable while cultivating dozens of little arts which win the confidence of his superior officers. He is clever and quick-witted, within his limitations; he knows what it behoves him to know; he has the skills that make for survival and coming out on top.

The opposite view of Iago's character, that he is a force of bottomless evil, derives mainly from Coleridge's phrase about 'the motive-hunting of a motiveless malignity'. It is a pity Coleridge ever permitted himself this phrase, which reveals clearly that his attention had wandered from the play. The very opening words of the first Act give us Iago's motive.

> RODERIGO. Tush, never tell me; I take it much unkindly
> That you, Iago, who has had my purse
> As if the strings were thine, shouldst know of this.

Know of what? Why, that Othello had eloped with Desdemona and married her. And Iago's answer is perfectly genuine.

> 'Sblood, but you will not hear me.
> If ever I did dream of such a matter,
> Abhor me.

As a non-commissioned officer, he is not in Othello's confidence. The whole thing has taken him by surprise. And now, as a result, he has to talk his way out of an embarrassing situation; for Roderigo, the rich and dissolute gull, has been waiting in the background, and handing out funds, on the understanding that Iago will lead him to the favours of Desdemona.

To keep Roderigo happy, Iago launches into a recital of his grievances against Othello. He has (of course!) been passed over for promotion. And — again of course — the choice has fallen on a better-educated, less experienced man.

> Forsooth, a great arithmetician,
> One Michael Cassio, a Florentine.
> A fellow almost damn'd in a fair wife
> That never set a squadron in the field,
> Nor the division of a battle knows
> More than a spinster.

And so on. Iago thus has what he considers a perfectly adequate motive for hating both Othello and Cassio. Then there is his dirty-mindedness. To keep Roderigo in good heart and get some more money out of him, he assures him that Desdemona can't be as innocent as she seems. But this may be only partly a blind. Sexual innocence is something he cannot comprehend. He sees the small proportion of deceit in Desdemona's behaviour — when before her marriage she dissembled her feelings and hid her intention from her father — and misses the overwhelming proportion of innocence and good faith.

In fact Iago's smuttiness, the seam of debased and unhealthy sexuality that runs through his character, is responsible for some curious blind spots in which his normal shrewdness fails to operate. This is very true to everyday observation. All such men are clear-sighted except where sexual relations are concerned, and then they will believe anything if it is disgraceful enough. Before the end of Act I, Iago utters an explanatory speech, in soliloquy, in which he makes the preposterous suggestion that Othello has been making love to Emilia.

> I hate the Moor;
> And it is thought abroad that 'twixt my sheets
> 'Has done my office. I know not if't be true;
> Yet I, for mere suspicion in that kind,
> Will do as if for surety.

If any such absurdity is in fact 'thought abroad', it can only be by someone of very much the same type as Iago — as Emilia herself points out later, when the subject comes up between them. By saying that he will react to suspicion by assuming that it is true, Iago is thus offering us a hideous parody of the state to which he will bring Othello. 'To be once in doubt Is to be once resolved.'

A little later, having begun his work by convincing Roderigo that Cassio and Desdemona are plotting adultery, we find him soliloquizing again, and now his fantasies are beginning to attach themselves to Desdemona.

> Now I do love her too;
> Not out of absolute lust, though peradventure
> I stand accountant for as great a sin,
> But partly led to diet my revenge,
> For that I do suspect the lusty Moor
> Hath leap'd into my seat; the thought whereof
> Doth like a poisonous mineral gnaw my inwards;
> And nothing can nor shall content my soul
> Till I am even'd with him, wife for wife.

Adultery conceived as an act of revenge! It is exactly the level on which Iago operates. And the stupidity, the complete failure to assess the situation, that can lead him to toy with the idea of involving Desdemona in a love affair, matches the grotesque unreality of his suspicion of Othello.

These are delusions, but they are commonplace delusions. All they indicate is that Iago, like so many outwardly bluff, manly fellows, is slightly ill in his sexual emotions. His main symptom is an incurable low-mindedness, mingled with deep-rooted envy and a suspiciousness that leads him to wander into fantasy. Such an outfit does not add up to a very powerful armoury. If we play the amusing fireside game of scrambling the characters in Shakespeare's plays, and imagine Iago trying to outwit Hamlet, or Benedick, or King Harry the Fifth, we get a sudden glimpse of Othello's vulnerability. Iago's lies are such as only Othello could be induced to believe. And the suspicion in which they involve Othello is such as only a Desdemona could fail to dispel at an early stage.

Othello has wandered into Venice from a world of incredible hardship and legendary strangeness. His life-story is what first captivates Desdemona; its romantic quality appeals to a city-bred girl who has been carefully tended and secluded. She really knows nothing about him, nor he about her; they have not yet come to terms with each other's characters; they have nothing except the fiercely blazing love that will ultimately settle down to this comfortable warmth. The time for a mischief-maker like Iago to intervene is now, before the lovers have spent much time together.

Othello is attracted by Desdemona's strangeness as much as she by his. She is a product of this sophisticated city world about which he knows nothing. His grandeur, and the large simplicities of his conduct, make him an albatross in Venice. Like Shylock, he enters the glittering Venetian scene throwing the enormous shadows of an older and more primitive world. When Iago tells him that he knows nothing of Venetian women, and must therefore accept his, Iago's, estimate of his wife's character, he can only acquiesce. And having acquiesced, he can imagine no remedy except to kill her. His nature is geared to action, and the only action he knows is his 'occupation'.

Shakespeare's drama, as we have said, is primarily an art of language. It depended on the direct transmission of words into visual images. So that a character who is set apart from the rest is always given a strongly contrasting idiom and rhythm. Shylock's language is different in weight, pace and *timbre* from that of the Venetian characters in the play, and he is given two arias ('When Jacob grazed his uncle Laban's sheep' and 'Signior Antonio, many a time and oft') part of whose function is to accustom our ears to his individual cadences.

Similarly with Othello. When we first see him, he is listening to Iago's excited description of the hue and cry that has been raised for him by Desdemona's father. Iago has of course provoked this hue and cry, and it is illustrative of the shallow nature of his plotting, the way he needs all his luck to keep one jump ahead, that he has completely misjudged the situation between Othello and the nobility of Venice. When the torches of the approaching officers are seen coming towards them, Iago prepares to savour the sight of Othello in retreat, and prompts him eagerly,

> Those are the raised father and his friends:
> You were best go in.

Othello, of course, refuses to run away from the officers, and answers in the vein of his grand simplicity,

> Not I; I must be found:
> My parts, my title, and my perfect soul
> Shall manifest me rightly.

It then turns out that the party, though they are indeed seeking Othello, have nothing to do with Brabantio. They bring an urgent message from the Duke, requesting Othello's presence; and the chief messenger is Iago's hated rival, Cassio. While Iago is digesting his spleen at the way things have turned out, Brabantio's party arrive, but the threatened brawl is at once averted by Othello's calm authority. His

> Keep up your bright swords, for the dew will rust them!

is one of the great signature-lines in Shakespeare, like Hamlet's 'A little more than kin, and less than kind,' or Falstaff's 'Now Hal, what time o' day is it, lad?' — lines which immediately strike the keynote of a character and give it a flesh and blood presence. Othello's slight contempt for these excited Venetians, who flash their nice new swords like toys, gives extra weight to his unforced authority. In a few moments we are in the council chamber, and Othello is making his speech to the Senators beginning 'Most potent, grave and reverend signiors'. This is his first aria. It stands out from the surrounding dialogue by virtue of its slower and more majestic rhythm, its sonority, and the romantic nature of its images.

> Wherein of antres vast and deserts idle,
> Rough quarries, rocks, and hills whose heads touch heaven,
> It was my hint to speak — such was the process;
> And of the Cannibals that each other eat,
> The Anthropophagi, and men whose heads
> Do grow beneath their shoulders.

The proud Senators of wealthy Venice sit attentive before this huge, kingly barbarian on whose generalship they rely for their protection; he speaks to them of the world that begins where theirs ends. (And indeed, even in the twentieth century one gets the impression at Venice of standing on the frontier where a different and mysterious way of life begins; the story couldn't, so fitly, have been set anywhere else, as Shakespeare must have realized.)

The essence of a kingly barbarian is that he has no middle range of conduct; when he is shocked out of his grand behaviour he falls straight to the level of cruelty and violence. So when Othello is driven mad by the suspicion of Desdemona's infidelity he does not stab her with an intellectual weapon, as Hamlet stabs Ophelia; he actually strikes her, and a few hours later throttles her to death. And all this without ceasing to speak in the high, sonorous idiom that Shakespeare employs to set him apart. This idiom is never better shown, in fact, than in the murder scene, where Othello's preliminary speech ('It is the cause, it is the cause, my soul') has a wonderful blend of the elegiac and the menacing.

Like his behaviour, Othello's language knows no middle range. When his agony is so intense as to forbid the use of his natural stately rhythm, he falls into delirium and utters broken fragments of speech.

> Lie with her — lie on her? We say lie on her when they belie her. Lie with her. Zounds, that's fulsome. Handkerchief — confessions — handkerchief! To confess, and be hang'd for his labour — first, to be hang'd, and then to confess. I tremble at it. Nature would not invest herself in such shadowing passion without some instruction. It is not words that shakes me thus — pish! noses, ears, and lips. Is't possible? Confess! Handkerchief! O devil!
>
> *(Falls in a trance.)*

Other devices are, of course, used to indicate Othello's distance from the other characters. The whole episode of Desdemona's handkerchief is one such device. Iago's motive in wanting to get hold of it is simply that he knows it to be 'her first remembrancer from the Moor'. To manipulate evidence to make it appear that Desdemona has given this handkerchief to Cassio — this is exactly the kind of thing he excels at. And, as usual, Othello's reaction is deeper than Iago can foresee. He does not merely value the handkerchief as a token of affection. He attaches magical significance to it.

> There's magic in the web of it.
> A sibyl that had numb'red in the world
> The sun to course two hundred compasses
> In her prophetic fury sew'd the work;
> The worms were hallowed that did breed the silk;
> And it was dy'd in mummy which the skilful
> Conserv'd of maidens' hearts.

Desdemona's reaction is a Western, rational one. If there is so much sacred mumbo-jumbo attached to the handkerchief, it would have been better not to give it as a present. The gulf between her anthropological background and Othello's is at once cruelly manifest.

DESDEMONA. I'faith! Is't true?
OTHELLO. Most veritable; therefore look to't well.
DESDEMONA. Then would to God that I had never seen't!
OTHELLO. Ha! Wherefore?
DESDEMONA. Why do you speak so startingly and rash?
OTHELLO. Is't lost? Is't gone? Speak, Is't out o' th' way?
DESDEMONA. Heaven bless us!
OTHELLO. Say you?
DESDEMONA. It is not lost; but what an if it were?
OTHELLO. How!
DESDEMONA. I say it is not lost.
OTHELLO. Fetch't, let me see't.
DESDEMONA. Why, so I can, sir, but I will not now.
This is a trick to put me from my suit:
Pray you let Cassio be receiv'd again.

Common sense, and a decent sense of the duty of helping a friend, lead the poor child to choose this moment to bring Cassio's name up again. The two simplicities confront one another. And we all know what happens when simplicities clash. Neither knows how to give way. So that the tragedy needs very little further assistance from Iago. From that point on, it hastens to its dreadful end, fed by its own fuel and obedient to its own inexorable laws.

IV

In his last full-scale treatment of this theme of lovers held asunder by the world, Shakespeare turned to the universally known story of Antony and Cleopatra. Here was a legend to call out his full powers. Once more it was a tale culminating in suicide, but this time the motives for suicide were far more wide-ranging than the simple emotional disappointment of Romeo and Juliet. Once more the union was between a magnificent barbarian and a product of ordered civilization. But this time the woman was the barbarian. And the quarrel in the background was no mere bicker between two Hellenic tribes over the defection of a princess, but the confrontation of the steady and legalistic civilization of Rome with the strange, beckoning world that lay over its eastern horizon.

Shakespeare seems to have had an instinctive understanding of the problems that were to confront his countrymen during the next three or four centuries. He divined, long before England became an imperial power, one of the most difficult problems of imperialism: how to stop your personnel from going native. The nineteenth-century British administrator who dressed for dinner in the jungle has become a figure of fun. Yet there is a sound psychological basis for such antics. Once the emissary of a civilization drops the conspicuous habits of that civilization, and begins to adopt those of the people he governs, his authority declines.

When the action of *Antony and Cleopatra* begins, the problem is not, as yet, much more than this. Julius Caesar is dead, and the Roman world is governed by the triumvirate, Octavius Caesar, Mark Antony, and Lepidus. Lepidus, a weak character, is already slipping down out of sight, and the effective rule is divided between Caesar and Antony: the one in Rome, the other attending to the far-flung responsibilities of empire in Egypt. And disturbing reports have come back to Rome which indicate that Antony, under the bewitchment of Cleopatra, has gone native. Demetrius, an officer newly arrived from Rome, is discussing the situation with Philo, a member of Antony's staff; and, as they watch, the lovers enter, sumptuously attended, and Antony, having brusquely refused to hear the messenger from Rome, proposes to Cleopatra that they should dismiss all thoughts except those of pleasure:

> and all alone,
> To-night we'll wander through the streets, and note
> The qualities of people.

In other words, he no longer cares to keep a proper distance between himself and the Egyptian populace. A little later, when the scene has switched to Rome and we hear Caesar angrily complaining of Antony's conduct, this indiscriminate gregariousness is one of the gravest of Antony's offences:

> to sit
> And keep the turn of tippling with a slave,
> To reel the streets at noon, and stand the buffet
> With knaves that smell of sweat . . .

It is true that Caesar is something of a prig, who feels no temptation to drink or be matey with anyone. But then he is another of Shakespeare's portraits of men 'that have power to hurt, and will do none'. As usual, this type comes out on top when anything to do with power and politics is afoot.

Antony, meanwhile, is in thrall: not merely to Cleopatra, but to what Cleopatra typifies. The East, with all those undertones of mysterious sensual abandonment which disintegrate the Westerner? Yes, partly. But beyond that, something deeper and more universal. Cleopatra is not only the picturesque and unfathomable Orient. She also contains within herself all those elements in women which make men willing to throw away rationality, toss aside careers and security, and end up in rags. She is 'the serpent of old Nile'. Her nature, as we see it in action in the play, cannot be simply described in a sentence. It is conveyed by a very strong current of imagery and symbolism.

Shakespeare's theatre used boy actors for female parts. He could not rely on having a real-life enchantress on the stage, to sway the audience into sharing Antony's feelings. Accordingly, the lady's beauty is, as usual, conveyed by verbal description. In this case, by one of the greatest of Shakespearean set-pieces: the speech of Enobarbus in Act II, Scene ii.

> The barge she sat in, like a burnish'd throne,
> Burn'd on the water. The poop was beaten gold;
> Purple the sails, and so perfumed that
> The winds were love-sick with them; the oars were
>   silver,
> Which to the tune of flutes kept stroke, and made
> The water which they beat to follow faster,
> As amorous of their strokes. For her own person,
> It beggar'd all description. She did lie
> In her pavilion, cloth-of-gold, of tissue,
> O'erpicturing that Venus where we see
> The fancy out-work nature. On each side her
> Stood pretty dimpled boys, like smiling Cupids,
> With divers-colour'd fans, whose wind did seem
> To glow the delicate cheeks which they did cool,
> And what they undid did.

AGRIPPA. O, rare for Antony!

ENOBARBUS. Her gentlewomen, like the Nereides,
> So many mermaids, tended her i' th' eyes,
> And made their bends adornings. At the helm
> A seeming mermaid steers. The silken tackle
> Swell with the touches of those flower-soft hands
> That yarely frame the office. From the barge
> A strange invisible perfume hits the sense
> Of the adjacent wharfs. The city cast
> Her people out upon her; and Antony,
> Enthron'd i' th' market-place, did sit alone,
> Whistling to th' air; which, but for vacancy,
> Had gone to gaze on Cleopatra too,
> And made a gap in nature.

This passage has been endlessly analysed and commented on, because it exemplifies the Shakespearean power in so many ways. To begin with, it is modelled with extreme closeness on the same description in North's translation of Plutarch, from which Shakespeare was taking the story. In a superb demonstration of economy of effort, Shakespeare substitutes verse for North's prose, and changes hardly anything else. His main contribution is dramatic. He puts the speech into the mouth of the hard-bitten Enobarbus, a tough and unsentimental officer of the line who has seen women come and go in a soldier's life. That it should be *he* who says, a few lines further on, that age cannot wither Cleopatra, nor custom stale her infinite variety, makes the description entirely convincing.

Enobarbus, for all that he has seen and done, cannot keep the wonder out of his voice as he describes Cleopatra's appearance in her barge at Cydnus. Yet if we look over the description again we see that it contains nothing at all about Cleopatra herself. What makes the impression is the parade of luxury, sensuality and mystery, so beautifully conveyed in the imagery with its languorous sexual undertones. It is taken for granted that Cleopatra is a beautiful woman. Yet no woman could make this impact with beauty alone. It is the barbaric lure of the world she represents, as much as her own attraction, that submerges Antony.

I say 'submerges' advisedly. Not for nothing is this first formal portrait of Cleopatra — the first full statement of how she looks when seen through a man's eyes — sited on a barge floating down a river. Cleopatra's element is water. Like water, she is unbiddable and unstable; immediately finds her own level; wins every battle not by fighting but by absorbing the strength of the assailant. This is no piece of arbitrary symbolism on Shakespeare's part. Water is universally accepted as the basic feminine symbol. Each of us begins his life as a small fish, floating in the amniotic fluid inside a woman's body; and from this physical basis, the symbolism rises to its full psychological inclusiveness. Cleopatra floats in a barge for the same reason that

Molly Bloom uses her chamber-pot in the final section of *Ulysses*.

Antony's absorption in Cleopatra is the absorption of earth in water. This is true at all levels, from the most superficial to the deepest. To take the superficial first, we need only note that when it comes to an open conflict between himself and Caesar, he loses, although he has adequate forces and more than adequate generalship. And the reason he loses is because, under Cleopatra's influence, he twice elects to fight at sea rather than on land. This decision is taken against the advice of everyone in his army, from Enobarbus to the anonymous soldier who appears and suddenly calls to him,

> O noble emperor, do not fight by sea;
> Trust not to rotten planks. Do you misdoubt
> This sword and these my wounds? Let th' Egyptians
> And the Phoenicians go a-ducking; we
> Have us'd to conquer standing on the earth
> And fighting foot to foot.

This soldier understands the Roman tradition: the firmness of earth typifies the heavy solidity of the Roman mind, leaving nothing to chance and thumping its way through to a predictable mastery. Water has no place in this way of life. But this is the Antony who, in the opening scene of the play, has exclaimed impatiently,

> Let Rome in Tiber melt, and the wide arch
> Of the ranged empire fall!

And by the end of the play Rome, in the person of her greatest general, has melted indeed: not in Tiber, but in the more treacherous waters of the Nile.

Towards the end of Antony's life, when he finally sees after his second defeat that the game is up, he calls his servant Eros and begins to talk about clouds.

ANTONY. Eros, thou yet behold'st me?
EROS.   Ay, noble lord.

ANTONY. Sometime we see a cloud that's dragonish;
    A vapour sometime like a bear or lion,
    A tower'd citadel, a pendent rock,
    A forked mountain, or blue promontory
    With trees upon't that nod unto the world
    And mock our eyes with air. Thou hast seen these signs;
    They are black vesper's pageants.
EROS.   Ay, my lord.
ANTONY. That which is now a horse, even with a thought
    The rack dislimns, and makes it indistinct,
    As water is in water.
EROS.   It does, my lord.
ANTONY. My good knave Eros, now thy captain is
    Even such a body. Here I am Antony;
    Yet cannot hold this visible shape, my knave.

On a 'realistic' level, this musing on clouds does no more to advance the action than Gertrude's botany-lesson when she is announcing the death of Ophelia in *Hamlet*. Both belong to the symbolic-poetic side of Shakespeare's armoury. Antony understands the fate that has overtaken him, and enables us to understand it, by describing his ruin in terms of vapour and deliquescence.

His element is earth: hers is water. When the two meet, the result is mud. Hence it is not surprising to find a consistent thread of imagery about mud and slime running through the play. For these, too, are symbols of Antony's predicament. His unrestrained enjoyment of Cleopatra, involving him in two broken marriages during the one play, is the mud into which a man dives when he cannot hold himself back. And mud, primeval slime, suggests fecundity and the warm, undiscriminating huddle in which all life begins. This is faithfully borne out by the imagery. In that same opening scene, impatient with the messengers from Rome, Antony has declared,

    Kingdoms are clay; our dungy earth alike
    Feeds beast as man.

In comparison with the rarified ecstasies of love, it is menial to concern oneself with empire, which is a mere matter of domination over so many miles of muddy earth. This is echoed at the end of the play, in the musing of Cleopatra when she welcomes the release of death.

> . . . it is great
> To do that thing that ends all other deeds,
> Which shackles accidents, and bolts up change,
> Which sleeps, and never palates more the dung,
> The beggar's nurse and Caesar's.

Many editors, from the eighteenth century to the present day, have substituted 'dug' for 'dung' in that passage; for instance the 'Oxford Shakespeare', published in 1892 and still widely current, reads 'dug'. So, more surprisingly, does Peter Alexander's 'Tudor' edition of 1951. But this is to substitute the wrong kind of logic for the right kind: the logic of consistent metaphor as against the deeper logic of the drift of imagery and emotion. All life comes from manure and dead things; what we call beautiful and good is rooted in what we call disgusting; as Hamlet says, 'Imperious Caesar, dead and turn'd to clay, Might stop a hole to keep the wind away:'. Cleopatra is very much aware of her own humanity and earthiness; her tastes have not been exactly ethereal; but now, in her last majestic hour, she finds the earth no longer to her taste.

> I am all fire and air; my other elements
> I give to baser life.

She renounces, that is, earth and water. And this is fitting enough as an exit line. But that same mixture of earth and water has made the fecund mud which has quickened under the hot sunshine of male passion.

Antony, at an exalted moment (Act I, Scene iii), has sworn constancy to Cleopatra by 'the fire that quickens Nilus' slime'. That is, by himself. Without the adoration of a man, Cleopatra is inert. And this links her to the play's serpent-imagery. It was a widespread traveller's tale in Shakespeare's day, inherited from the Middle Ages and no doubt ultimately from Pliny, that large snakes such as the python, which had no obvious means of procreation, were in fact generated by the action of the sun on tropical mud. Small wonder that Cleopatra finds pleasure in recalling that Antony calls her his 'serpent of old Nile'. She is brought to life in the same way. And her consciousness remains close to these dark origins. Stung by anger and loss, she bursts out (Act II, Scene v) 'Melt Egypt into Nile! And kindly creatures Turn all to serpents!' And later, appalled by the thought of being taken captive by Caesar and exhibited in Rome, she cries,

> Rather a ditch in Egypt
> Be gentle grave unto me! rather on Nilus' mud
> Lay me stark naked, and let the water-flies
> Blow me into abhorring!

Such images carry the central symbolism through the play like an artery. To note their all-pervading presence we need only look at the banquet-scene (Act II, Scene vii) at which Caesar, Antony and Lepidus celebrate a short-lived amity with Pompey. (A little later it is casually remarked by someone that Pompey has been murdered; a few toasts round a table do not protect anyone in this world of imperial power-politics.) The four men sit down to some serious drinking (on board a ship, be it noted) and do not break off until Caesar insists that things have gone far enough.

> Gentle lords, let's part;
> You see we have burnt our cheeks. Strong Enobarb
> Is weaker than the wine, and mine own tongue
> Splits what it speaks. The wild disguise hath almost
> Antick'd us all.

What Caesar objects to is the loss of self-command, definiteness, identity: those qualities he prizes most and which are his instrument for subduing the world. The symbol of the interrupted feast is always an important one in Shakespeare; there are many ways in which he might have made this particular one break off, but he chose to end it in drunkenness, i.e. the dissolution of consciousness. As Caesar distastefully remarks,

> It's monstrous labour, when I wash my brain
> And it grows fouler.

North, whom Shakespeare follows so closely, has no mention of drunkenness at this feast. Clearly, Shakespeare introduced it to chime in with the central theme of dissolution and blurring.

It should, therefore, come as no surprise to us, when we engage more deeply with the play, to find that there is a deeper uncertainty, a more crucial blurring of outlines, at the very heart of the story. The love of Antony and Cleopatra, powerful and conspicuous though it is, seems curiously distanced from reality. It has a vein of — what shall we call it? illusion? vagueness? fanciful distortion? running right through to its centre. Perhaps this is because it is a middle-aged love affair. Antony is a grizzled veteran, Cleopatra is 'wrinkled deep in time'. Not that middle-aged people do not have wild love affairs. But such affairs are, in Antony's striking phrase, 'black Vesper's pageants'. They represent the brief glory of sunset. And this is where the smoky atmosphere of illusion and fantasy creeps in, for it is only Romeo and Juliet who have the right to believe that love will take care of everything.

Othello and Desdemona had settled for domesticity. She asks nothing better than to be the neat little housewife to her great husband, as in the touching moment when she says to him,

> 'Tis as I should entreat you wear your gloves,
> Or feed on nourishing dishes, or keep you warm.

Even with this bridge, they could not set up a mutually recognizable reality that would be proof against Iago's misrepresentations. What chance, then, have Antony and Cleopatra, wrenched apart by the exigencies of empire, and with nothing to hold them together except 'the poor benefit of a bewildering minute'? Hence the pervasive unreality in which they grope, so beautifully and lightly underscored by the imagery of mud and vapour.

This imagery is performing so many functions at once that it is with a shock of admiration that we realize, finally, that it is unobtrusively holding the entire play together. For mud is not merely the fertile, clinging element into which everyone enjoys a dive. It is also apt to get in one's eyes.

This magnificent and stately unreality continues to build up throughout the play's latter stages. Antony kills himself because he is at Caesar's mercy, and there is no other way to rise above his defeat. But the immediate spur which drives him to the deed is the report that Cleopatra has killed herself in despair at his anger and the breakdown of their love. This report is false. ('Bring me how he takes my death.') After the touching self-sacrifice of Eros, who stabs himself rather than look on the death of his master, Antony falls on his sword, but his skill fails him and he dies slowly, so that he and Cleopatra have time to exchange farewells.

After his death, Cleopatra is bent on suicide. She declares this at once ('Let's do it after the high Roman fashion, And make death proud to take us'), and when surprised and taken captive she whips out a dagger and tries to stab herself. Then follows the feigned submission to Caesar; she listens to his promises of safety and generous treatment, but without belief. Dolabella, who wishes her well, has managed to gain access to her before the interview with Caesar, and told her that Caesar will make a triumphal captive of her; when it is over, he slips back again, and confirms that the decision has been definitely taken. The news hardens her in her resolution to die, but for all I can see there is no evidence in the play that she would have done anything else even if Caesar's intention had been good. After a life nourished by the passion of great lovers, culminating in Antony, it is not likely that she could face twenty years on a widow's pension.

So much for the realities. Both Antony and Cleopatra have their own valid reasons for suicide. They have lost one another, and a dreadful fate is about to overtake them. But over these bare facts Shakespeare throws a great mound of flowers. Never before or afterwards did he lavish the resources of his poetry as he lavishes them here. Page after page of utterly unforgettable verse, perfect in cadence, perfect in metaphor — it is the most dazzling display of the world's most dazzling poet. One has no misgivings about such writing — except, perhaps, the misgiving as to whether it has not outgone the reality it starts from. The deaths of Antony and Cleopatra receive the full tragic treatment. Yet they are not tragic in the full sense, as the deaths of Cordelia or Hamlet are tragic. They are deaths of exhaustion, rather than brutal interruptions of a natural life.

But if there is a puzzle here, it is only momentary. The discrepancy between the prosaic logic of these deaths and the high poignancy with which they are celebrated, is no more than the working-out of that unreality, that confusion of outline, which has from the beginning characterized the passion of Antony and Cleopatra. And in case anyone doubts that this is so, Shakespeare has written in a beautifully delicate — yet entirely conclusive — scene in which it is made clear. When Dolabella gains access to Cleopatra for the first time, he finds her musing on Antony; having just been prevented from killing herself, she is still not quite back in the world, and he has great difficulty in bringing her to attend to his brisk and common-sense message.

DOLABELLA. Most noble Empress, you have heard of me?
CLEOPATRA. I cannot tell.
DOLABELLA. Assuredly you know me.
CLEOPATRA. No matter, sir, what I have heard or known.
　　　　　You laugh when boys or women tell their dreams;
　　　　　Is't not your trick?
DOLABELLA. I understand not, madam.
CLEOPATRA. I dreamt there was an Emperor Antony ——
　　　　　O, such another sleep, that I might see
　　　　　But such another man!
DOLABELLA. If it might please ye ——
CLEOPATRA. His face was as the heav'ns, and therein stuck
　　　　　A sun and moon, which kept their course and lighted
　　　　　The little O, the earth.

DOLABELLA. Most sovereign creature ——
CLEOPATRA. His legs bestrid the ocean; his rear'd arm
Crested the world. His voice was propertied
As all the tuned spheres, and that to friends;
But when he meant to quail and shake the orb,
He was as rattling thunder. For his bounty,
There was no winter in't; an autumn 'twas
That grew the more by reaping. His delights
Were dolphin-like: they show'd his back above
The element they liv'd in. In his livery
Walk'd crowns and crownets; realms and islands were
As plates dropp'd from his pocket.

At this point Dolabella, unable to stand any more, breaks in with a sharp interruption, addressing her unceremoniously by her name, instead of as 'most noble empress' or 'madam'. He is determined to break the trance which is leading her to pile up hyperbole on hyperbole. She knows, too, that this is what she is doing. When she finally turns and addresses him, her question reveals that she has been deliberately outraging his hard Roman common sense, in a mocking spirit, as it might be the mockery of a god for a mortal creature.

CLEOPATRA. Think you there was or might be such a man
As this I dreamt of?
DOLABELLA. Gentle madam, no.
CLEOPATRA. You lie, up to the hearing of the gods.
But if there be nor ever were one such,
It's past the size of dreaming. Nature wants stuff
To vie strange forms with fancy; yet t' imagine
An Antony were nature's piece 'gainst fancy,
Condemning shadows quite.

This exchange, thrown in so lightly amid a bustle of great actions, is one of the supreme moments in Shakespeare. Dolabella, humbled and awed by the queen's passion and constancy, is still a grave, sensible Roman officer. There is a wonderful tenderness and pity in his firm, 'Gentle madam, no'. And, after one line of almost perfunctory dismissal of his point of view, a mere spark of the old fire, she falls back into her musing vein, but with a new clarity. Truth is inadequate; it does not satisfy the demands of our nature; we need, and therefore must invent, a greater reality. 'Nature wants stuff To vie strange forms with fancy' means 'Nature lacks the material to compete with fancy in the devising of strange forms'. Yet even to imagine an Antony is to call into being a reality which could never be confused with mere fancy. 'Nature's piece 'gainst fancy' means 'the weapon which nature brings into the field against fancy'; the trump card, as it were, that nature deals, making all 'shadows' look trivial. And there is always that 'if' to hook the whole thing safe above the bruising to-and-fro of mere evidences. 'If' Antony ever existed, his was a greatness that could never have been merely dreamed. The needs of love are deeper than the universe can satisfy. And if these needs call into being a magnificence that the everyday world cannot admit ('Gentle madam, no'), where, in the end, is the true reality?

Confronted by this kind of thing, we cease to use the conventional categories. This is not 'tragedy', nor is it 'love poetry', as either is ordinarily understood. It is the working of the richest and most delicate imagination in all literature, utterly absorbed in its own concerns.

V

BLINDNESS

IT is perhaps naïve to speak of Shakespeare, or any artist, as moving into a 'tragic period'. Tragedy is not a compartment, like comedy or historical writing. It is the inevitable result of taking a complete view of the human situation. Some human lives know precious little comedy; for the unreflective there is no history, and for the insensitive no lyricism; but every life knows tragedy. As the poet Robinson Jeffers remarked, 'It seems to me that every personal story ends more or less in tragedy; comedy is an unfinished story.' This is not mere pessimism; it is sound sense. An account of human life that misses out the tragic element is untrue because incomplete. And the failures in Shakespeare's comedies, the places where intention and meaning fall apart, are exactly those places where the fragile, uncompleted structure of comedy is pushed aside by the drive towards completeness; the irresistible impulse to make Shylock a truthful portrait, or to have Beatrice exclaim, 'Kill Claudio!'

Shakespeare's 'tragic period', which extends from the composition of *Hamlet* (1600) to that of *Timon of Athens* (probably 1606), is not, in any simple sense, a period of gloom. His view of the world did not suddenly turn sombre, and then become rosy again when the appropriate lighting was switched on. These were the years of his mightiest efforts, in which he gave us the plays which engage most deeply with the essential nature of man. That nature is tragic, since the conflicts within human nature are not, finally, reconcilable. And therefore these plays are

'tragedies'. But one of the first things we see when we approach
them is that they differ among themselves in the extent to which
they are tragic. At the one extreme we have *Othello*, a study in
pure pain and loss; at the other, we have *Hamlet*, which ends
with the death of the hero but also with his triumph and the
sanctification of his memory. *King Lear*, the most gigantic of
these plays, contains some elements of pure tragedy, notably the
death of Cordelia; but on the whole it is an upward movement
that is described, since cruelty and error are much less in the
ascendant at the end than at the beginning. *Macbeth* is tragic if
one looks at it from a Christian point of view, for it is, like the
Faust-legend, the story of the damnation of a great soul. In
political terms, however, it is much less tragic, since it describes
how a country fell into the power of a murderer and tyrant,
groaned for a while, then gathered its strength and shook him
off to place a just and rightful king on the throne. *Coriolanus*, a
story of vengeful pride giving way to heroic self-sacrifice, is tragic
only in the technical sense that the hero dies. And even *Timon of
Athens*, for all the maniacal fury of its denunciations of mankind,
is not wholly a tragedy. It is at least partly a cautionary tale.

I

I do not know what the typical modern person carries in his
head as a picture of the universe — some savage, meaningless
quarrel of protons or neutrons, perhaps, against a background of
universal frozen darkness. But Shakespeare, in common with the
men of his time, had a mental picture of the universe as an ordered
structure. It was built up in a series of rungs, like a ladder, and
every created thing, whether living or not, had its appointed
rung. At the highest point was God, the creator and judge; at the
lowest, the utterly inanimate. The midpoint on this long stretch
was man, who occupied a splendid but vulnerable position at the
point where the animal world met the angelic. At any moment
his animal nature could lead him to plunge downwards into
degradation — or, if he fought free of this temptation, there was

the even more deadly sin of Pride, waiting to incite him to claim a higher place than he had been allotted, and to set up his judgment above God's.

As long as the natural tie, the *pietas*, is observed, the universe is basically a happy one; not free of misfortune, of course, but warmed by kindness and irradiated by love. As soon as *pietas* is broken, however, all unnaturalness and cruelty are set loose.

Harmony, 'degree', natural subordination of the lower to the higher — this is the key to all life. The great symbols of this unity are music and dancing. It is no accident that in *The Merchant of Venice*, when the disruptive element represented by Shylock has been removed, and the young lovers are left alone with their happiness, they begin to talk about music.

> Here will we sit and let the sounds of music
> Creep in our ears; soft stillness and the night
> Become the touches of sweet harmony.
> Sit, Jessica. Look how the floor of heaven
> Is thick inlaid with patines of bright gold;
> There's not the smallest orb which thou behold'st
> But in his motion like an angel sings,
> Still quiring to the young-ey'd cherubins;
> Such harmony is in immortal souls,
> But whilst this muddy vesture of decay
> Doth grossly close it in we cannot hear it.

And before long, a few lines later, we get the expected reference to Orpheus, the symbol of music's power to impose harmony on warring natures. The Christian joins hands with the classical. Both systems put harmony at the centre, and make the richness and beauty of life depend on a balance, a sense of touch and proportion, like that which guides the fiddle-bow across the strings.

This mediaeval and Renaissance thinking about harmony and degree could be amusingly simple: as in the case of King Henry VII, who once, doubtless in half-serious mood, ordered the death of some dogs who had killed a lion, their 'kindly king'. ('Kind' meant 'nature', though it was just beginning to have its modern meaning; hence the richness of the famous line with which Hamlet makes his entrance.) But the philosophy of hierarchy could also be beautifully subtle, an affair of delicate and creative thinking. It differed from modern styles of thinking chiefly in the extent to which it was analogical. To the Renaissance, as to the Middle Ages, analogy was a natural method of perceiving truth. 'Just as' this happens in one sphere, 'even so' that happens in another sphere. (Some features of Elizabethan English writing, such as the vogue for 'Euphuism', can only be understood against the background of this analogical thinking.)

So the Renaissance mind saw three interlacing kinds of order. Order within the universe; order within the political commonwealth; order within the human system. These three were in a relationship essentially analogical. The universe was a vast series of mirrors. What went on in one sphere was paralleled in the others. Not in the simple sense that cause in one sphere was immediately followed by effect in another, but in the analogical sense that the introduction of disorder at any point was a surrender, an admission of the power of the destructive principle, which constituted a general threat. Thus when Shakespeare shows Lear as committing a terrible act of political and human destructiveness, breaking up his realm and also renouncing his daughter, he naturally follows it by making him go mad (disruption of order within the human mind and body) amid a raging storm (disruption of order within the natural elements). Not that Shakespeare imagined in any naïve literal way that whenever a king went mad the heavens obliged with thunder and lightning. Of course, they sometimes did, and this was taken as a very natural omen. But Shakespeare's thinking on these matters was what we should call symbolic. The storm in *Lear* is like the sudden outbreak of unnatural events on the night Duncan is murdered by Macbeth. Or the similar disturbances on the night before Caesar is killed by the conspirators. In the later plays, the symbol of the storm reappears, but with a new significance; the tempest which drives the mariners to Prospero's island, or the wild weather in

which the shepherds discover Perdita's cradle, are signs of an
upheaval ultimately life-giving, the scrambling of an existing
unsatisfactory pattern out of which a new pattern will emerge.
But in the tragedies the function of the storm-symbol is analogical.

> Take but degree away, untune that string,
> And hark, what discord follows!

And all Shakespeare's symbols of disorder — the storm, the interrupted feast, madness, the onset of the prodigious — are illu-
strations of that 'discord'.

We have said that much Renaissance thinking was analogical
in character. In addition to proceeding step by step towards a
logical conclusion, as modern thought seeks to do, it proceeded
by building up layers of meaning. Shakespeare's art is multiple
in this analogical sense. It works by parallelism, analogy, juxtaposition. Hamlet is seeking to avenge his father: two other young
men in the same play are also seeking to avenge their fathers. Lear
suffers at the hands of his unnatural children: Gloucester also
suffers at the hands of his unnatural children; in each case one
loyal child brings final solace. Timon is driven from Athens by
the ingratitude of the citizens; so, in the same play, is Alcibiades.
This wealth of juxtaposition, this art of telling the same story
twice with different emphases and different endings, is already to
be seen in the comedies. But in the tragedies Shakespeare exploits
its full range. The result is an art of subtle and continuous inter-
weaving. No one can begin to interpret a Shakespearean tragedy
until he has accustomed himself to the minuet of plot and sub-plot.

Shakespeare's view of the world, the fulness and urgency of
his statement of the case for 'degree', is nowadays very well
understood. Such books as Lovejoy's *The Great Chain of Being*,
Spencer's *Shakespeare and the Nature of Man* and Tillyard's *The
Elizabethan World Picture*, have been widely read and have placed
this idea firmly before the modern student. The result has been
beneficial in so far as Shakespeare's plays are no longer studied
purely in terms of 'character', as if they were nineteenth-century

novels. But there has been one back-handed effect. The idea has somehow got about that Shakespeare was content to be the spokesman for generally accepted Renaissance ideas, and that once we have excogitated these ideas and discussed them, we have wrapped up his work. This attitude could prove to be as harmful as the eighteenth-century view of Shakespeare as a semi-literate poacher.

The idea of a hierarchical universe, a 'great chain of being', is of course obsolete. Nobody now holds it. And if we link Shakespeare's work too literally to this scheme, we are in danger of having to throw them both away together. For this reason it may be as well to say here and now that I, personally, accept Shakespeare's world-view as completely truthful. Its basic tenet, that all life depends on observance of the natural order, is one whose validity I can see for myself in every area of my experience. Take, as an amusingly simple example, the difficulties that have resulted from the well-meant efforts of biologists to stamp out this or that 'pest'. A chemical is introduced which, over a given area, causes the disappearance of a certain insect. The result is the breaking of a food-chain, leading various species to prey on one another, and by the time the disturbance has run its course it is found to have caused trouble in hundreds of unforeseen ways. This is an example of that unpredictability which, in Shakespeare's work, is one of the most terrible features of the act of disruption.

In the political sphere, wars and revolutions spawn wars and revolutions. In the human body, one imbalance leads to over-correction followed by another imbalance. These examples are of course too simple to be capable of seriously engaging our interest. For the working of this principle in its full range, we turn to Shakespeare. All that is necessary is to rid our minds of any idea that 'order', as Shakespeare conceives of it, is in any way related to an obsolete astronomy, and obsolete physics, an obsolete political science, or (if we are not Christians) an obsolete religion. In working out his idea of order, Shakespeare used the imagery provided by these systems. But the order he desiderated is entirely independent of them. In recent times we have tended to describe this order in terms widely different from Shakespeare's. We have called it 'integration of the personality', for instance. Or we have accepted the Lawrentian demand for a full instinctual life which would render mankind immune to the withering effects of modern industrialization. We have spoken with pitying scorn of the Organization Men, the Exurbanites and other categories of the damned — meaning, in each case, people whose lives are split and compartmented along lines that have no human meaning. But always, what we are talking about is order. The natural harmony that makes for health and peace.

When we contemplate the terrible disasters of our own century they seem very similar to the tragic disasters we meet in Shakespeare. The whole rise and fall of a man like Hitler, for instance. First the violent fever of the First World War, leaving the moral sense of all Europe weakened and wasted. Then the torture of Germany by means of inflation, insult, starvation. Then the bitterness, bringing with it a twisted malignity that would tolerate any cruelty at home and any aggressiveness abroad. And this bitterness was met by no positive qualities among the so-called 'Allies'. A diseased situation created further areas of disease, exactly as in *Hamlet*; until, finally, matters came to a conflict which claimed the life of a new generation, a generation uneasily aware that it was called on by history to suffer for the sins of its fathers. Again, exactly as in *Hamlet*.

Before we go on to a consideration of this play, there is one more general point that remains to be made about Shakespearean tragedy: we must note the absence of large-scale villains. Shakespeare's tragic world contains evil and cruelty enough. But it does not site these qualities within the psychology of certain hand-picked characters and dub them 'villains'. The Shakespearean tragic villain is inevitably on a smaller scale than the hero. Such figures as Edmund and Claudius are mere creatures of the plot. They have selfish desires, which they gratify in a way that unleashes disorder and ruin. But this ruin comes from outside themselves. Their fault is that they lack the vision to see the true consequence of their actions. Lady Macbeth, for example, nags her husband into murdering a king because she cannot see beyond her own commonplace ambition. When it is too late and she sees the true nature of the action she made him undertake, she cannot bear the knowledge, breaks down and kills herself.

The terror and suffering unleashed by the Shakespearean wrongdoer is too huge to come from within any human being. The villains who drive the plot along are not in themselves terrible figures. They are like. children, let loose in some great power station, who in sheer wilfulness pull the forbidden switch — and cause an avalanche of disruption in which they themselves perish almost unnoticed.

II

The action of *Hamlet* takes us into a royal household, a court and a country, all stricken with a mortal sickness. Claudius has committed murder in order to get the throne. More, his murder has been that of a brother and has been followed by marriage to that brother's wife. The bond of kinship as well as the political bond has been dragged asunder. Claudius is tainted with the unnaturalness of Goneril and Regan as well as the blood-spilling ambition of Macbeth.

From this central ulcer, the infection spreads outwards. Every relationship, every enterprise is touched with disease. Finally the illness is cured by the violent surgery of the last act. But only at the cost of Hamlet's own life among the others.

Hamlet, a man more deeply sensitive than any of the other Shakespearean tragic heroes, feels this all-pervading corruption intuitively from the beginning. When we first see him, he has been recalled from his studies at Wittenberg by the death of his father and the subsequent marriage of his mother to Claudius. For this marriage he feels a disgust which seems disproportionate. His mordant irony plays over the situation like bitter lightning: 'Thrift, thrift, Horatio! The funeral baked meats Did coldly furnish forth the marriage-tables.' Hasty, unseemly, the marriage may be: but Hamlet's disgust goes much deeper than could be warranted by anything he knows. Knows with his conscious mind, that is.

But Hamlet's knowledge lies deeper. It is picked up by the invisible antennae of imaginative sympathy. Even before he hears the news that his father's ghost has appeared to the soldiers on their watch — a sure sign of unrest in the general state — he is already visited by the despair and death-wish that makes him long to escape from his 'too solid flesh'. After his first meeting with the ghost, who tells him of Claudius's crime and enjoins on him the duty of revenge, he sees beyond doubt that fate has planted him in the middle of a cobweb of evil and that his own life is caught in the net. He knows that the time is out of joint: being the son of a king, next in line to the throne, he knows also that he is 'born to set it right'. However much he may rebel in his heart against this royal destiny, it never occurs to him to opt out. As in the English historical plays, kingship is not a business, to be taken up and put down at will. It is a destiny that sets a man apart, whether for triumph or for disaster, and it cannot be refused.

Hamlet is certain of these things. But there his certainties end. Everything else is wrapped in doubt and suspicion. The whole play is enveloped in a thick fog, in which Hamlet gropes as uncertainly as everyone else. He knows that Claudius is guilty of murder and usurpation, and he accepts the obligation laid on him by his father's ghost, to murder Claudius in his turn. But this acceptance is an affair of the surface. It does not permeate his character. He wanders through the action, trying to clear a path along which he can 'sweep to his revenge', and indulging in sudden random action; but he is defeated by the general confusion, which has entered his own mind. Indeed, there is a vein of contradiction running through the commands of the ghost himself. Telling Hamlet that his death was not natural, but the result of murder, the ghost adds,

Murder most foul, as in the best it is;
But this most foul, strange, and unnatural.

If murder is 'most foul' even under the 'best' and most extenuat-
ing of circumstances, what right has the ghost, already suffering
(in purgatory, one gathers) for the unshriven sins committed
during life, to demand that Hamlet burden his soul with it?

Not that Hamlet's soul is spotless. He does not escape the general
taint of evil that rises into the air from the 'something rotten'
that is at the heart of Denmark. Hamlet is certainly to blame in his
neurotic torturing of his mother, and again in his impulsive stabbing of Polonius in mistake for Claudius. Far worse than either
of these is his treatment of Ophelia. Overruled by her father's
senile authority and by lack of steady support from Hamlet himself, Ophelia withdraws into shyness and reserve, and makes a
timid attempt to return the presents Hamlet has given her. This
evidently makes Hamlet decide that she has joined the forces of
the enemy, and his brutality to her, under the guise of a partly-
feigned outburst of madness, sends her into a decline in which she
meets her death. The concentrated jets of venom which Hamlet
shoots at Ophelia are not at all closely related to the character or
actions of the girl herself; they arise from that neurotic sexual disgust from which Hamlet is suffering when we first see him. His
attack on her reveals the same ambivalence as everything else in
the play; with part of his mind he is furious at her for being a
woman, and therefore a perpetual temptation to the uncleanness
of the animal act; with another part, he is shocked at the tragic
fate that will lead her purity into the general mire. His savagely
repeated 'Get thee to a nunnery!' carries the full charge of this
ambivalence, for the word was used in Elizabethan slang to mean
a brothel. He does not, finally, know whether he wants Ophelia
to be a nun or a whore, to rise entirely above his orbit or fall
entirely below it. All he knows is that he cannot bear her presence.

The uncertainty within Hamlet's mind leads him not only into
moral but also strategic errors. He does not really know what to

make of his father's ghost, deeply though it affects him during its actual visitations; as soon as he is left alone, doubts reassert themselves. The whole play-within-a-play episode is contrived by Hamlet, as he tells Horatio (Act III, Scene ii), to test the genuineness of the ghost's story. When it is over and Claudius has revealed the turmoil within him by his unforgettable cry — 'Give me some light! Away!' — Hamlet exults, 'O good Horatio! I'll take the ghost's word for a thousand pound'. This is a strange way to talk about a ghost, especially a 'majestical' one; we half expect him to go on to say that he will get it to foretell the next Derby winner. The ambivalence persists, even though Claudius has acted convincingly the part of a guilty man.

In any case, the whole ruse of staging the play has failed. If Hamlet could have controlled his terrible inner agitation sufficiently to sit quiet and watch the king's face, other people would have done the same, and the business of undermining Claudius would have begun without Hamlet's having to show his hand. As it is, Hamlet cannot keep silent for a moment. He chatters to Ophelia during the dumb-show, gets in a vicious dig at his mother before the play itself has lasted five minutes, and to Claudius's brief query 'What do you call the play?' answers with a babbling mixture of threats and nervousness. His 'your majesty and I have free souls; it touches us not,' might just pass as an innocent remark, but when the poisoner enters he immediately adds, 'This is one Lucianus, nephew to the king'. Since there is no evidence in the play itself that the poisoner is in fact the king's nephew, the detail is evidently invented by Hamlet — or, more precisely, forced out of him by the pressure of his hatred for Claudius, the usurper who sits so temptingly close by on the throne that should be Hamlet's, side by side with Hamlet's mother who has forgotten his father. Under these circumstances, it amounts to a threat. Altogether, Hamlet's behaviour during the whole episode is such as to draw attention to himself and therefore away from Claudius, and in addition to arouse Claudius's suspicions. Hamlet is no plotter. Deeply meditative, he cannot gear his meditation to action; he acts only in rash, bounding sorties.

III

In common with so many Shakespearean plays, the basic flavour of *Hamlet* is military. It begins with the watch on the castle walls and it ends with the words, 'Go, bid the soldiers shoot'. The ghost appears in armour, 'with martial stalk', and the officers at once realize that the apparition is related to the flurry of warlike preparation that is going on. Denmark is threatened with invasion from Norway; not official military invasion, since the king of Norway is old and feeble, and accepts directives from Claudius, but marauding guerrilla activity directed by young Fortinbras, whose father was killed in single combat by Hamlet *père*, after which his lands, which would otherwise have gone to Fortinbras junior, were confiscated. So that Fortinbras has reason to hate the memory of Hamlet's father for having killed his own father and dispossessed him. This is exactly what Claudius has done to Hamlet. And to complete the pattern, Laertes, another man of the same generation, loses his father during the action, felled by the sword of Hamlet himself. The action is thus from the start a tangled mass of interconnecting motives. Hamlet is very much aware of this. He says of Laertes (Act V, Scene ii) 'by the image of my cause, I see The portraiture of his.' As for Fortinbras, Hamlet names him in his last breath as the best successor to the throne of Denmark. So clearly is the duty of making restitution to these wronged men, suffering from the actions of his father and himself, present to his mind.

Hamlet recognizes himself as both sinned against and sinning: that, far more than his sympathetic wit and modesty, his quickness of mind and depth of reflection, is the key to the emotional hold he has over us. No other Shakespearean hero invites such complete identification. In discussing Hamlet, we are always discussing ourselves. Deeply wronged, he is drawn step by step into a position in which he cannot help wronging others. And this is exactly how we all see our own situation. The nature of human life makes Hamlets of us all. George Rylands has appositely pointed out the lineage, in theatrical terms, of the Hamlet-figure:

'In the mediaeval Morality plays there is a central figure — his name may be Humanum Genus or Lusty Juventus or Everyman — in whom we see ourselves, symbolic victim of the conflict of Good and Evil, of Life and Death. Hamlet is such a one in this Renaissance Morality; courtier, soldier, scholar — a young man growing up.'

Such characters are found likewise in modern literature; every little girl identifies with Alice, and the doomed intelligentsia of Central Europe in the 1930s, menaced on the one hand by Hitler and on the other by Stalin, knew, each one, that the faceless heroes of Kafka's nightmare stories wore his own face. *Hamlet* is popular because it is the greatest of these works which place the reader or spectator at the suffering and reacting centre. What happens to Hamlet happens to us. That is why C. S. Lewis could declare, 'I would go a long way to meet Beatrice or Falstaff. . . . I would not cross the road to meet Hamlet. It would never be necessary. He is always where I am.'

Even so, the play would not have won its unique place in world literature if it had not been powered by the full strength of Shakespeare's verbal imagination. The sheer *writing* of Hamlet is what strikes one as miraculous. There is a special flavour in every line of it, a marvellous aptness and memorability. No wonder that line after line of it has passed into the language, so that hardly any English-speaking person goes through life without quoting *Hamlet* consciously or unconsciously — for who is there who has never said 'hoist with his own petar', or 'murder most foul', or 'more honoured in the breach than the observance', or 'to be or not to be', or 'the funeral baked meats', or 'a consummation devoutly to be wished'?

But let us not be carried away. The most influential literary critic of the twentieth century, Mr. T. S. Eliot, has said that

Hamlet is 'most certainly an artistic failure'. And what is more, Mr. Eliot is quite right.

IV

Mr. Eliot's famous essay on *Hamlet* (1919) contains his theory of the 'objective correlative'. He introduces it as follows:

'The only way of expressing emotion in the form of art is by finding an "objective correlative"; in other words, a set of objects, a situation, a chain of events which shall be the formula of that particular emotion. . . .'

The word 'formula' dates this passage very clearly as belonging to the period when, for various reasons, it was felt that literary criticism should borrow a few terms from the laboratory. All it means is an event, a concrete situation or happening, which shall produce in the onlooker the required emotion and not some other. If we want to produce anger and revulsion in the audience we must show a character kicking an old-age pensioner, rather than, say, drinking a cup of tea. Let us continue; this formula must be:

'. . . such that when the external facts, which must terminate in sensory experience, are given, the emotion is immediately evoked.'

'Terminate in sensory experience' means that if we wish to show a character in revolt against a tyrannical landlady, we have him throw a bucket of whitewash over her on the stage. When Shylock, in anticipation of claiming his pound of Antonio's flesh, sharpens his knife before our eyes, the action produces in us the same attitude to Shylock that Antonio and Bassanio have. The Cockney woman in Mr. Eliot's own *Waste Land*, who felt ill and unable to welcome her demobbed husband because of 'them pills I took . . . to bring it off', and who had frittered away the money he gave her on his last leave to get her decayed teeth replaced by bright false ones, provides an objective correlative for the sufferings of the poor in the modern spiritual desert; her false teeth, horrible in themselves and yet an object of hope by comparison with her real decayed stumps, an impossible hope now that she

has lost the money, are on the same level of desperate unfulfil-
ment as the cheap abortion pills she buys at a back-street chemist's.
Mr. Eliot himself gives two examples, both from *Macbeth*, of
perfectly achieved objective correlatives, leading to 'exact
equivalence', and goes on:

'The artistic "inevitability" lies in this complete adequacy of
the external to the emotion; and this is precisely what is deficient
in *Hamlet*. Hamlet (the man) is dominated by an emotion which
is inexpressible, because it is in *excess* of the facts as they appear.
And the supposed identity of Hamlet with his author is genuine
to this point: that Hamlet's bafflement at the absence of objective
equivalent to his feelings is a prolongation of the bafflement of
the creator in the face of his artistic problem.'

This gives us the essential clue. When a writer sits down to
begin a new work, he has in mind a theme which he has chosen
for reasons of his own, reasons that are fundamentally emotional.
He is drawn to this theme because he finds in it something that
corresponds to his own wishes, fears and impulses. But occasionally he makes a mistake. He chooses a story that seems, at first
sight, to measure up to his emotional drives, to contain the
energies they liberate. But as he works on he finds a growing imbalance. His emotions may change; or they may be revealed as
deeper, more complex, more powerful than he had imagined.
The story he has chosen may come to seem thin and unreal. The
charge of feeling he has running through it may burn it up. As
Mr. Eliot says earlier in the same essay,

'*Hamlet*, like the sonnets, is full of some stuff that the writer
could not drag to light, contemplate, or manipulate into art.
And when we search for this feeling, we find it, as in the sonnets,
very difficult to localize.'

An artist's work is powered by his emotional energies. But it is
not always possible for him to tell in advance exactly what form
these will take. Shakespeare, on beginning *The Merchant of Venice*,
could not have foreseen his involvement with the character of
Shylock. Hamlet, too, was wrenched apart, but in a more com-

plex way and by subtler and swifter forces. The position is further complicated by the fact that a writer cannot foresee his own development. This proceeds not in a steady curve but by a series of jumps. Work that is planned in one stage of development may be no longer feasible by the time it is actually begun: but in most cases the writer does not know this until he is well into the work and is committed to it for financial or other reasons. Then begins the struggle. Either the material has to be adapted to fit what the writer really wants to say *now*, or he has to hold the material steady while he casts his mind back to what he wanted to say *then*. There is no more exhausting work than this, and in fact if we look at *Hamlet* we can see the marks of colossal labour on Shakespeare's part. It is much longer than any of the other plays and bears the marks of stitching and re-stitching. This, I take it, is what Mr. Eliot is referring to when he speaks of Shakespeare's 'artistic problem'. And in describing the play as 'an artistic failure', Eliot is not dismissing it as without interest. He is indicating that the problem was, finally, never completely solved.

That this is so, we must surely agree. C. S. Lewis has a fine burst of indignation against Eliot's judgment:

' "Most certainly an artistic failure." All argument is for that conclusion — until you read or see *Hamlet* again. And when you do, you are left saying that if this is failure, then failure is better than success. We want more of these "bad" plays. From our first childish reading of the ghost scenes down to those golden minutes which we stole from marking examination papers on *Hamlet* to read a few pages of *Hamlet* itself, have we ever known the day or the hour when its enchantment failed?'

But this is beside the point. In the world of art, as in the world of human character, a fascinating failure is generally better loved than a routine success. Of course we are all deeply drawn to *Hamlet*, with its hypnotic glitter and its deep interior echoes. But the play's lack of a unified impression, its obscurity, the hospitality it seems to offer to every lunatic interpretation, all point to a deep failure.

F*   157

What happened is fairly evident. Shakespeare (either on his own initiative or at the request of his fellow-players) decided to write an example of that ever-profitable standby of the Elizabethan theatre, the 'tragedy of revenge'. The basic ingredients of this *genre* were the ghost of a wronged man, an insolent tyrant, and an avenger who feigns madness in order to disarm suspicion. The audience invariably responded well to a story of revenge, as do the audience for present-day Western or gangster TV sagas. To identify with the revenger is balm to the inward hurts we all suffer from.

Whether Shakespeare was starting from scratch or (more probably) reworking a formerly popular revenge-play that needed to be brought up to date, matters little. The main objective — at first — was to write an exciting and popular play about murder and suspense. We can see this impulse at work in the opening scenes. Never has a play started at a higher dramatic pitch. It begins with an attack of nerves on the eerie ramparts of a castle. The wrong man makes the challenge: the soldier coming on guard is so keyed-up that he calls 'Who's there?' to the man who is still at his post. The answer, equally tense, is 'Nay, answer *me* — stand, and unfold yourself'. Bernardo, about to take up his duties and fearful of being left alone, says:

> If you do meet Horatio and Marcellus,
> The rivals of my watch, bid them make haste.

Obviously there is some special cause of anxiety in the minds of these men. And in the play's twenty-first line Marcellus is already asking,

> What, has this thing appear'd again to-night?

At once we are launched into the ghost-story, and the soldiers, their watch done, hurry away to find Hamlet. No more dramatic build-up, for the entrance of a play's main character, could be imagined. But when we meet Hamlet we find ourselves suddenly in another play. The adventure story dies away and we are deep in a psychological study of jealousy and melancholia. We wait to see these two strands woven into one, but they never are. As the play goes on, it has more and more brilliant and unforgettable scenes which pull outward, away from its centre, rather than inward towards it. In the end no one can say what this centre is, except that it must be something that concerns Hamlet, whose character gives the play so muchof its special flavour that 'Hamlet without the prince' has passed into the language as a proverbial description of anything that lacks its *raison d'être*.

I myself believe the best way to get *Hamlet* into perspective is to look at it in conjunction with *Timon of Athens*. The one stands at the entrance to the great tragic period, the other at its exit. Both contain some of Shakespeare's most miraculous writing. And in *Timon*, as in *Hamlet*, the relatively simple plot is devastated by the enormous power that is made to flow through it. Both are masterpieces, but equivocal masterpieces. They fall apart, yet have such vitality in their dismembered limbs that they compel attention where more unified wholes do not. In both, Shakespeare's art was thrown out of control by the sheer force it was trying to organize. He was, to use a homely illustration, in the same position as the amateur mechanic who tunes up a stock engine to deliver twice its normal power and then finds himself unable to keep all four wheels on the ground. It is usual to regard *Timon* as an unfinished play, though it has a beginning, a middle and an end. Many scholars (E. K. Chambers, for a notable instance) have felt that the combination of power and rawness in that work represents the breaking of a wave: that Shakespeare, after the titanic labours of his tragic period, which lasted for six or seven years, had some sort of nervous crisis, after which he emerged into the comparative calm of the final plays. This may well be. But I believe that if *Timon* is the product of a period of crisis, so is *Hamlet*. Not a crisis of exhaustion, but of acceleration. The sudden realization of new powers must have been as disturbing as the feeling, seven years later, of having drained those powers away.

This was the force that pulled *Hamlet* apart: the sudden discovery by Shakespeare that there was no longer any limit to his strength. No technical problem need remain unsolved. In verse, he could draw on the Marlovian grandeur of *Richard III*, as well as on the lyricism of *Twelfth Night*. In prose, he could combine the richness of the Falstaff scenes with the dry elegance of a speech by Benedick. And while gathering into a new unity the strength he had already shown, Shakespeare was at the same time able to draw on the strength he had not yet shown. Verse with a colloquial, sinewy rapidity, a psychological penetration that reveals the inner nature of a man's mind in half a dozen sentences — these are the marks of the mature Shakespeare, and we find them for the first time in *Hamlet*. Along with this abrupt enlargement of powers we see a willingness to juxtapose styles and to mingle experimental with traditional elements. The opening scene on the ramparts is in the well-tried vein of the revenge thriller. The scene with the players is in the vein of a prose comedy of manners like *Much Ado*. Whereas the scene of Ophelia's funeral — the suspicion of suicide, the unforgiving priest, the maimed rites, the horrible scuffle in the grave — might, as Mr. Rylands acutely remarks, have come from a novel by Thomas Hardy.

In a word, *Hamlet* is too much. The endlessly burgeoning material breaks out of the commonplace mould. Where the conventional revenge-play hero is kept from fulfilling his vow only by material difficulties, Hamlet hesitates because of 'conscience'. Where the simple revenge-code demands a life for a life, Hamlet in his suit of black walks among skulls and philosophizes incomparably on death. Where the conventional villain of the play is a self-satisfied brute, Claudius is as fully convinced of his own wickedness, and as horrified by it, as Hamlet is. At other points, folk-tale material intrudes; Fortinbras with his emblematic name ('Strong-in-Arm') resembles some hero of fairy-tale; but Gertrude, who might well have been on this plane (the murderous mother) turns out to be another psychological study, the weak woman among strong men.

In one respect, and one only, is *Hamlet* rock-steady. It is completely true to the mature Shakespearean concept of tragedy, whereby the destructive power of evil is set going by an initial offence against *pietas*: the murder of a brother, the violent usurpation of a crown. From then on, disorder spirals outward. The initial act of brutal folly is finally expiated at a cost far beyond its own range of reference. Claudius is punished by death, but we may well feel that death is merciful compared with the desperate loneliness of his brief reign. Having renounced the natural tie, he is cut off from God and man: he knows neither prayer nor friendship. The tempest that is stirred up by his defiance of 'the primal eldest curse' cannot be stilled until it has claimed other lives than his own, those of Ophelia, Polonius, Gertrude, Laertes, Hamlet himself: just as Macbeth's crime will cost the lives of Banquo and of Macduff's wife and children, or Lear's will cost the life of Cordelia. Once 'order' is jarred, the shock will run through everything. Already, on the threshold of Shakespeare's tragic period, we see his concept of wrong-doing: the wilful child puts his hand on the switch, and suddenly a world of terror is upon us.

V

King Lear begins, like *Hamlet*, at a tremendous pace. Within two minutes we have been launched into the sub-plot, and within five into the main plot. Both stories begin with offences against the natural order. Gloucester, whom we first see in conversation with the more austere Kent, is *l'homme moyen sensuel*, a rib-digging clubman with a fat chuckle. We see him introducing to Kent his illegitimate son Edmund, with a mixture of ruefulness and pride; he makes his confession in a man-to-man, joking fashion ('I cannot conceive you.' 'Sir, this young fellow's mother could'), and incidentally lets slip that he has 'a son, by order of law, some year elder than this'. We might expect a man's illegitimate son, product of a rootless period of his life, to be older than his legitimate, not younger; Gloucester's code has evidently permitted a self-indulgence that goes beyond the ordinary masculine casualness. Kent turns aside Gloucester's uneasy bluffness with, 'I cannot wish the fault undone, the issue of it being so proper', and greets the young man with grave courtesy. Already, the nature of Gloucester's offence is clear to us.

Immediately afterwards, Lear enters, and announces his 'darker purpose,' which is to give up the duties and cares of kingship while retaining 'the name, and all th' addition to a king'. He does not see the obvious dangers of this; after a lifetime of autocratic power, he cannot imagine a world in which he would no longer be deferred to as a king. His personal folly is matched only by his political *naïveté*, since he intends to split England into three and divide it among the husbands of his three daughters.

As if this giddy plunge were not enough, Lear proceeds to gratify his vanity by engaging his daughters in a flattering-contest. The more eloquently they can express their love for him, the larger will be their share of the kingdom. (This part of the story has been called unrealistic, or defended as one defends a Grimm fairy-story; but not by anyone who has any experience of ageing men who have enjoyed too much power for their own good.) Goneril and Regan pass this test easily, but Cordelia dries up, and Lear's rage and disappointment come welling out in a terrible curse.

LEAR.   So young and so untender?
CORDELIA. So young, my lord, and true.
LEAR.   Let it be so! Thy truth, then, be thy dower!
          For, by the sacred radiance of the sun,
          The mysteries of Hecat and the night;
          By all the operation of the orbs
          From whom we do exist and cease to be;
          Here I disclaim all my paternal care,
          Propinquity and property of blood,
          And as a stranger to my heart and me
          Hold thee from this for ever. The barbarous Scythian,
          Or he that makes his generation messes

To gorge his appetite, shall to my bosom
Be as well neighbour'd, pitied, and reliev'd,
As thou my sometime daughter.

Lear's peculiar blend of impetuosity, obstinacy and emotional self-indulgence is hideous in its anti-human destructiveness. Having banished Kent for trying to intervene, made an enemy of the king of France at the moment of losing Cordelia to him, divided his realm and given himself up to the mercies of Goneril and Regan, he has in a few wild moments destroyed the basis of everyone's happiness and cleared the way for greed and cruelty to roam unchecked. His vengefulness is such that when France offers to take Cordelia without a dowry, he repeats that she is no longer his child: 'for we Have no such daughter'.

The scene ends, and within a few minutes we see Gloucester deceived by Edmund's plan to discredit and supplant Edgar; a little later (Act II, Scene ii) we hear him exclaim indignantly, 'I never got him!' and call Edmund 'loyal and natural boy'. Thus the tragic chain of events is set in motion: the two fathers have renounced the children who love them, and elected to trust the children who will betray them. Each has repudiated the natural bond and, horribly erring, cited 'nature' herself as the authority for his action. To Lear, Cordelia is 'a wretch whom nature is ashamed Almost t' acknowledge hers'. To Gloucester, Edgar is an 'Unnatural, detested, brutish villain! Worse than brutish!'

Both men have sinned against 'nature', the vital principle in all things; and the revenge of nature will be a terrible one. They will be cut adrift from the ordinary kindness and protection which human beings extend to one another: they will be sent wandering in a storm, the great Shakespearean symbol of disorder; in the end, one must be blinded in order to see, the other must go mad in order to understand.

VI

The punishments inflicted on these two suffering fathers are parallel, but not really similar. Gloucester is the weaker character.

His sins have been passive rather than active. He has indulged himself, neglected deeper responsibilities, let things slide. The nature of his tragedy is (almost) adequately summed up in the tit-for-tat moralizing of Edgar's words to Edmund in Act V, Scene iii:

> The gods are just, and of our pleasant vices
> Make instruments to plague us:
> The dark and vicious place where thee he got
> Cost him his eyes.

Characteristically, the sin into which Gloucester most readily falls, when calamity overtakes him, is that of despair. By pushing back in time to a pre-Christian Stonehenge Britain, Shakespeare was probably trying to give himself a metaphysical freedom that could only come from dealing with characters who had not heard of original sin, redemption, and the other specific Christian doctrines; but the scene in which Edgar, acting the part of an anonymous countryman, pretends to assist his father in his suicide-leap from Beachy Head, and then, assuming another voice, picks him up and talks of his miraculous deliverance from the power of a 'fiend' with 'a thousand noses, Horns whelk'd and waved like the enridged sea' —— this is an injection of pure Christianity, and an interesting contribution to the dialectic of the play.

Gloucester, in the end, dies off-stage; too faint a character to be allowed the pomp of a tragic death, he is led away to be 'bestowed with a friend', and we learn later that, on his being reunited with Edgar, his heart, torn between grief and joy, has 'burst smilingly'.

Lear's punishment, like his crime, is altogether bigger and more complex. It is in two stages. First he has to be educated to the point at which he is fit for the full purgation. Not every silly old man is good enough to be punished on this Promethean scale.

This initial, educative phase is represented by Lear's wanderings in the storm. His spiritual growth during these scenes is rapid and clearly marked. We start at rock-bottom. Lear has

gone on from stupidity to stupidity. He has made himself in-
tolerable at his first anchorage, with Goneril and her husband.
At the first sign of impatience on the part of his hosts, he im-
periously calls Oswald, the steward (who, admittedly, is a horrible
creature) and thrusts at him the question which cannot be
answered as he wishes and expects it to be.

> O, you, sir, you! Come you hither, sir. Who am I, sir?
> OSWALD. My lady's father.

The clash of wills is now provoked, and very soon we see Lear
uttering his hideous curse on Goneril.

> Hear, Nature, hear; dear goddess, hear.
> Suspend thy purpose, if thou didst intend
> To make this creature fruitful.
> Into her womb convey sterility;
> Dry up in her the organs of increase;
> And from her derogate body never spring
> A babe to honour her! If she must teem,
> Create her child of spleen, that it may live
> And be a thwart disnatur'd torment to her.
> Let it stamp wrinkles in her brow of youth,
> With cadent tears fret channels in her cheeks,
> Turn all her mother's pains and benefits
> . To laughter and contempt, that she may feel
> How sharper than a serpent's tooth it is
> To have a thankless child.

The 'dear goddess', Nature, is that same Nature invoked by
Edmund ('Thou, Nature, art my goddess') in his declaration of
war against humanity. Edmund will have his way, whatever the
cost to others; he recognizes no humane impulse towards mercy
or truthfulness. The Nature he invokes is the Nature of the serpent's tooth, and he sees in her nothing but the sanction of his
ruthless egotism. Animals prey on one another; if he preys on his
brother and his father, he is obeying the same Nature — that is
his view of the matter. Lear, at the beginning of his Purgatorio,
holds much the same views. Though he has brushed aside the

claims of this same Nature in declaring Cordelia no daughter of his, he does not hesitate to call upon her to act out his fantasies of vengeance on Goneril.

A similar encounter with Regan follows, and during this scene Lear makes his first faltering step towards better spiritual health. Goneril, who has followed him across country, now confronts him and helps to poison his already sick welcome from Regan. Lear turns on her, and we expect another renunciation and another curse. But what he actually says is,

> I prithee, daughter, do not make me mad.
> I will not trouble thee, my child; farewell.
> We'll no more meet, no more see one another.
> But yet thou art my flesh, my blood, my daughter;
> Or rather a disease that's in my flesh,
> Which I must needs call mine; thou art a boil,
> A plague-sore, or embossed carbuncle
> In my corrupted blood. But I'll not chide thee;
> Let shame come when it will, I do not call it;
> I do not bid the Thunder-bearer shoot,
> Nor tell tales of thee to high-judging Jove.
> Mend when thou canst; be better at thy leisure;
> I can be patient.

Disease though she is, Goneril is Lear's daughter, 'whom I must needs call mine'. This, at any rate, is an improvement on the state represented by his renunciation of Cordelia, 'my sometimes daughter', or Gloucester's 'I never got him'.

However, if step at all, it is a tiny one. The castle gates swing shut, and Lear wanders off over the heath, accompanied by the Fool and trailed by Kent, as the storm gathers its full terrible force. Very soon (Act III, Scene ii) we see him buffeted by the weather, and challenging it with bombastic rhetoric to do its worst; the sight of universal destruction can be nothing but welcome to a man so cruelly wronged as he.

> Crack nature's moulds, all germens spill at once,
> That makes ingrateful man.

As he becomes more distracted, he sees the storm as an instrument of divine vengeance — on other people. He has, still, no inkling that his own sins are as bad as anyone else's.

> Let the great gods,
> That keep this dreadful pudder o'er our heads,
> Find out their enemies now. Tremble, thou wretch,
> That hast within thee undivulged crimes
> Unwhipp'd of justice. Hide thee, thou bloody hand;
> Thou perjur'd, and thou simular man of virtue
> That art incestuous; caitiff, to pieces shake,
> That under covert and convenient seeming
> Hast practis'd on man's life. Close pent-up guilts,
> Rive your concealing continents, and cry
> These dreadful summoners grace. I am a man
> More sinn'd against than sinning.

His heart is still stony with self-righteousness. But the lessons of adversity are crowding in fast. Within a few minutes we hear him say, 'My wits begin to turn'. And immediately he goes on to utter the first unselfish sentiment we have yet had from him.

> Poor fool and knave, I have one part in my heart
> That's sorry yet for thee.

The significant thing there is the identification of madness with a fresh view of his situation. Both begin to gain upon him in the same moment. And this should prepare us for an appreciation of the complex and subtle use of madness throughout this section of the play. Lear, whose wits are genuinely breaking down, is flanked on one side by the Fool and on the other by Edgar. The Fool, as we saw in our discussion of Feste and Touchstone, is descended from a line of visionary simpletons. His speech is wild, rambling, full of strange juxtapositions; his humour is frequently surrealist. ('This prophecy Merlin shall make, for I live before his time.') Edgar, for his part, is feigning madness as a disguise. Thus three kinds of madness are woven into a strange pattern before our eyes. And the result is a fresh look at the human being in a setting of 'Nature'. For madness, if it means derangement, also

means the breaking of that constricting mould of habit and acquired information which keeps our perceptions dull. If the Fool
is, as I have suggested, a Surrealist, he embodies that lesson which
the Surrealists of the early twentieth century were to teach — the
so-called 'paranoid method' which simulated insanity in order to
break down the crust of familiarity which keeps us from perception.

Madness means destruction of the past. The madman has no
memory. He cannot reason from his experience, nor be held to
account for his actions of yesterday. Shakespeare has already
shown us Hamlet taking advantage of this freedom. Now, in an
infinitely more complex pattern, he shows us the breakdown of
reason producing illumination as the three wild figures reel across
the stage.

But this is to anticipate. We left Lear saying 'Poor fool and
knave, I have one part in my heart That's sorry yet for thee.'
Before the encounter with Edgar, that is, some spiritual progress
has already been made. A brief scene between Edmund and
Gloucester, inserted both as plot-feeding and as a kind of punc-
tuation, comes next; then we see Lear, led by Kent and the
Fool, arriving at the hovel which offers some pitiful shelter. He
insists that the Fool should enter first, and gently propels him
with 'Nay, get thee in. I'll pray, and then I'll sleep'.

What will be the nature of this prayer? Another horrible curse,
another cry for vengeance on his daughters? On the contrary,
what he offers up is a prayer to poverty; a plea for forgiveness
from 'a fellow that never had the ache in his shoulders'.

> Poor naked wretches, wheresoe'er you are,
> That bide the pelting of this pitiless storm,
> How shall your houseless heads and unfed sides,
> Your loop'd and window'd raggedness, defend you
> From seasons such as these? O, I have ta'en
> Too little care of this! Take physic, pomp;
> Expose thyself to feel what wretches feel,
> That thou mayst shake the superflux to them,
> And show the heavens more just.

Lear has, in fact, arrived at the state of illumination represented by Kent's remark in the stocks: 'Nothing almost sees miracles but misery'. Reduced to a state below the level even of his fallen fortunes, insulted and left in the stocks, Kent opens the letter he is carrying, and from it learns that the King of France is planning an invasion. The joy he feels at this news is greater than if he had been in his former state; when we sink to a low enough level, he says to himself, we are fit ground for the seed of miracles to fall on. Lear echoes this when he acknowledges that bareness and poverty have opened his mind and been 'physic' to his 'pomp'.

The Fool, meanwhile, has obediently crawled into the hovel, only to come scuttling out in terror at Edgar's blood-curdling shriek. This is a turning-point in the play; if we examine the tone of Lear's speeches before and after this moment, we shall find that he crosses, just here, the hair-line between great strain and actual madness. Edgar, when questioned by Kent, naturally invents a feigned history for himself; but his invention is not random. It is dovetailed into the main theme of this section of the play. He declares that he has been a serving-man, full of the fashionable arts of pleasing, corrupt in every way and especially in sexual matters. He curled his hair and wore gloves in his cap; his life was at the furthest possible remove from the simplicity of Nature. Yet now, he has become the very emblem of humanity reduced to the state of the animals. And Lear, with the vision of his madness, sees this at once. To him, the naked figure crouching in the straw is 'the thing itself'. Wretched as they are, he and his two companions are still 'sophisticated', removed from Nature by a layer of artificiality.

Why, thou wert better in a grave than to answer with thy uncover'd body this extremity of the skies. Is man no more than this? Consider him well. Thou ow'st the worm no silk, the beast no hide, the sheep no wool, the cat no perfume. Ha! here's three on's are sophisticated! Thou art the thing itself: unaccommodated man is no more but such a poor, bare, forked animal as thou art. Off, off, you lendings! Come, unbutton here.

Lear is at last brought face to face with the bedrock human condition. If men do not protect themselves by association and alliance, if they do not unite to rob the animals of fur, hide and silk, they fall to this condition of pitiable helplessness. This is the Nature to whom he has prayed in his outbursts of spite, seeing her as the instrument of his vengeful will. Yet terrible as she is, naked Nature is holy and purifying; those who have confronted her have earned a kind of wisdom. His madness helps Lear to perceive this, and he immediately becomes attached to Edgar and insists on questioning him as a 'philosopher'.

The whole central section of the play concerns itself with this confrontation of Nature. Lear's exposure to the storm, the savage blinding of Gloucester, the lust that invades the minds of Goneril and Regan and turns them into deadly enemies — this is that uncontrolled fury into which Nature leads human beings who have forgotten their Nature. For humanity includes *pietas*. To be set on nothing but rapine and slaughter is to deny humanity. Gloucester, already bound fast in the chair, urges on Regan the wickedness of sending her father out into the storm.

> If wolves had at thy gate howl'd that dern time,
> Thou should'st have said, 'Good porter, turn the key.'

A full humanity will not behave wolfishly even to a wolf. Human nature must rebel against itself before such cruelties are possible. This is the question at which Lear's broken mind is gnawing when he slumps beside the fire in the shelter provided by Gloucester, and mutters,

> Then let them anatomize Regan; see what breeds about her heart.
> Is there any cause in nature that makes these hard hearts?

The play's answer to this question is No. Unnaturalness, not nature, breeds hard hearts. Ordinary humanity, not turned from its course by the injection of some evil element, is faithful to the human bond of mutual support and kindness. And to underscore this point, Shakespeare has written in an episode, in the very middle of the play's murkiest passage, which affirms the decency of ordinary humanity. When Cornwall has put out one of Gloucester's eyes, and is just about to attack the other, one of the serving-men releases his hold on the victim and draws his sword against his master. They fight, and though the servant is killed by a stab from behind, administered by Regan, he has already given Cornwall a wound that will prove mortal. This is a pivotal episode in the play, for it is the death of Cornwall that leaves Regan without a mate and turns her thoughts towards Edmund, already the lover of her sister; and this leads directly to the murderous jealousy which renders their alliance unworkable and finally claims the lives of both.

Just before going back into his castle to meet his cruel punishment, Gloucester has seen to it that Lear is carried away to Dover to seek the protection of the invading army. Kent and the Fool carry Lear away on a litter, and with their exit this section of the play ends. The Fool's last words, 'I'll go to bed at noon,' signal his departure from the action; we hear nothing further about him except that he is hanged, so that his exit line has a melancholy prescience, for to go to bed at noon is symbolic of a life cut short in youth. Edgar's role, too, changes from this point on; he becomes more and more of a power in the plot, dispensing comfort and justice, and at the end it is, fittingly, on his shoulders that the authority of government rests.

For Lear there remains the supreme agony. Scarcely has he grown into the power to love another human being, and fixed his love entirely upon Cordelia, when she is murdered and he dies of grief. Shakespeare took the story of King Lear from a number of sources, but the basic version is that given in Holinshed's *Chronicles*. In that account the wicked daughters are foiled, and Lear is restored to the throne and lives for two more years. Cordelia succeeds him, but five years later she is deposed by her nephews, who have presumably inherited the wickedness of their mothers, and kills herself in prison. In Shakespeare's handling of the plot, Cordelia's death is brought forward and made directly consequent on Lear's initial act of destructive folly. At last, having attained to the dignity of tragic suffering, Lear is plunged into the gigantic agony which links him in world literature with Oedipus and Prometheus.

We noted at the beginning of this chapter that Shakespeare's tragedies differ from one another in the extent to which they are tragic. *King Lear*, which ranges across the field of tragedy more widely than any other work in English, contains elements of pure tragedy blended with an optimism which finally triumphs. For when all is over, the picture of human nature we find in this play is not entirely dark. Goneril and Regan, Cornwall and Edmund, behave savagely, but their savagery has been released by the folly of Lear and Gloucester. They are the instruments of Nature's revenge for the disturbance of *pietas* — a revenge, admittedly, which sweeps far beyond the bounds of the original offence and includes innocent beings in its wrath. Nevertheless, average humanity, the play insists, is not corrupted; it remains true to that Nature which lifts man above the beasts. The structural importance that Shakespeare has given to the revolt of Cornwall's anonymous serving-man, as we have seen, reminds us of this; so does the merciful attitude of the equally anonymous 'Old Man' who leads the blinded Gloucester to Edgar, and who, believing as he does that Edgar is the merest riff-raff, 'madman and beggar too,' determines to clothe him so that he can be of better service to Gloucester :'I'll bring him the best 'parel that I have, Come on't what will.'

Ordinary humanity recognizes the nature within it as well as the nature without. The reckless cruelty of the elements is not paralleled in fully human hearts. Kent and the Fool stick by Lear from first to last; Albany is an upright man; Edgar strives consistently for ends higher than his own self-preservation. Swinburne's remark, that Gloucester's

> As flies to wanton boys are we to th' gods:
> They kill us for their sport

sums up the whole spirit of the play, shows that even a poet can study *King Lear* without the slightest comprehension. Shakespeare did not assemble all the varied materials of this mighty play to leave us, at the end, with a capsule of facile pessimism. In this story of a great offence, expiated by a great suffering, we end at a higher point than we began. Lear, as he staggers in carrying the body of Cordelia, is blessed by comparison with the savagely limited figure we see at the beginning; he knows, at last, what love means.

All this titanic expenditure of effort and suffering to teach two stupid old men how to love? Yes: and rightly; for the colossal extravagance of means, the cosmic excess of upheaval and waste, celebrates the range and importance of the nature of man. At such times, even the supreme powers of the universe (whatever and wherever they may be) humble themselves before man, and bow to him, for

> Upon such sacrifices, my Cordelia,
> The gods themselves throw incense.

VII

The crime of Macbeth is a shockingly multiple violation of *pietas*. Like Claudius, he commits murder, and the murder of a kinsman, in order to seize the throne. But his action throws an even darker shadow than Claudius's. As a host, he kills the guest who is depending on his protection. As a husband, he allows his wife to over-rule him for an evil purpose. As a soldier enjoying the special gratitude of king and people for having saved them from a dangerous enemy, he tosses that gratitude aside by murdering the king and oppressing the people.

Macbeth's greatness is never in doubt. From a great national hero, he becomes a great tyrant. He acts on a grand scale. And the sublimity of his tragedy lies in the heroic fatalism with which he accepts his damnation. Having, against his own judgment, plunged into a career of destruction, having embraced the cause of disorder and identified himself with that anti-nature represented by the witches, he recognizes that there is no longer any route back to order, *pietas* and goodness. Just as Faustus at last realizes what it is to be in the clutches of Hell, just as Othello sees himself finally as one

> whose hand
> Like the base Judaean, threw away a pearl
> Richer than all his tribe,

so Macbeth knows from the very moment of stabbing Duncan that he has 'given to the common enemy of mankind' his 'eternal jewel'.

In this he is tragically clear-sighted, but in other respects he is progressively misguided and deceived. In particular, he accepts too simple-mindedly the division between natural and unnatural. He himself plays by the rules of hell and expects everyone else to play by the rules of heaven. Although he has thrown in his lot with the witches, called their sorcery to his aid, and announced that he wishes to throw off his human nature and his place in the ordered scale of created beings, he is insanely confident that these forces will never boomerang. When it is prophesied that Birnam Wood must come to Dunsinane before he can be overthrown, and even then only by a man not born of woman, he accepts this as a guarantee of earthly protection. And when, finally, these two prodigies are fulfilled, but in a natural framework — when, that is, he is defeated by apparent but not real violations of order — the play's strong and beautiful symbolism has described its full circle.

VIII

Of all Shakespeare's plays, *Macbeth* has the closest verbal texture. Its imagery is so densely knit that almost every phrase echoes or anticipates another. In this unified organization, it provides a show-case example of 'dramatic poetry'. It is equally poem and drama. The two forces are in perfect harmony.

The characterization of both the Macbeth couple is floated on a tide of imagery that speaks of destructiveness, violation and blindness. There is no need to give such obvious examples as Lady Macbeth's 'unsex me here' speech, or Macbeth's 'stars, hide your fires', uttered during his first encounter with Duncan. Obviously they both embrace darkness and violence. At the first sign of hesitation on Macbeth's part, Lady Macbeth renounces her womanhood even more decisively.

> I have given suck, and know
> How tender 'tis to love the babe that milks me —
> I would, while it was smiling in my face,
> Have pluck'd my nipple from his boneless gums,
> And dash'd the brains out, had I so sworn
> As you have done to this.

He has, of course, not 'sworn' at all; the sacred oath, so strong that it takes precedence over the human bond, exists only in her imagination. I say 'imagination', but of course the key to Lady Macbeth's actions is that she has no imagination. A blinkered, fiercely acquisitive woman, she has no eyes for anything except the golden prize that seems to have fallen within her grasp. Savagely scolding Macbeth, driving him on with exactly the same arguments as a suburban housewife nagging her husband to apply for a rise, she never lifts her head to the horizon. As she trots about busily making preparations for the murder, drugging the grooms' drink, laying out the daggers, arranging this and contriving that, she has no time to think what she is really doing; like Iago, she is satisfied to keep one jump ahead of the action. Only at one point does something like illumination break in: coming down from Duncan's chamber, she says, 'Had he not resembled my father as he slept, I had done 't.' But she turns away from the offered revelation. Duncan resembles her father — very well! Macbeth must kill him; she cannot quite do it herself. Even at this moment, the little fool hasn't the imagination to see that to kill Duncan is the same thing as killing her father.

The crime proceeds from her blindness. It leads Macbeth into the murk represented by witchcraft, ambiguous prophecies, and the eclipse of the mind's natural daylight. The theme of uncertainty and deceptiveness, introduced at the very beginning by the wounded sergeant, is echoed by Duncan in his grief at being deceived by the thane of Cawdor ('There's no art To find the mind's construction in the face') and continued right up to Macbeth's despairing cry in the last scene of the play,

> And be these juggling fiends no more believ'd
> That palter with us in a double sense;
> That keep the word of promise to our ear,
> And break it to our hope.

It follows that darkness and blindness are obsessive themes. Macbeth, in the 'stars, hide your fires' speech, says 'let that be Which the eye fears, when it is done, to see.' In his first access of horror and remorse, immediately after the murder, he cries out, 'What hands are here? Ha! They pluck out mine eyes.' When arranging the murder of Banquo, he tells the murderers his reason for 'masking the business from the common eye.' The murder of Duncan takes place at night, that of Banquo just as the light is fading. The witches, who 'hover through the fog and filthy air,' are addressed by Macbeth as 'secret, black and midnight hags'. To Macbeth and his queen, light is the enemy. All this is magnificently contained within the terrible invocation to the powers of darkness which Macbeth utters as he stares out through the window, oblivious for the moment of the bewildered figure of his wife standing beside him, into that dusk through which Banquo will ride to his death.

>   Come, seeling night,
> Scarf up the tender eye of pitiful day,
> And with thy bloody and invisible hand
> Cancel and tear to pieces that great bond
> Which keeps me pale. Light thickens, and the crow
> Makes wing to th' rooky wood;
> Good things of day begin to droop and drowse,
> Whiles night's black agents to their preys do rouse.

This is an echo of the similar prayer to 'thick night' made by Lady Macbeth before the murder of Duncan:

> pall thee in the dunnest smoke of hell,
> That my keen knife see not the wound it makes,
> Nor heaven peep through the blanket of the dark
> To cry 'Hold, hold!'

But there is a significant difference of emphasis. Lady Macbeth will not actually have to inflict a wound with a keen knife; her invocation has a certain theatricality about it; she wants to make a large gesture towards bloody-mindedness, whereas Macbeth has a terrible and sombre knowledge of just what it is that he is doing. She is content to ask heaven to look the other way, and let matter rest there; he knows that the murder he plans will put him finally outside the human family. His monstrous prayer, 'Cancel and tear to pieces that great bond Which keeps me pale', is the exact equivalent of the moment when Faustus, under the guidance of Mephistopheles, signs away his soul.

By contrast, the play's 'good' characters — those who are on the side of life and positiveness — constantly use the imagery of green and growing things. Duncan, greeting Macbeth on his return from the battlefield, says, 'I have begun to plant thee, and will labour To make thee full of growing.' Banquo uses this kind of imagery naturally; he has already said to the witches

> If you can look into the seeds of time,
> And say which grain will grow and which will not,
> Speak then to me.

And when Duncan, turning to him after greeting Macbeth, says 'let me infold thee And hold thee to my heart,' Banquo replies, 'There if I grow, The harvest is your own.' It is he, on the party's first arriving at Macbeth's castle, who notices the 'procreant cradles' of the house-martins. He has a natural reverence for, and interest in, all forms of life.

This imagery is confirmed in the play's visual symbolism. When Macbeth is driven by desperation to call on the witches for aid, in reading his future, the third and most riddling apparition they show him, the one who utters the prophecy about Birnam Wood and high Dunsinane hill, is 'a Child crowned, with a tree in his hand'. This tree signifies the fecund royal line of Banquo's succession, and also hints at the 'leafy screen' which will be carried by the advancing English soldiers as they move towards Dunsinane. It is a pity that most stage directors approach this latter scene in a depressed, let's-get-it-over frame of mind; the steady forward march of ten thousand men, each carrying a green bough, is a wonderful visual symbol of the great tide of nature flowing over the scene of Macbeth's crime, bringing healing and renewal. Similarly the Caesarean operation which brought Macduff into the world is a better plot-pivot than, say, the legalistic quibble with which Portia entraps Shylock, since such an operation is one of the ways in which the hand of man ('the great assay of art') comes to the aid of nature for a creative purpose.

When the play is all but over, and Malcolm speaks the closing lines, we find the note of green and living things sounded once more, when the new king promises to attend faithfully to the many tasks that await him: 'What's more to do, Which would be planted newly with the time . . . We will perform.' The new life of Scotland will be 'planted' on the soured and trampled soil; growth, continuity and nature will come back into their own.

IX

One of the most important characters in *Macbeth* is one who has no lines and does not even appear on the stage. In Act IV, Scene iii, we find Macduff visiting Malcolm at the court of the English king, Edward the Confessor. This is one of the crucial passages of the play, and any stage production which allows the interest to slacken at this point is failing to interpret the story properly. Edward the Confessor is a king who is the opposite of Macbeth: saintly, much loved, he is the intermediary between his subjects and the mercies of heaven. He has the power to heal scrofula by the laying on of hands:

> How he solicits heaven,
> Himself best knows; but strangely-visited people,
> All swoln and ulcerous, pitiful to the eye,
> The mere despair of surgery, he cures,
> Hanging a golden stamp about their necks,
> Put on with holy prayers; and 'tis spoken,
> To the succeeding royalty he leaves
> The healing benediction. With this strange virtue
> He hath a heavenly gift of prophecy;
> And sundry blessings hang about his throne
> That speak him full of grace.

These lines, admiringly spoken by Malcolm, heir to the throne of
Scotland, establish Edward the Confessor as one of the play's
positive forces. Like the witches, he can prophesy, but his is 'a
heavenly gift', not derived from the powers of evil as theirs is,
and therefore not deceiving men or inciting them to wickedness.
His gift of healing, moreover, is left 'to the succeeding royalty';
and we recall that the ceremony of 'touching for the King's
Evil' lasted through many reigns, and was not finally abandoned
by the English monarchy till the death of Queen Anne.

Edward heals: Macbeth poisons and wounds. Macduff, disillusioned by the self-condemnation of Malcolm, asks when Scotland shall see her 'wholesome days again'. And when the Scot
lords join with the English power to drive Macbeth out, one of
them, Caithness, says,

> Well, march we on,
> To give obedience where 'tis truly ow'd;
> Meet we the med'cine of our sickly weal,
> And with him pour we in our country's purge
> Each drop of us.

The imagery of a laxative is carried on by Macbeth himself, who,
in bitter mockery of the doctor who has failed to cure Lady
Macbeth ('Canst thou not minister to a mind diseas'd?') asks him
to use his skill where it might do some good:

> If thou couldst, doctor, cast
> The water of my land, find her disease,
> And purge it to a sound and pristine health,
> I would applaud thee to the very echo,
> That should applaud again. — Pull't off, I say —
> What rhubarb, senna, or what purgative drug,
> Would scour these English hence?

Reverting for a moment to the scene at the English court, it is of course here that Shakespeare draws together the audience's feelings of revulsion from Macbeth and gives them a focus. We begin with a very considerable sympathy for Macbeth; even after the murder of Banquo, this has not quite dispersed; but the decision to sack the castle of Macduff and butcher his family, which is taken rapidly and with no hint of inward struggle, indicates that he has now become a monster. The touching scene with Lady Macduff and her children is immediately followed by the conversation at King Edward's court, at which Macduff learns of Macbeth's brutal retribution. All this passage is remarkably modern-sounding to twentieth-century ears; during the Second World War, London was full of *émigré* governments, working from temporary headquarters and issuing *their* version of what was happening in their countries; and all twentieth-century tyrants have found it convenient, when an opponent of the regime has managed to get away to safety, to punish him by murdering the relatives who remain behind. Macduff's grief, slowly hardening into anger, is essential for the play's effect; and his cry 'He has no children' brings out with superb economy, the gulf between Macbeth (or a Hitler, or a Stalin) and the ordinary, human man who loves and is loved. Since Lady Macbeth has 'given suck', some people have seen a contradiction here; but it is not deeply felt as a contradiction. The Macbeths may have had children at some time or another, but as we see them in the play they are lost to any such creative purpose; they stand against life.

Dramatically, the core of the play is the contrast between the spiritual states of Macbeth and his wife. Her crime is shallowness; she does not understand what it is that she is involving them both in, and when knowledge at last breaks in, she cannot bear it and goes to pieces almost at once. This contrast is very clear in the play's opening scenes. When Macbeth first meets the witches, and later when he is amazed to hear that their prophecies are already beginning to come true, he is tossed this way and that by violent emotions. Before he has spoken a line in answer to their predictions, Banquo is already asking

> Good sir, why do you start, and seem to fear
> Things that do sound so fair?

Almost immediately comes the news that the first of these predictions is fulfilled, and at once Macbeth is plunged into renewed agitation.

> . . . why do I yield to that suggestion
> Whose horrid image doth unfix my hair
> And make my seated heart knock at my ribs,
> Against the use of nature?

When Lady Macbeth first reads his letter, there is no comparable hesitation, since her nature is superficial and opportunistic. Her first line expresses a determination already completely formed.

> Glamis thou art, and Cawdor, and *shalt be*
> That which is promised.

And at once she states to herself the major problem; how to get Macbeth to act against his own nature. He is too full of the milk of human kindness. We shall be reminded of that milk later, when she makes her frightful declaration about dashing out the brains of a baby as it 'milks' her; and again when Malcolm, representing himself as a monster in order to test the good faith of Macduff, says

> had I pow'r, I should
> Pour the sweet milk of concord into hell,
> Uproar the universal peace, confound
> All unity on earth.

After the murder, Macbeth is already numbed. By an unforgettable dramatic irony, he makes a speech to Lennox which has the double function of keeping up his deceit — it is just the speech that a coolly unscrupulous ruffian would make — and expressing, with a masked but complete sincerity, his own remorse.

> Had I but died an hour before this chance,
> I had liv'd a blessed time; for, from this instant,
> There's nothing serious in mortality —
> All is but toys; renown and grace is dead;
> The wine of life is drawn, and the mere lees
> Is left this vault to brag of.

All he can think of is his bitter, overwhelming regret and self-disgust. It is Lady Macbeth who organizes everything, throws a skilful faint when the questions turn awkward, and begins at once to set up the social life of the new royal couple by issuing invitations to a banquet. The exact point at which she begins to break down is a problem for producer and actress to work out between them. That the Macbeths do not have a scene together after Act III, Scene iv, immediately after the banquet, has struck some commentators as an omission, perhaps traceable to the fact that the text of the play which has come down to us is very short and may represent a cut acting copy. To me, it seems natural enough. They have nothing more to say to each other; communication between them is over, and each retires into a separate world of pain.

Macbeth, so full of anguished awareness of what he is doing, has had nerves before committing the murder; afterwards, seeing that there is no other way but downward into greater hardness and cruelty, he becomes immovable and rock-like, shedding his humanity along with his hope of eternal salvation. We see this very clearly if we look at the three soliloquies which precede each of his three murders. Before killing Duncan, he utters the great speech beginning 'If it were done when 'tis done, then 'twere well It were done quickly' (Act I, Scene vii), the most convincing portrayal in all literature of a man struggling with his conscience before a dreadful act. Conscience wins, and Lady Macbeth has to apply the goad once more to drive him on.

By the time it becomes necessary to murder Banquo, Macbeth has already made rapid progress into hardness; in fact he has reached the point where his progress seems to him not rapid enough; and he makes the speech (Act III, Scene ii), which we have already noted, requesting 'seeling night' to plunge everything in blackness and liberate him from his human bond. This hideous prayer is answered, and his next murder, that of Macduff's family, is introduced with a soliloquy that does no more than curtly announce his intention.

> The castle of Macduff I will surprise,
> Seize upon Fife, give to th'edge o' th' sword
> His wife, his babes, and all unfortunate souls
> That trace him in his line. No boasting like a fool:
> This deed I'll do before this purpose cool.

His next words, the agonized cry, 'But no more sights!', indicate, of course, that he is still in torment. But the torment is now the ignorant suffering of an animal. The agony of decision-making is over. He now has to live with his destiny, which he sees — rightly — as an endless vista of blood and hatred.

During the earlier stages of their complicity, Lady Macbeth has several times taunted Macbeth with being less than a man. When she is savagely mocking him with the contemptuous allusion to 'the poor cat i' the adage' (who loved fish, but was afraid to wet his feet), Macbeth replies,

> Prithee, peace.
> I dare do all that may become a man;
> Who dares do more, is none.

She comes back at him immediately, of course, with 'What beast was 't, then, That made you break this enterprise to me?' Later, during the scene of the interrupted feast, the same dramatic irony occurs again. After calming the amazement of the guests, she approaches him with a hiss of 'Are you a man?' This sticks in

Macbeth's mind, perhaps because he has used the same taunt against the murderers of Banquo to prevent their hesitating.

> Are you so gospell'd,
> To pray for this good man and for his issue,
> Whose heavy hand hath bow'd you to the grave
> And beggar'd yours for ever?
>
> IST MURDERER. We are men, my liege.
> MACBETH. Ay, in the catalogue ye go for men;
> As hounds, and greyhounds, mongrels, spaniels, curs,
> Shoughs, water-rugs, and demi-wolves, are clept
> All by the name of dogs.

A few minutes after his wife's challenge to his manhood, when the ghost appears for a second time, he raves at it,

> What man dare, I dare.
> Approach thou like the rugged Russian bear,
> The arm'd rhinoceros, or th' Hyrcan tiger;
> Take any shape but that, and my firm nerves
> Shall never tremble. Or be alive again,
> And dare me to the desert with thy sword;
> If trembling I inhabit, then protest me
> The baby of a girl. Hence, horrible shadow!
> Unreal mock'ry, hence!

At this stage, he is still a man; a man conscious of mortal sin, aghast at his own cruelty, but still feeling himself tied to the human race if only by the dying agonies of his conscience. The dividing-line comes, it seems to me, in the scene (Act IV, Scene i) when he seeks out the witches and swears the oath which binds him to them.

> I conjure you by that which you profess ——
> Howe'er you come to know it — answer me.
> Though you untie the winds and let them fight
> Against the churches; though the yesty waves
> Confound and swallow navigation up;
> Though bladed corn be lodg'd and trees blown down;
> Though castles topple on their warders' heads;
> Though palaces and pyramids do slope

Their heads to their foundations; though the treasure
Of nature's germens tumble all together,
Even till destruction sicken — answer me
To what I ask you.

With the words 'I conjure you by that which you profess,' Macbeth has announced his defection from the human camp and his new allegiance to the power which the hags also serve. The rest of the speech gives rein to that recklessness which Lear felt when he urged the storm on to greater mischief — 'Strike flat the thick rotundity o' the world'. But where Lear's progress is upward, to a greater humanity, Macbeth's is downward.

Finally Macbeth reaches the stage of complete spiritual death represented by the two speeches he makes one after another in Act V, Scene iv. The chilling cry of the women, offstage, stirs him only to the extent of asking what it is; while Seyton goes to find out, Macbeth comments almost idly on the fact that nothing any longer has the power to horrify him; his human nerves are atrophied.

I have almost forgot the taste of fears.
The time has been my senses would have cool'd
To hear a night-shriek, and my fell of hair
Would at a dismal treatise rouse and stir
As life were in't. I have supp'd full with horrors:
Direness, familiar to my slaughterous thoughts,
Cannot once start me.

Seyton then reappears with the announcement that Lady Macbeth, once his 'dearest partner in greatness,' is dead. And in the lines beginning 'She should have died hereafter,' Macbeth once more reveals the icy loneliness of that darkness we enter once we have severed the human bond. His loneliness at this moment is the loneliness of Iago or Claudius as they contemplate their crimes. He has done with human feeling, and as a result can have no share in the grief and joy of the world. Small wonder that to him life is meaningless, 'a tale told by an idiot'. These lines have become possibly the most famous in Shakespeare, and one sometimes hears them quoted (like the similarly pessimistic lines of Gloucester in *King Lear* about flies and wanton boys) as if they somehow represented Shakespeare's own point of view. Anyone who could think so after reading *Macbeth*, or seeing an honest production of it, would do better to leave great poetry alone.

In the battle, which now breaks out, we see Macbeth, in his last solitary moment, facing the knowledge that, as far as this world is concerned, he is no more than an animal. 'They have tied me to the stake; I cannot fly, But bear-like I must fight the course.' His descent from humanity is complete. The play is over.

x

Macbeth is the most Christian of Shakespeare's works. The basis of Shakespearean morality, in all the plays, is Christian, but in this play it becomes fairly explicit. The virtues of the good kings, Duncan and Edward the Confessor, are specifically Christian virtues ('Such sanctity hath heaven given his hand'), Macbeth is conscious of damnation, and Malcolm's promise to set the realm in order, which concludes the action and points towards the future, has a Christian flavour ('by the grace of Grace we will perform'). Even so, there is no easy version of Christian doctrine preached here. Banquo, one of the play's principal heroes, father of a line of kings, providing in his uprightness the example Macbeth ought to have followed, vows to devote himself to discovering the murderer of Duncan and upholding truth and order, with the words

> In the great hand of God I stand, and thence
> Against the undivulg'd pretence I fight
> Of treasonous malice.

But the great hand of God doesn't prevent Banquo from being murdered by Macbeth's paid ruffians. The good are cut off in their prime; Heaven's blessings (*pace* the miraculous powers of the saintly Edward) are not of this world: we are, inevitably, left

with the tragic question which Lear puts to the dead body of
Cordelia:

> Why should a dog, a horse, a rat have life,
> And thou no breath at all?

Once again, the tragic action has started a whirlwind which
carries away the innocent. And our consolation must be that,
however savagely the frame of things has been wrenched apart,
it is finally pushed back into its proper shape. The 'dead butcher
and his fiend-like queen' have been beaten down and dismissed
to their punishment; Banquo, appearing to Macbeth in a vision,
'smiles' at him, from a new serenity out of reach of crime and
misfortune; Scotland is restored to peace and health. Malcolm,
like Fortinbras, like Edgar, will pick up the pieces and repair
the damage — in human terms. The questions that remain in our
minds are metaphysical only. And in order that they may reverberate more strongly, Shakespeare has kept the play at a certain
distance from formal Christianity. The witches, for instance, are
not really figments of the religious imagination; they belong to
folk-lore. (They are, of course, never described in the play as
'witches', but as the 'weird sisters', and they carry a distinct suggestion of the three Fates, or the Norns of Scandinavian mythology.) Agents they certainly are of the Prince of Darkness, but
their function in the play is not so much to bring a whiff of brim-
stone across the stage as to symbolize the murky, unexplored
reaches of the human mind. Macbeth is responsive to them,
Banquo is coolly wary; their first appeal is not to anything directly evil in Macbeth's nature but rather to the indecision, be-
wilderment and error which is their element and which they find
echoed in his perplexity.

> The earth hath bubbles, as the water hath,
> And these are of them.

The play's first quarter of an hour sets the tone of this perplexity.
It is one huge question mark, and the characters seem to communicate entirely by interrogation. *When shall we three meet again?*

What bloody man is that? Dismay'd not this our captains?
Whence cam'st thou, worthy thane? Where hast thou been, sister?
How far is 't called to Forres? Speak, if you can: what are you? And
then, capping all the others, the two most important questions:

> Good sir, why do you start, and seem to fear
> Things that do sound so fair?

and,

> Were such things here as we do speak about?
> Or have we eaten on the insane root
> That takes the reason prisoner?

Questioning, probing; darkness, uncertainty — this is the play's
atmosphere, and it never lifts until the last few minutes. Even in
the scene at the English court, Malcolm is so surrounded by
danger that he has to put on a fake character to test honest
Macduff. Even Edward the Confessor is mysterious. ('How he
solicits heaven Himself best knows.') And this atmosphere is
wonderfully conveyed by the play's language, which is everywhere concrete and tactile. Our minds are constantly directed
not to things we can see, but to things we can touch. We respond
to the imagery of *Macbeth* not so much with our visual imagination as with our hands, teeth, throats, our very skin, hair and
nails.

> Till he unseam'd him from the nave to the chaps.

> A sailor's wife had chestnuts in her lap,
> And munch'd, and munch'd, and munch'd . . .

> Nor heaven peep through the blanket of the dark . . .

> . . . upon this bank and shoal of time,
> We'd jump the life to come.

> . . . they rise again,
> With twenty mortal murders on their crowns,
> And push us from our stools.

> Make the gruel thick and slab . . .

                        . . . new sorrows
Strike heaven on the face . . .

                            . . . Now does he feel
His secret murders sticking on his hands. . . .

It is against this background of continuously tactile language that
we see the force of Macbeth's horrified cry:

> Is this a dagger that I see before me,
> The handle toward my hand?

It would be superfluous to remark on the sheer skill and ap-
positeness of this. Quite apart from its spiritual range and depth,
Macbeth is a brilliant demonstration of Shakespeare's prowess as
a writer. Search where you will, the art of literature can show no
more dazzling performance.

XI

The core of all Shakespeare's tragedies is his sense of the sacredness of the bonds which hold human beings together. In the state,
the political bond; in the personal life, the bond of blood-re-
lationship. And the tragic series closes with two plays in which
the chief character turns his back on this network of relationships.
In the case of Coriolanus, the voice of nature prevails, and the hero
is won back, at dreadful cost to himself. In the case of Timon, he
stays outside.

Coriolanus, like *Julius Caesar*, is basically an enquiry into man's
political nature. Shakespeare had taken the discussion of power and
responsibility as far as he could in the English historical plays —
as far, that is, as he could without coming into collision with the
doctrine of the Divine Right of Kings, which tended to fence off
the discussion at its further boundary. Ancient Rome offered an
obvious attraction; a society about which the Elizabethans knew
a good deal, which had been very politically conscious, and
which afforded many striking examples of how men had succeeded and failed in the very tasks which Englishmen were now
to face. How much rope to give the populace at home, how best

to govern overseas possessions, and above all in what circumstances it was permissible to overthrow one's ruler by violence — these were problems whose answers the Elizabethans sought eagerly in the pages of Plutarch and Livy.

In *Julius Caesar*, Shakespeare had produced a play not altogether unlike *Richard II*; the cause of freedom may quite probably be best served by getting rid of Caesar, yet the deed is so frightful that much expiation, and much time, is needed before things are stable again. In this pattern, Octavius Caesar fills the role of Henry V; a cold, efficient character, he drives through to power, stability and an impersonal justice; but this consummation has to wait until *Antony and Cleopatra*. All we are shown in *Julius Caesar* is the mixed motives of the assassins and the swift retribution that falls on them. *Coriolanus*, the last of the three Roman plays, goes back to an earlier period of Roman history and takes a new grip on the old questions: how should a republic be governed? Is a man of war, who has earned the people's gratitude by protecting them from enemies, a suitable governor in peacetime?

The problems are all met very honestly; there is no minimizing the complexity of the situation. Volumnia, mother of Coriolanus, is a character on whom Shakespeare expended much thought; she is hardly mentioned in the source, Plutarch's *Lives*, until she goes to plead with Coriolanus at the head of his avenging army. Shakespeare makes her as anti-democratic, as implacably contemptuous of the people, as Coriolanus himself; but she is quite ready to advise her son to hide his feelings in the interests of his political career.

> Because that now it lies you on to speak
> To th' people, not by your own instruction,
> Nor by the matter which your heart prompts you,
> But with such words that are but roted in
> Your tongue, though but bastards and syllables
> Of no allowance to your bosom's truth.
> Now, this no more dishonours you at all
> Than to take in a town with gentle words,

> Which else would put you to your fortune and
> The hazard of much blood.

The attitude of the conservative aristocratic politician was never
better summed up: throw the dogs a little insincere flattery, till
you are safely in possession of their votes. Obviously Volumnia
is not intended as a likeable woman; she is as tough and ruthless
as her son; but it is she, nevertheless, who in the play's most
important scene is made the mouthpiece of a power so sacred
that even Coriolanus bows to it, and in doing so redeems himself.
And, indeed, Volumnia's haughtiness is necessary to the play's full
effect. If she were a gentle, tender-hearted woman, her plea to
Coriolanus would have to be more softly phrased and accompanied by tears such as might bring on a rush of emotion in a
hardened soldier, which he might afterwards disavow. It is the
very marmoreal dignity of her appeal that makes it impossible for
him to resist.

> Say my request's unjust,
> And spurn me back; but if it be not so,
> Thou art not honest, and the gods will plague thee,
> That thou restrain'st from me the duty which
> To a mother's part belongs. He turns away.
> Down, ladies; let us shame him with our knees.
> To his surname Coriolanus 'longs more pride
> Than pity to our prayers. Down. An end;
> This is the last. So we will home to Rome,
> And die among our neighbours. Nay, behold 's!
> This boy, that cannot tell what he would have
> But kneels and holds up hands for fellowship,
> Does reason our petition with more strength
> Than thou hast to deny't. Come, let us go.
> This fellow had a Volscian to his mother;
> His wife is in Corioli, and his child
> Like him by chance. Yet give us our dispatch.
> I am hush'd until our city be afire,
> And then I'll speak a little.

Coriolanus's next words are his capitulation. And among the
significant silences in Shakespeare hers is not the least, when he

assures her that the success of this plea will be the means of his own destruction.

> But for your son — believe it, O, believe it! ——
> Most dangerously you have with him prevail'd,
> If not most mortal to him.

Volumnia says nothing, for she has always known that to have a hero for a son is to be ready at any time to sacrifice him to the demands of honour. Put in these stark terms, her appeal to the tie of blood is unanswerable; Coriolanus knows what treatment awaits him if he returns to Antium (the various phases of his relationship with Aufidius, incidentally, are shown with an economical skill as good as anything in Shakespeare), but there is no other way; to renounce these ties would be to enter the lonely hell of Macbeth, and Coriolanus rises to full heroic stature at the moment when he perceives this and understands that death is preferable.

With *Timon of Athens* we reach the end of the tragedies. Shakespeare's mind, after the years of titanic struggle with ultimate problems, was in a curious state, if we are to judge by this play. On the one hand, a certain fatigue had set in; on the other, new energies seemed to be gathering. Everyone has noticed that in the last plays, the 'romances', Shakespeare the poet rises to new heights, while Shakespeare the portrayer of character and contriver of dramatic situations is content to spare himself. The last plays are full of freshness and originality, in fact they create a new *genre* and explore its furthest limitations, but they contain no drama so intensely perceived and strongly constructed as, say, the relationship of Iago and Othello. Their achievement is imaginative and mythopoeic rather than dramatic. In *Timon of Athens* I believe we see the beginning of this process. The story of Timon is simple, and Shakespeare has been content to leave it in its simplicity rather than enrich it with extra characters and incidents. This would indicate a willingness to save his strength, to turn aside from some of the challenges and incitements offered by the fable. On the other hand, the actual writing of the play shows Shakespeare at the peak of his strength, in a display as dazzling as anything in the better-known tragic plays. Not even in *Hamlet* or *Lear* do we find more powerful writing than in Act IV, Scene iii, of *Timon of Athens*. This five-hundred-line stretch is one of Shakespeare's showpieces. And the rest of the play is not far beneath it. The poet's imagination is soaring higher and faster than ever. Not only in the matchless handling of imagery and rhythm, but in the choice of visual symbols, this play bridges the gap between the tragedies and the romances, between the greatness of *Macbeth* and the greatness of *The Tempest*. The ruined Timon, in the wilderness, digging for roots and finding a hoard of gold, which he throws away in disgust; or his final choice of a resting-place, a tomb on the sea-shore which 'once a day with his embossed froth The turbulent surge shall cover' — these are symbols of the non-verbal kind to which Shakespeare's mind, in the last groups of plays, increasingly turned.

The story, as I have said, is simple. Yet its simplicity has not protected it from misinterpretation. The impact of the great rhetoric in this play is so strong that many readers and spectators have been moved to take Timon's case at his own valuation. He sees himself as a generous man betrayed, in his hour of need, by those on whom he has lavished kindness and bounty. In a bitter, black despair, he takes to the woods and lives like an animal to show his hatred and contempt of man. Various people visit him in his seclusion, ranging from robbers and prostitutes to upright and worthy men; but none is able to change Timon's despair into hope, and as a final act of rejection he wills his own death. And more than one perceptive critic has been ready to accept his bitter tirades at face-value. Even so shrewd a commentator as John Masefield, whose short book *Shakespeare* (1911) is full of illumination and wisdom, calls Timon 'the great-hearted, truly generous man, whose mind is as beneficial as the sun,' and says that 'the flaming out of his anger against whatever is parasitic in life makes the action of the last two acts'. But this is to dignify

Timon by overlooking the element of sheer pettishness in his rejection of mankind. Dr. Johnson is much nearer the mark: 'the
catastrophe', he says, 'affords a very powerful warning against
that ostentatious liberality which scatters bounty, but confers no
benefits, and buys flattery, but not friendship.'

Timon's generosity resembles lust rather than love. It does not
see its object with joyful exactness. It is a blind, indiscriminate
drive, expressing itself in mechanical fashion. Everyone who
comes to him must be feasted and rewarded — not for the sake
of relieving distress or encouraging merit, but simply because
Timon is Timon and this is his form of vanity. When his honest
steward Flavius tries to jog his elbow and draw his attention to
the rapidly emptying coffers, Timon brushes him aside. Finally,
when his creditors throng the house and his bankruptcy is forced
on his attention, Timon tries to blame the situation on Flavius.

TIMON. You make me marvel wherefore ere this time
          Had you not fully laid my state before me,
          That I might so have rated my expense
          As I had leave of means.
FLAVIUS. You would not hear me
          At many leisures I propos'd.
TIMON.   Go to;
          Perchance some single vantages you took
          When my indisposition put you back,
          And that unaptness made your minister
          Thus to excuse yourself.
FLAVIUS.   O my good lord,
          At many times I brought in my accounts,
          Laid them before you; you would throw them off
          And say you found them in mine honesty.
          When, for some trifling present, you have bid me
          Return so much, I have shook my head and wept;
          Yea, 'gainst th' authority of manners, pray'd you
          To hold your hand more close. I did endure
          Not seldom, nor no slight checks, when I have
          Prompted you in the ebb of your estate
          And your great flow of debts.

This generosity is a form of self-indulgence; it is a parody of real love, just as the fawning thanks of his neighbours are a parody of true gratitude. They have no sympathy for him when his funds are gone, and after one frenzied gesture of contempt and hatred — the banquet, mounted with all the old magnificence, at which the dishes when uncovered contain nothing but warm water — Timon turns his back on 'all feasts, societies, and throngs of men'. Pausing outside the gates of Athens for one last look, he calls down such hideous curses on the inhabitants, and beyond them on mankind in general, as to convince us that his hatred is neurotic and self-feeding:

> Let me look back upon thee. O thou wall
> That girdles in those wolves, dive in the earth
> And fence not Athens! Matrons, turn incontinent.
> Obedience, fail in children! Slaves and fools,
> Pluck the grave wrinkled Senate from the bench
> And minister in their steads. To general filths
> Convert, o' th' instant, green virginity.
> Do't in your parents' eyes. Bankrupts, hold fast;
> Rather than render back, out with your knives
> And cut your trusters' throats. Bound servants, steal:
> Large-handed robbers your grave masters are,
> And pill by law. Maid, to thy master's bed:
> Thy mistress is o' th' brothel. Son of sixteen,
> Pluck the lin'd crutch from thy old limping sire,
> With it beat out his brains. Piety and fear,
> Religion to the gods, justice, truth,
> Domestic awe, night-rest, and neighbourhood,
> Instruction, manners, mysteries, and trades,
> Degrees, observances, customs and laws,
> Decline to your confounding contraries
> And let confusion live.

Where have we heard this kind of language before? In the reckless speeches of those characters in the tragedies who embrace chaos to gratify their own lust for power or vengeance: Lear's 'all germans spill at once', Macbeth's 'cancel and tear to pieces this great bond'. This is not the language Shakespeare would ever put into the mouth of a 'great-hearted, truly generous man'. Timon is mad with rage because his neighbours did not dance to his tune; he had imagined that his undiscriminating generosity would give him first place in their hearts, and now that he finds it did not, he is ready to curse all mankind.

The rest of the action shows Timon's attitude to the various people who happen on him, or come to seek him, in the woods. (*A Midsummer Night's Dream*, we recall, also takes its characters into 'a wood near Athens' — what a distance we have travelled!) Some of the characters Timon sees are destructive types and therefore welcome to him; he urges the robbers to pursue their calling vigorously, in the interests of chaos, and of course the two whores who accompany Alcibiades are a gift to him:

> Consumptions sow
> In hollow bones of man; strike their sharp shins,
> And mar men's spurring. Crack the lawyer's voice,
> That he may never more false title plead,
> Nor sound his quillets shrilly. Hoar the flamen,
> That scolds against the quality of flesh
> And not believes himself. Down with the nose,
> Down with it flat, take the bridge quite away
> Of him that, his particular to foresee,
> Smells from the general weal. Make curl'd-pate ruffians bald,
> And let the unscarr'd braggarts of the war
> Derive some pain from you. Plague all,
> That your activity may defeat and quell
> The source of all erection. There's more gold.
> Do you damn others, and let this damn you,
> And ditches grave you all!

Of the sympathetic characters, however, he can make nothing. Alcibiades is another Coriolanus, a notable soldier who has been driven away from his city by what he takes to be its ingratitude; his case is better than that of Coriolanus, inasmuch as in the immediate dispute the fault is really the senators' and not at all his. Timon has no interest in the rights and wrongs of the case; he sees Alcibiades simply as an instrument of vengeance on the

Athenians; when, later, two senators come to beg him to join his voice to theirs in deprecating the wrath of Alcibiades, Timon takes a vicious pleasure in telling them that he cares nothing if they are all butchered. Flavius is a more difficult case; he has followed Timon out of pure loyalty and love, wishing to go on seeing him without hope of gain. Timon's reception of him (Act IV, Scene iii) is a convincing proof of the sick nature of his misanthropy. He admits that he was mistaken in cursing all mankind; evidently one just man does exist; but he makes the admission grudgingly ('How fain would I have hated all mankind!') and even insults Flavius by asking whether his kindness is genuine or inspired by some devious hope of gain. Convinced, finally, that Flavius really is what he seems, Timon hastily dismisses him; giving him some of the gold he has found, he cautions him not to employ it to spread happiness among mankind:

> Go, live rich and happy,
> But thus condition'd: thou shalt build from men;
> Hate all, curse all, show charity to none,
> But let the famish'd flesh slide from the bone
> Ere thou relieve the beggar. Give to dogs
> What thou deniest to men; let prisons swallow 'em,
> Debts wither 'em to nothing. Be men like blasted woods,
> And may disease lick up their false bloods!
> And so, farewell and thrive.

The mockery of bidding a man live 'happy' and 'thrive', while enjoining him to this meanness and wickedness, is a new peak in Timon's misanthropy; at last he has managed to twist the encounter with loyalty and honesty into something that suits his own diseased purposes; evidently wishing to stop the game while he is winning, he bundles Flavius off the stage.

FLAVIUS.   O, let me stay
    And comfort you, my master.
TIMON.   If thou hat'st curses,
    Stay not; fly whilst thou are blest and free.
    Ne'er see thou man, and let me ne'er see thee.

The encounter with Apemantus, which comes just before, is excellent bitter farce. Timon has renounced human status and embraced the life of a beast. This irritates Apemantus, since it poaches on his professional territory; he is a cynic, and the word is of course derived from Greek κυων, meaning a dog; a cynic is a man who acknowledges no human restraint to his impoliteness; he will lift up his leg and make water on anything. To him, Timon's misanthropy is 'a poor unmanly melancholy, sprung From change of fortune'. It is undignified to go to these lengths merely because one has been flattered and let down. Timon's retort is that, on the contrary, people like Apemantus who are born poor and unlucky have no right to hate mankind; that privilege is reserved for people like himself, who have known glory and been robbed of it by human ingratitude.

> Why should'st thou hate men?
> They never flatter'd thee: what hast thou given?
> If thou wilt curse, thy father, that poor rag,
> Must be thy subject; who in spite put stuff
> To some she-beggar and compounded thee
> Poor rogue hereditary.

Timon is especially enraged by Apemantus's claim to reject humanity and identify with the animals. He even descends from his high denunciatory verse to explain in prose exactly what kind of mistake Apemantus is making.

A beastly ambition, which the gods grant thee t' attain to! If thou wert the lion, the fox would beguile thee; if thou wert the lamb, the fox would eat thee; if thou wert the fox, the lion would suspect thee, when, peradventure, thou wert accus'd by the ass. If thou wert the ass, thy dulness would torment thee; and still thou liv'dst but as a breakfast to the wolf. If thou wert the wolf, thy greediness would afflict thee, and oft thou shouldst hazard thy life for thy dinner. Wert thou the unicorn, pride and wrath would confound thee, and make thine own self the conquest of thy fury. Wert thou a bear, thou wouldst be kill'd by the horse; wert thou a horse, thou wouldst be seiz'd by the leopard; wert thou a leopard, thou wert german to the lion, and the spots of thy kindred were jurors on thy life. All thy safety were remotion, and thy defence absence. What beast couldst thou be that were not subject to a beast? And what a beast art thou already, that seest not thy loss in transformation!

The claim to prefer animal life to human life is absurd when anyone makes it but himself. Here, as in the case of the visit of Flavius, Timon is offered illumination and refuses it. He might have learnt from the ugly and commonplace spite of Apemantus, as he might have learnt from the generosity and self-sacrifice of Flavius, had he not been too far gone, too sunk in self-pity and the luxury of hatred. And in that spirit he dies.

That is the story, and it is clear that Shakespeare resisted any temptation to enlarge its scope. Where, for instance, is Timon's family? Has he a wife and children, or parents? Evidently not; to bring in such characters would be to pose him with the choice that had to be faced by Coriolanus. (And even Alcibiades is not faced with this choice.) Timon's bond with mankind is purely societal. He joins with his fellow beings solely in their joint role as consumers. He has no colleagues, since he does not work; he has no child or woman to grieve over his departure; the only women in the story are whores, and Flavius is an employee. Shakespeare, in other words, was content to duck some of the implications that were there *in posse* in the story. As a full-scale portrait of a human being in a certain situation it lacks the completeness of the greater tragedies. Where it makes up this lack is in the unforgettable power of the writing. It is clear that what Shakespeare really wanted to do was to write magnificent gloomy speeches. Perhaps after the years of deep, exhausting imaginative exploration of the dark places, he had an accumulation of bitterness and pessimism which demanded expression. He tried to contain it within a fable — and, we must insist, a fable in itself not bitter or pessimistic, but, as Johnson calls it, a 'warning'. But, by no means for the first time, he found that the dramatic framework sagged and splintered under the weight of the poetic statement. We can see the outlines of the story, but what stays in our minds is the language. The Timon we remember is the character whose pessimism finds expression in such lines as,

> My long sickness
> Of health and living now begins to mend,
> And nothing brings me all things.

This, like Macbeth's description of life as a tale told by an idiot, or Gloucester's 'flies to wanton boys', lingers in our minds and gives us a strange pleasure, so that we are often tempted to describe these statements, quite wrongly, as the key utterances in the plays in which they occur. It is difficult to explain why such gloomy statements should exert such power over us; but the fact is that pessimism, when memorably expressed, is always very attractive to the human mind. Perhaps it is because the average human being cannot afford pessimism, must keep struggling on and hoping for the best, that he so eagerly embraces the pessimistic in art. It gives an outlet to the side of his nature that cannot be indulged in daily life. As Philip Brockbank has remarked, with *Timon* in mind: 'Renaissance pessimism might well serve to qualify and refine our own, with Shakespeare supplying the most instant points of contact; some pessimisms are more vital than others.' Certainly the contemplation of a pessimism like Timon's is not depressing; on the contrary, we find it, like the pessimism of *A Shropshire Lad* or *Waiting for Godot*, rather exhilarating; something final, extreme and rather bracing has been said. And truly Timon's pessimism is one of Shakespeare's ultimates. After exhausting the possibilities of rhetoric in his great curses and diatribes, he rejects rhetoric itself with 'Lips, let sour words go by, and language end', and goes off to seek his death.

Timon of Athens, like Hamlet, is a broken portal. Through it, we pass out of the realm of tragedy, as through *Hamlet* we came into it. It is the equal of *Hamlet* in power, though not in attractiveness. Above all, it points forward to the next phase. Seen on the stage, *Timon* offers wonderful opportunities for the visual sense.

The contrast between the first three acts, full of colour and bustle, with magnificent surroundings and rich costumes, and the utter bareness of the last two, foreshadows the kind of physical contrast we find in the romances — the switch from a king's court to a Welsh mountainside, from the deck of a sinking ship to the shore of a peaceful island. And the sight of Timon handling gold after he had rejected wealth and society, as if unable to shake off its curse, is the kind of symbol that comes out wonderfully on the stage. Perhaps the most telling symbol of all is the grave by the sea-shore. Not only will the salt sea-water give Timon, twice a day, that brine he sought in vain in the eyes of those who heard of his misfortune; its sterile bitterness will keep anything green and growing away from his tomb, so that his savage rejection of life will be perpetuated. In the presence of this energy and freshness still undimmed in Shakespeare, we take leave of the tragedies, and turn with a new sense of expectancy towards the masterpieces that are still to come.

VI

'IN MY END IS MY BEGINNING'

IN May 1609 a fleet of nine ships carrying five hundred colonists set out from England with the purpose of strengthening Captain John Smith's colony in Virginia. In command of the operation were Sir George Summers and Sir Thomas Gates, who sailed together in the vessel *Sea-Adventure*. On 25 July a storm arose and the *Sea-Adventure* was carried away from the other eight ships, which continued their voyage and, with one exception, reached the American mainland. Their news of the disappearance of the *Sea-Adventure* was in due course carried back to England, and no one who heard the story could doubt that the ship had gone down and Summers and Gates perished with their crew.

About a year later, however, an astonishing tale found its way to England. Summers and Gates were alive, and safe in Florida with all hands. The gale had driven the *Sea-Adventure* to the coast of the Bermudas, where, in taking the desperate risk of running her ashore, the crew managed to drive her between two rocks, so that she stuck fast. All on board got safely to shore, together with supplies and equipment, and the following summer they re-floated the ship and sailed triumphantly to America.

In the absence of newspapers, the Elizabethan journalist cashed in on news scoops by writing pamphlets, and a number of such pamphlets appeared which told the story of the wreck and merciful deliverance of the *Sea-Adventure*, and of the strange island to which she was driven by the storm. Of these pamphlets, Shakespeare is generally considered to have had particular interest in three: Sylvester Jourdain's *Discovery of the Bermudas* (1610), the Council of Virginia's *True Declaration of the state of the Colonie in Virginia* (also 1610) and William Strachey's *True Reportory of the Wrack*, written in the form of a letter and dated 15 July 1610, but not printed till 1625. That Shakespeare knew Strachey's account has been fairly established, and the fact that he should in this way take the trouble to get hold of unpublished material points to a special interest in the story.

The Council's *True Declaration* is an official publication which naturally plays down the marvellous, and represents the passage to Virginia not as a desperate enterprise but as something that hard-headed men might reasonably undertake. Strachey's account is more affecting, with its pathetic account of the violence of the storm, the confusion of the crew and the terror of the passengers. He also gives prominence to an extraordinary sight which amazed the already hard-pressed sailors:

'During all this time, the heavens look'd so blacke upon us, that it was not possible the elevation of the Pole might be ab-served: nor a Starre by night, nor Sunne beame by day was to be seene. Onely upon the thursday night Sir George Summers being upon the watch, had an apparition of a little round light, like a faint Starre, trembling, and streaming along with a sparkel-ing blaze, halfe the height upon the Maine Mast, and shooting sometimes from Shroud to Shroud, tempting to settle as it were upon any of the foure Shrouds: and for three or foure houres together, or rather more, halfe the night it kept with us; running sometimes along the Maine-yard to the very end, and then return-ing. At which, Sir George Summers called divers about him, and shewed them the same, who observed it with much won-der, and carefulnesse: but upon a sodaine, towards the morning watch, they lost the sight of it, and knew not what way it made.'

That this kind of detail was helpful to Shakespeare in taking a firm imaginative grip on the idea of a shipwreck, we see at once from the exchange between Prospero and Ariel.

'In My End is My Beginning'

— Hast thou, spirit,
Performed to point the tempest that I bade thee?

— To every article.
I boarded the king's ship; now on the beak,
Now in the waist, the deck, in every cabin,
I flamed amazement. Sometime I'd divide
And burn in many places; on the topmast,
The yards, and bowsprit, would I flame distinctly,
Then meet, and join. Jove's lightning, the precursors
O' th' dreadful thunder-claps, more momentary
And sight-outrunning were not. . . .

But if any member of the original audience, in 1611, with the story of the *Sea-Adventure* fresh in his mind, expected a merely topical treatment, his mind would very soon be led away from such channels. 'It is as well to be clear,' says Frank Kermode in his Introduction to the 'Arden' edition of the play, from which the information above was taken, 'that there is nothing in *The Tempest* fundamental to its structure of ideas which could not have existed had America remained undiscovered, and the Bermuda voyage never taken place.' Shakespeare was interested in long and dangerous voyages, unknown shores, miraculous escapes, and encounters with aboriginal inhabitants not for their own sakes but because of the new perspective in which such reports could set the familiar Renaissance problems of Nature *versus* Art, the rights and duties of governors, the nature of Divine Providence, and beyond them his own personal struggle to reconcile the discordant elements in human experience, to imagine a reconciliation powerful enough to bring sin and evil under its sway and unite all life in a deeper harmony. His sea-adventure was not a real-life action yarn but a symbolic structure whose episodes reverberate with the overtones of myth. The news-story is steeped in the life-giving waters of folk-tale and legend until it suffers a sea-change. What began as prodigy ends as symbol.

Shakespeare's art is from the beginning an art of blending and fusing, of making a single complex reality out of disparate simple realities. But this is his crowning achievement: to take a piece of contemporary history — a news-story that is also a dramatic contribution to a debate that is in full swing — and integrate it with his symbolic dream-world. That world is the last, and in some ways the richest, of the worlds he created. Character and dramatic tension are relaxed; vision and poetry control everything. It may be that Shakespeare was working in Stratford, away from the bustle of the London stage, free to meditate his plots among quiet lanes and gardens. This would be a liberation. But it was no slackening of energy. On the contrary, the late Shakespeare is in many ways the most daring and original. As G. K. Chesterton remarked, an artist, as he goes through life, realizes more and more clearly what it is that he has to do, so that the older he grows as a man, the younger he grows as an artist. In *The Tempest*, with his world of mythical dream (or dream-like myth?) fully developed, Shakespeare was able to turn his eyes back to the ordinary world of contemporary events, and bring the two into a majestic harmony. This is the peak of his marvellous 'final period'. The steps by which he climbed up to that peak can be traced through the preceding three plays: *Pericles, Cymbeline* and *The Winter's Tale*.

I

Pericles is almost certainly a work of collaboration between Shakespeare and some unidentified fellow-dramatist. It was not included in the First Folio of 1623, and the text as we have it is taken from a Quarto edition of 1609, from the press of one Henry Gosson, which is certainly a corrupt version. Shakespeare's characteristic hand is seen most clearly in the last three acts; the first two are written at a lower level, though even in their jog-trot one gets a moment or two of Shakespeare's manner, such as the lines in the first scene:

> For vice repeated is like the wand'ring wind,
> Blows dust in others' eyes, to spread itself;

And yet the end of all is bought thus dear,
The breath is gone, and the sore eyes see clear
To stop the air would hurt them. The blind mole casts
Copp'd hills towards heaven, to tell the earth is throng'd
By man's oppression, and the poor worm doth die for 't.

Such lines could hardly have been written by any poet but Shakespeare; they show his characteristic boldness of rhythm and concreteness of imagery. In the last three acts, such writing is more the rule than the exception, and we rise now and again to a peak such as the lament of Pericles over the supposed death of his wife Thaisa, whose coffin is given to the waves:

A terrible childbed hast thou had, my dear,
No light, no fire. Th' unfriendly elements
Forgot thee utterly; nor have I time
To give thee hallow'd to thy grave, but straight
Must cast thee, scarcely coffin'd, in the ooze;
Where, for a monument upon thy bones,
And aye-remaining lamps, the belching whale
And humming water must o'erwhelm thy corpse,
Lying with simple shells.

However, there are better reasons for turning to *Pericles* than the hope of pulling out occasional plums from the verse. The play is important as ushering in the main subject-matter of these late works, and in its leisurely, semi-narrative approach to the story. Whether Shakespeare wrote most of *Pericles*, or only some of it, he was sufficiently interested in the play to take a hand in it; perhaps he suggested the story, which was a widespread one; its most familiar version was in Book viii of Gower's *Confessio Amantis*, and therefore the play brings the half-forgotten four-teenth-century poet on to the stage to act as narrator. Altogether, the mode of presenting the action is worth special notice. It is a first step towards the method of *The Winter's Tale* and *The Tempest*. Dramatization is only part of this method. It relies just as much on narrative. Either in the theatre or by the fireside, it holds our attention with the immemorial spell of the story-teller. The truth it aims at is not the truth of realistic character-portrayal or closely

observed and probable action. It is the truth of fable, which expresses things close to the heart of man by means of symbolic
action. Just as *Henry V* blended the Virgilian epic poem with the
chronicle play, so *Pericles* is a first step in the art of blending the
romance with a drama of pageantry, masques and stage-illusions.
For by now the London theatre was more sophisticated than in
the days of Shakespeare's youth. Admission prices were higher;
visual effect was no longer limited to bright costumes and fine
presences. The new drama had masque-like elements which
proved ideally suited to the dream-like, almost cinematic turn
that Shakespeare's imagination was taking. It has been suggested
that, in falling in with this mode, Shakespeare was tamely following a fashion set going by younger men. I believe myself that it
was the final sublimation and refinement of his early influence
from Ovid.

The story of *Pericles* tells of a man who loses his wife and, a
little later, his daughter, and after many adventures is reunited
with them. Shakespeare, at the very beginning of his career, had
treated a story of much this kind in *A Comedy of Errors*; but now
he took it up again as a vehicle for the central poetic and psychological insights of his later years. Thaisa, the wife of Pericles,
appears to die in childbirth, during a sea-voyage; a storm blows
up, and during it she goes into labour and apparently succumbs.
Her coffin is thrown overboard; washed ashore, she is revived
by a saintly magician. Meanwhile Pericles leaves his baby girl,
christened Marina, to be brought up by Cleon, governor of
Tharsus, and his wife Dionyza. Marina's royal qualities shine out
so much in girlhood that Dionyza is jealous on behalf of her own
daughter, and plots against Marina's life. She falls into the hands
of pirates and is carried away and sold to a brothel in Myteline.
Here, her innocence strikes pity from a man who is brought to
her as a customer, and ultimately from the owners of the place, so
that, as Gower's narrative rather perfunctorily says,

> Marina thus the brothel scapes, and chances
> Into an honest house.

Here she is respectfully entertained, and presently re-united with her father; in obedience to the goddess Diana, who appears to Pericles in a vision, they make a journey to Ephesus and there find Thaisa alive and well, serving as a nun in the temple of Diana. The story ends with the marriage of Marina to a young prince, amid general joy and thanksgiving.

The action of *Pericles* thus takes us, at one stride, into the heart of the dream-territory of Shakespeare's last plays. Its plot is complex and improbable, as befits a 'romance'; its tone is in the main high and visionary, with sudden disconcerting descents into the ugly and vicious; and it ends with the rediscovery of a precious thing taken for lost. Like *King Lear*, it has a storm at its centre. But the storm in *Lear* is a terrible vengeance, an ordeal in which the characters find their true nature under the stress of agony. In *Pericles*, the storm is an apparent disaster which in the end proves fruitful; it is like the storm that drove the *Sea-Adventure* to the shores of Bermuda; and Pericles, like Ferdinand, can say in grateful surprise:

> Though the seas threaten, they are merciful;
> I have curs'd them without cause.

II

Cymbeline, the next play in the series, is an astonishing piece of work, in the most literal sense. Astonishment is the feeling we chiefly experience as we read or see it, and that Shakespeare evidently set himself to arouse in us. It is extravagantly experimental, showing Shakespeare at what we should nowadays call his most 'modern'. It must have struck its original audiences in very much the way that a poem like *The Waste Land* struck readers of the 1920s: as a staggering juxtaposition of disparate and contrasting elements, flung together with no regard for conventional notions of unity. Old age is, of course, a period of reckless experimentation for many artists; and, while Shakespeare was never what we should call old — he died at fifty-two — the men of the Renaissance often burnt out quickly, and Shakespeare himself seems to have regarded everyone over about fifty as a dotard; witness Juliet's father, who, though he has a daughter of only fourteen, is represented as totally senile. Shakespeare's romances are his equivalent of Beethoven's late quartets or the *Last Poems* of Yeats. But in none of them is there so much experimental daring as in *Cymbeline*. It is his most *avant-garde* work.

To begin with, there is the startling blend of elements. The groundwork of the plot, dealing with British history and the repulse of the Romans, Shakespeare took from Holinshed's *Chronicles*, that old mainstay of his English historical plays. The story of Iachimo's treachery, on the other hand, came from Boccaccio. Holinshed and Boccaccio! — there, for a start, is one of those scarcely imaginable mixtures; one might as well say 'Disraeli and Rimbaud' or 'Tolstoy and Martial'. In switching between England and Rome, and showing both Britons and Romans as having sterling qualities, Shakespeare was meeting a contemporary taste, since heroic Britons were a Jacobean fashion, while Ancient Rome was revered as the lawgiver, the nurse of civilization and order. In this play, the two are very much in equipoise; Caius Lucius, the Roman ambassador who comes to demand tribute in Caesar's name, is a match for King Cymbeline in *gravitas* and courtesy, and, when, in the last act, he thinks he is certain to be executed, he shows the stoical dignity that was traditionally expected of an 'antique Roman'. In the end, the two standards fly side by side over a Britain reconciled with Rome. But the play has a third point of reference, modern Italy. Shakespeare makes Iachimo a contemporary Italian; the Rome *he* comes from is no antique world capital of eagles and classic pillars, but lies in the hot, corrupt, Machiavellian Italy which bred, so the Elizabethan English believed, 'devils incarnate'.

Then there is the sophistication of the play's visual element. For this, of course, Shakespeare may have been only partly responsible. The days had gone by when the stage was ruled by the dramatist alone. Stage-designers like Inigo Jones, composers like

Ferrabosco, had crowded in and transformed the simpler drama of the 1590s into a rich mixture of music, spectacle and symbolism. Shakespeare, with his usual readiness, produced something to meet this need. When Posthumus, taken for a Roman soldier, is in prison awaiting execution, he falls asleep and sees a vision in which his father, mother and two brothers all return from the shades and pray to Jupiter to spare his life. Jupiter comes down astride his sacred eagle, rebukes the suppliants and says that Posthumus is quite safe in his hands. The verse of this scene is strongly stylized, and many critics, including Johnson, have thought it an interpolation by some other hand. Personally I believe that Shakespeare knew what he was doing. On the page, this verse reads flatly; but set it against a background of solemn music and pageantry, and it has exactly the right stiff, brocaded dignity. Furthermore, it is thematically in harmony with the rest of the play. Cymbeline's father has been an heroic British warrior, his brothers have died in battle, and in appealing to a (Roman) deity to spare the last survivor of their family, these visionary figures are participating in the historical action; the best British stock must be left alive to breed, or what will become of the nation? And it is worth noticing that as soon as Jupiter has re-ascended to the clouds, the verse once more takes on the rhythm of speech and has a characteristically Shakespearean ring:

> SICILIUS. He came in thunder; his celestial breath
> Was sulphurous to smell: the holy eagle
> Stoop'd, as to foot us. His ascension is
> More sweet than our blest fields. His royal bird
> Prunes the immortal wing, and cloys his beak,
> As when his god is pleas'd.
> ALL.   Thanks, Jupiter!
> SICILIUS. The marble pavement closes, he is enter'd
> His radiant roof. Away! and to be blest
> Let us with care perform his great behest.

Shakespeare was thus able to gratify the demand for music and spectacle while enforcing one of the central themes of the play:

the rise of the Ancient Britons, fortified by contact with Rome, into an heroic nation.

But, beyond all these things, the chief mark of the experimental imagination in *Cymbeline* is to be found in its verse. Here, it is obvious, Shakespeare simply threw aside all caution and enjoyed himself. Take one feature only: the rhythms. For many years, Shakespeare had been moving towards a more complex counter-point in his dramatic verse. Not since *Richard III* had he relied mainly on a chiming, one-line-at-a-time progression of ten-syllable statements. Increasingly, he had set the rhythms of realistic human speech running across the beat of the decasyllabic metronome, so that the result was a rapid, subtle music in which we can always hear two rhythms at once: on the one hand, the

ti TUM ti TUM ti TUM ti TUM ti TUM

of the 'iambic pentameter', and on the other the mood (urgent, or lazy, or aggressive, or bantering, or mournful) of the human speaker. In order to approach the verse of *Cymbeline*, we must have before our eyes an example of the normal manner of Shakespeare's blank verse. Almost anything will do. Take, at random, the speech of Helena in *All's Well that Ends Well*, on discovering that her bridegroom, to avoid her, has stolen away to risk his life in the wars:

> Poor lord! is't I
> That chase thee from thy country, and expose
> These tender limbs of thine to the event
> Of the none-sparing war? And is it I
> That drive thee from the sportive court, where thou
> Wast shot at with fair eyes, to be the mark
> Of smoky muskets? O you leaden messengers,
> That ride upon the violent speed of fire,
> Fly with false aim; move the still-piercing air,
> That sings with piercing; do not touch my lord.
> Whoever shoots at him, I set him there;
> Whoever charges on his forward breast,
> I am the caitiff that do hold him to't;

And though I kill him not, I am the cause
His death was so effected. Better 'twere
I met the ravin lion when he roar'd
With sharp constraint of hunger; better 'twere
That all the miseries which nature owes
Were mine at once. No; come thou home, Rousillon,
Whence honour but of danger wins a scar,
As oft it loses all. I will be gone.
My being here it is that holds thee hence.
Shall I stay here to do't? No, no, although
The air of paradise did fan the house,
And angels offic'd all.

What is noteworthy about this passage — and there are hundreds like it — is that the extreme freedom and flexibility of the verse is achieved with an absolute minimum of metrical licence. Except for the line ending with 'Rousillon', which is a borderline case, since the word is almost a dissyllable, there is only one line that breaks out of the strictness of the ten-syllable pattern, i.e.

Of smoky muskets? O you leaden messengers,

And even this line, with its strong pause after the question mark and its air of beginning again, is not felt as a metrical licence, but rather as a breathing-space.

This, as I say, was the norm of mature Shakespearean verse. Turn now to the rhythms of *Cymbeline*.

                     With fairest flowers,
Whilst summer lasts and I live here, Fidele,
I'll sweeten thy sad grave. Thou shalt not lack
The flower that's like thy face, pale primrose; nor
The azur'd hare-bell, like thy veins; no, nor
The leaf of eglantine, whom not to slander,
Out-sweet'ned not thy breath. The ruddock would
With charitable bill — O bill, sore shaming
Those rich-left heirs that let their fathers lie
Without a monument! — bring thee all this;
Yea, and furr'd moss besides, when flow'rs are none,
To winter-ground thy corse.

Shakespeare's late verse is sometimes said to be 'loosened'. But this is not loosened. If anything, it is tightened. The words are packed densely; instead of flowing out in sentences, they seem to break off individually, like chips of quartz under the hammer; they reach the ear in a rhythm that is abrupt and yet elegiac, angular yet gentle. This strange, haunting rhythm is the hallmark of *Cymbeline*, the feature that remains in our minds longest when everything else fades. (Not surprisingly, the play has always fascinated poets. It was Tennyson's favourite play, and his beloved copy was buried with him in the grave.)

For a full-scale example of the almost perverse originality that Shakespeare put into the verse of *Cymbeline*, a good passage to examine is the long speech of Posthumus in Act V, Scene iv, describing the fight in the narrow lane; taking it, say, from line 14 ('Close by the battle, ditch'd, and wall'd with turf') down to line 51 ('the mortal bugs o' th' field'). This speech is rather too long to be quoted here, but it shows the qualities of this extraordinary verse to perfection. How an actor is meant to manage it on the stage I do not know — particularly an English actor, who has in all probability been given no training in the speaking of verse and is playing to an audience who regard Shakespeare's habit of using verse as, at best, an amiable weakness. ('Should the works of Shakespeare be put into modern prose . . . ?') It belongs to an epoch of magnificent experimental audacity; it is designed to be spoken before an audience of highly cultivated people, capable of appreciating its extravagant brilliance. And to those readers and playgoers who have no relish for such qualities, one can only say, 'Keep away from *Cymbeline*. You are well catered for in many, indeed most, of Shakespeare's other plays. Let this corner of his work be for the amateur of literary virtuosity.'

The subject-matter of *Cymbeline*, however, is as central to the concerns of the later Shakespeare as its manner is far out. All its strands are found woven into the other romances. Imogen, an innocent woman separated from her husband by jealousy, foreshadows Hermione. Like Marina, she is exposed to the danger of ravishment; like both Thaisa and Hermione, she is taken for dead by her husband; and, for good measure, she also recalls the heroines of the earlier comedies by putting on boy's clothes and being taken on as a page.

Another central theme is that of 'Nature *versus* Nurture'. After his years of facing tragic issues, of contemplating man's wickedness and irresponsibility, Shakespeare in this last phase was much taken up with the question, 'What makes men good?' — or, turning it to catch the light in a different way, 'What makes good men?' In particular, he was interested by the question of natural *versus* instilled virtue. Will the explorers of the New World find the noble savage of European imagination? Or will they find a much fallen creature, brutal and ignorant, asking to be raised by training and education? Again, is virtue carried in the bloodstream? Can it be inherited, so that the children of noble families are naturally noble in their turn? *Cymbeline* suggests many answers to this. Posthumus is easily the superior of the brutal Cloten, though Cloten is the son of a king and queen. On the other hand, the king's two sons, who have been carried away by an exiled courtier as an act of revenge, and brought up by him in a Welsh mountain cave, show their royal blood in everything they do, even though they scarcely know that such a thing as royalty exists; so that their guardian, old Belarius, murmurs

> 'Tis wonder
> That an invisible instinct should frame them
> To royalty unlearn'd, honour untaught,
> Civility not seen from other, valour
> That wildly grows in them, but yields a crop
> As if it had been sow'd.

The boys might make the same complaint to Belarius as Orlando made to his brother Oliver in *As You Like It*:

> My father charg'd you in his will to give me good education; you have train'd me like a peasant, obscuring and hiding from me all gentleman-like qualities. The spirit of my father grows strong in me, and I will no longer endure it.

In the romances this theme is taken up with a deep seriousness In *Cymbeline*, the characters change their clothes, and adopt disguises, almost as often as in *Twelfth Night*, but the emphasis is different; in the golden comedies, the rapid changing of disguises symbolizes the search for the self, whereas in the romances it relates more to the question of nobility, which makes itself known through rags or advertises its want through cloth of gold.

As we should expect, *Cymbeline* plays with this idea in an unusually audacious fashion. In the scene where Imogen once and for all rejects Cloten's advances (Act II, Scene iii) she tells him that Posthumus's 'meanest garment' is better in her eyes than 'all the hairs above thee, Were they all made such men'. Cloten is outraged by this, and can do nothing but gobble 'His garment! Now, the devil——' 'His garment!' 'You have abus'd me: His meanest garment!' and, as he goes off, 'I'll be reveng'd: His meanest garment! Well.' In due course, hearing that Imogen has stolen away from the protection of the court, he forms the hideous scheme of getting hold of a suit of clothes belonging to Posthumus, finding Imogen, and ravishing her while wearing it, having first killed Posthumus before her eyes.

> He on the ground, my speech of insultment ended on his dead body, and when my lust hath dined (which, as I say, to vex her I will execute in the clothes that she so prais'd) to the court I'll knock her back, foot her home again.

After Cloten's head has been cut off by one of the noble boys, Imogen comes upon his headless corpse and naturally takes it for that of Posthumus. This is one of those *outré* pieces of visual symbolism that we associate with the late Shakespeare. Cloten is perfectly fitted by the clothes of Posthumus (as he himself remarks, 'The lines of my body are as well drawn as his'), so that only the head — the seat of intelligence and character — differentiates the two. This has a direct bearing on the argument about Nature and Nurture, since of course to be strong and well-formed does not of itself confer a noble character, as it might it men were animals.

Cymbeline, then, makes much the same statements as the other romances, but it makes them in its own strange, experimental, *avant-garde* idiom. It is not surprising, in view of all this, to find that when we reach the expected multiple happy ending, what we find is something very close to parody. The problems are solved with the speed of a Model-T chase in a Mack Sennet comedy. It was doubtless this kind of thing that Johnson had in mind when he wrote his famous dismissal; to enumerate all the absurdities in the play, he said, 'were to waste criticism upon unresisting imbecility, upon faults too evident for detection, and too gross for aggravation'. And of course if we thought all the extravagances in *Cymbeline* were due to careless incompetence, this snort would be justified. But that would be like expecting Picasso's 'Guernica' to have the literal recognizability of an aerial photograph. The sophistication of *Cymbeline*, properly taken, is a source of joy and exhilaration. Shakespeare's imaginative power is operating here with a peculiar freedom, and under cover of the incongruities and impossibilities, he is bringing off miracles of detail-work.

To take one example: everyone knows the superb dirge spoken by Guiderius and Arviragus over the body of Imogen when they take her for dead. The main import of those beautiful verses is that the dead person is now beyond reach of misfortune: 'Fear no more the heat o' th' sun'. Nor, indeed, any other enemy. 'To thee the reed is as the oak'. A little later, Posthumus, also in disguise and also regarded as a dead man — for he is being led off to execution — is told by his gaoler, 'A heavy reckoning for you sir: but the comfort is you shall be called to no payments, fear no more tavern-bills. . . . Indeed, sir, he that sleeps fears not the toothache.' Almost the same message, even to the repetition of the key phrase, but from two utterly contrasted areas of the play; the one entirely idealized, employing the lyrical language of romance, the other from an odd corner of that realistic disenchantment that gave us the brothel in *Pericles* and will give us the Stephano–Trinculo scenes in *The Tempest*. As Johnson said in another connection, 'The most heterogeneous elements are yoked by violence together.' But it is the violence of a great artist, deeply engaged in what he is doing.

IV

The Winter's Tale assembles the same materials as the two preceding plays. But, once again, the presentation is so different as to amount to a new experience. The unflagging interest in new techniques is still one of Shakespeare's motives. But by this time the desire for naked, work-bench experimentation has gone. There is a mellowness here which *Cymbeline* lacks. It is the first perfectly realized masterpiece among the final group.

The ingredients of *The Winter's Tale* present no surprises. An initial act of jealous spite; wanderings; the patience of a good woman; a storm out of which deliverance comes; a balance poised between Nature and Nurture. Just as Imogen in *Cymbeline* recalled a play like *Twelfth Night* with her page's clothes, so Perdita in *The Winter's Tale* becomes a shepherdess and takes us back to the world of *As You Like It*. But we must not talk as if there were no new element here. One major step is taken. The powers of reconciliation and regeneration are now squarely vested in the young people who represent a new generation. At mid-point, the action skips sixteen years. The two kings, Leontes and Polixenes, brought up together like brothers, have quarrelled in maturity, the issue being Leontes's sexual jealousy; in the end what brings them together is that the son of Polixenes falls in love with the lost daughter of Leontes, and, fleeing from the wrath of his father who opposes the lowly match, comes to seek refuge at the court of Leontes, who greets them with the words 'Welcome hither, As is the spring to the earth'. That is indeed what they represent; as Northrop Frye has put it, 'The symbolic reason for the sixteen-year gap is clearly to have the cycle of the year reinforced by the slower cycle of human generations.'

It is the young people who put right the trouble caused by their elders, and these young people are associated with 'nature', just as the older generation put their trust chiefly in 'nurture'. Cymbeline tried to make his daughter Imogen marry Cloten, as being a suitable match with royal blood. She preferred the worthier Posthumus. That was preferring nature to nurture. Her brothers, showing their royalty in a barbarous cave, were also demonstrating the powers of nature; but not quite unambiguously, since after all their royal blood was the result of selective breeding. Shakespeare avoids coming down on either side; he shows us the range of the question, and stands back. So in *The Winter's Tale*. When Leontes suspects his wife Hermione of playing him false with Polixenes, he has her hustled away to prison, and orders that the child she is about to bear shall be ·exposed in 'some remote and desert place'. Antigonus, the old courtier who undertakes this task, lands on the sea-shore of Bohemia [*sic*], lays the baby down with a bundle containing gold, and, seeing a storm coming on, hastens back to the ship, but on the way is attacked and torn to pieces by a bear. Both bear and storm seem to typify the intervention of that 'nature' which humbled Lear and Gloucester, the pitiless power which beats men to their knees. But, whatever we may think about the bear, the storm proves to be a fruitful turmoil like that in which Marina was born. Two rustic characters appear; a clown, who has seen the ship wrecked and Antigonus killed by the bear, and an old shepherd, who finds the baby girl. 'Now bless thyself,' says the shepherd; 'thou mett'st with things dying, I with things new born.'

Sixteen years go by, during which Perdita grows up in the shepherd's cottage. Her rustic simplicity combines with her royal blood to give her an irresistible grace and beauty, which win the heart of Florizel, the prince. Polixenes, hearing of this, comes among the shepherds in disguise; he arrives in the middle of the annual sheep-shearing feast, and Perdita, as queen of the day, makes him and his companion a pretty speech of welcome. At once, however, he finds it necessary to contradict her views on horticulture, and the two of them engage in a debate which is central to the meaning of the play.

POLIXENES.   Shepherdess ——
A fair one are you — well you fit our ages
With flow'rs of winter.

PERDITA.   Sir, the year growing ancient,
Not yet on summer's death nor on the birth
Of trembling winter, the fairest flow'rs o' th' season
Are our carnations and streak'd gillyvors,
Which some call nature's bastards. Of that kind
Our rustic garden's barren; and I care not
To get slips of them.

POLIXENES.   Wherefore, gentle maiden,
Do you neglect them?

PERDITA.   For I have heard it said
There is an art which in their piedness shares
With great creating nature.

POLIXENES.   Say there be;
Yet nature is made better by no mean
But nature makes that mean; so over that art,
Which you say adds to nature, is an art
That nature makes. You see, sweet maid, we marry
A gentler scion to the wildest stock,
And make conceive a bark of baser kind
By bud of nobler race. This is an art
Which does mend nature — change it rather; but
The art itself is nature.

PERDITA.   So it is.

POLIXENES. Then make your garden rich in gillyvors,
And do not call them bastards.

PERDITA.   I'll not put
The dibble in earth to set one slip of them;
No more than were I painted I would wish
This youth should say 'twere well, and only therefore
Desire to breed by me.

The frank use of the word 'breed' shows that this is no drawing-room argument. What is at stake is no mere question of the tending of a garden, but the management of the human generations who will make or mar the happiness of the world. The eager, unspoilt girl is all for Nature; the *rusé* old king inclined to Nurture. But even so, the argument is complicated by the fact that she is of royal birth; no ordinary shepherdess, the play implies, would have these qualities. Hence the irony of Camillo's remark to Polixenes as they watch the young couple. 'He tells her something That makes her blood look out: good sooth, she is The queen of curds and cream.' The irony is reinforced by the fact that Perdita, being of royal blood, is unconsciously serving the ends of Nurture (i.e. selective breeding) in accepting the love of Florizel.

Perdita has no use for 'gillyvors' (i.e. wallflowers) because she has heard that 'there is an art which in their piedness shares With great creating nature.' ('Art', of course, meant to Shakespeare everything that was not 'nature', including not only the arts of imagination but the experimental sciences and an empirical skill like horticulture.) She wishes to put herself entirely in the hands of great creating nature, and only on that basis to give her love to the young man who 'desires to breed' with her. This may be a suitable strategy for Eden, but Eden was a long time ago. Polixenes, recalling the early attachment between himself and Leontes, has described their life then in terms appropriate to a Golden Age:

> Two lads that thought there was no more behind
> But such a day to-morrow as to-day.
> And to be boy eternal.
> HERMIONE. Was not my lord the verier wag o' th' two?
> POLIXENES. We were as two twinn'd lambs that did frisk i' the sun,
> And bleat the one at the other: what we chang'd
> Was innocence for innocence; we knew not
> The doctrine of ill-doing, nor dream'd
> That any did.

This is to trust Nature further than is warranted by experience. The very title of the play is a reminder of the vulnerability of innocence. Mamillius, the young son of Leontes and Hermione, is exactly such a frisking lamb, snatched from his mother's arms just when he is about to whisper in her ear his 'sad tale', 'best for winter'. In an exchange of dialogue full of a beautiful and

creative tenderness, Hermione affectionately challenges him to
try to frighten her with his story of 'sprites and goblins'. Mamillius begins, softly, 'There was a man dwelt by a churchyard'.
He gets no further; the furious Leontes comes bursting in, Hermione is dragged off to prison, and Mamillius is so bewildered
and grieved that he goes into a fever and dies. He 'knows not the
doctrines of ill-doing', but his innocence does not save him.

Leontes sends to Delphos to get the word of the Oracle, which
he expects will confirm his suspicions and make his righteousness
clear to everyone. In the event, the Oracle clears Hermione and
Polixenes completely, but by that time Mamillius is dead, Perdita
presumed so, and Hermione, carried off in a dead swoon, is
hidden away and Leontes is given to understand that she, too,
has died. Under this threefold blow, Leontes, his life given over
to repentance, becomes 'the man [who] dwelt by a churchyard'
and acts out the sad winter's tale.

> Prithee, bring me
> To the dead bodies of my queen and son:
> One grave shall be for both. Upon them shall
> The causes of their death appear, unto
> Our shame perpetual. Once a day I'll visit
> The chapel where they lie; and tears shed there
> Shall be my recreation.

The play on that last word is probably intentional. The tears shed
by Leontes, his repentance when he realizes what he has done,
prove in the end to be his recreation; they re-create him; after
a sixteen-years' penance, he is led to a statue of Hermione before
which he bends in adoration, whereupon the statue descends and
proves to be his living wife, hidden from him till now in the
house of the widowed Paulina.

That there is a symbolic intention here is obvious to the most
unreflective playgoer. But to disentangle the complex threads of
this symbolism may well prove beyond the subtlest critic. Sixteen
years earlier, the oracle, in vindicating Hermione's innocence,
has said, 'The King shall live without an heir, if that which is lost

be not found'. The sixteen years that pass before Perdita finds her way back to her father's court are the time it takes her to grow up and become nubile; and she is then led back to her father by the man of her choice, who of course knows nothing of the relationship and sees Leontes simply as a possible source of mercy, understanding and protection. In that sense, Leontes has earned the restoration of Perdita. The springs of life are unclogged, and everything is free to start moving again. Naturally there were many plot devices that Shakespeare might have used to bring Hermione and Leontes together again; that he chose this one indicates something deeper than the concern with visual symbolism and stage-effect that mark his last period. His schoolboy reading of Ovid would have made him familiar from the beginning with the story of Pygmalion and Galatea, whose inner significance seems to be a vindication of the claims of art. The imagination can re-make the world in what shape it pleases. Pygmalion's is the art that 'gives to airy nothing A local habitation and a name'; it 'shares With great creating nature' in the making of everything that lives. For the contemplating eye modifies the object.

Polixenes, in his debate with Perdita, argues for Art against Nature, unaware that since the girl is a princess she is unwittingly behaving according to his principles as well as her own, in picking out Florizel as a mate; he confronts, that is, an Art disguised as Nature. Now Leontes, in his turn, confronts a Nature disguised as Art. And whereas Polixenes had — mistakenly — intervened to forbid the love of Perdita and Florizel in order to give Art its way over Nature, Leontes now has the impression that he has turned Art into Nature by the sheer force of his longing and penitence; he has obeyed the injunction of Shelley's Prometheus,

> to hope till hope creates
> From its own wreck the thing it contemplates.

His living, breathing queen is restored to him because his penance is fully worked out. He goes to see the statue in the company of

Polixenes, with whom he is now reconciled, and perhaps this recalls to his mind the unfallen state of innocence in which he and his friend ('two twinn'd lambs') passed their childhood, for on first seeing the supposed statue he exclaims,

> Chide me, dear stone, that I may say, indeed
> Thou art Hermione; or rather, thou art she
> In thy not chiding; for she was as tender
> As infancy and grace.

He thus links the memory of Hermione with the memory of that Eden from which he and his friend were expelled by the mere fact of growing up and developing adult passions; but he adds another ingredient, 'grace', to the softness of infancy. This is in resonance with the undertone of religious feeling that has been present throughout in the story of Hermione. When the disaster first breaks on her, and she is led away to prison, she comforts her weeping attendants with, 'this action I now go on Is for my better grace'. If it were not repeated at a crucial moment by Leontes, this use of the word 'grace' might be a mere chance, of no great significance; but the two occurrences of the word reinforce each other. And there is also Paulina's significant remark, just before Hermione steps down from the pedestal, 'It is requir'd You do awake your faith'.

The religious atmosphere is very strong in this scene. Hermione embraces her husband silently, but when Paulina presents the kneeling figure of Perdita, she speaks, and the first words her husband hears from her after sixteen years are in the form of a prayer:

> You gods, look down,
> And from your sacred vials pour your graces
> Upon my daughter's head!

That Hermione's prayer should be for her daughter, for the happy and virtuous continuation of the natural line of descent, is very true to the central import of the play. And we may note that in this high religious fervour, Nature and Art are reconciled; for, as

Yeats puts it, 'Both nuns and mothers worship images'. The mind in worship makes use of both Art and Nature and transcends them.

Meanwhile, the everyday characters are still living out their comic or unremarkable lives; even such moments of high symbolism do not make us quite forget the existence of Autolycus, the snapper-up of unconsidered trifles, or the old shepherd and the young clown, both of them so delighted by their flattering reception at court. Earlier on, Autolycus has patronized them, in just the way that Touchstone patronized the rustics in the Forest of Arden; but now they know that they are better than he. Autolycus has his own parody of the Nature-*versus*-Art debate, as when he preeningly reflects on his own superiority to the countrymen: 'How blessed are we that are not simple men! Yet nature might have made me as these are.' Like Perdita, he owes his superiority to a more generous endowment by Nature, yet he chooses to appear before them as a courtier, owing his attainments to upbringing, politeness and Art generally.

Art — the intervention of Paulina, the prophecy of the oracle, and the needs of spiritual discipline — kept Hermione hidden away from her husband during the slow maturing of another human harvest. Then, when their daughter had grown to womanhood in the course of Nature, Leontes was shown a statue which presently lived and moved. In other words, Art, having done what it could, handed over to Nature. But such a handing-over cannot be casual or simple. It needs an atmosphere of profound reverence. And it needs the presence of 'grace'. *The Winter's Tale* contains elements of debate, of question and counter-question, but it would be quite false to represent it as a discussion-play like, say, *As You Like It*. It is a profound lyrical meditation on the theme of forgiveness and renewal, full of delicacy and beauty, yet always close to the earth and the human heart-beat. Shakespeare never wrote a more perfect work.

In *The Tempest*, we come straightaway upon two striking differences from the pattern as it has become familiar to us. The preserving and creative storm comes at the very beginning instead of at mid-point; and it is caused not by Nature but by Art. Prospero, ousted from his dukedom by his brother Antonio, has been thrown on the mercy of the seas in a leaky hulk with his infant daughter. Miranda is thus, like Marina and Perdita, a child of the sea; and Prospero has undergone his own sea-ordeal before imposing it on the other characters. All this was years ago (sixteen years?), and the intervening time has been filled with study and meditation — a counterpart to the long repentance of Leontes.

But Prospero is not another Leontes. To begin with, he is not repentant. Though his loss of the dukedom is obviously to some extent his own fault — this appears even in his own account of it, to Miranda at the opening of the play — he sees his magical studies primarily as an instrument of power, by which he may win back his position. And during the years on the island he has likewise used his knowledge in the service of power. He has, as we should say, 'colonized' it. And here the story links up with the contemporary world, with the strange deliverance of the *Sea-Adventure*, the colony in Virginia, and the argument over Nature and Nurture.

One of the few books we can say with fair certainty that Shakespeare owned (as distinct from the many we know he must have read) is John Florio's translation of Montaigne's *Essays* (1603), for the British Museum has a copy of this book with what looks like Shakespeare's signature in it. There, Shakespeare would have taken particular note of the essay 'Of the Caniballes', which argued that these fortunate beings are the unspoilt children of Nature:

> They are even savage, as we call those fruits wilde, which nature of her selfe, and of her ordinarie progress hath produced: whereas

indeed, they are those which our selves have altered by our artificiall
devices, and diverted from their common order, we should rather
terme savage.

And again:

> . . . there is no reason, art should gaine the point of honour of our
> great and puissant mother Nature. We have so much by our inven-
> tions surcharged the beauties and riches of her workes, that we have
> altogether overchoaked her: yet where ever her puritie shineth, she
> makes our vaine and frivolous enterprises wonderfully ashamed.

This is a strong point of view; it is exactly in line with Perdita's
distrust of the art which shares with great creating nature; and if
Shakespeare had intended to agree with it, he would have made
Caliban beautiful and innocent, instead of (as the Dramatis
Personae firmly calls him) 'a savage and deformed Slave'. Does
Shakespeare, then, clash head-on with Montaigne and those who
think like him? No, not head-on. It is not Shakespeare's way to
give neatly defined answers that can be taken away and applied
independently of the works in which they occur. He will teach
general lessons, but he will not give blackboard answers to
specific problems.

Caliban is a symbolic figure, coming from the same region of
Shakespeare's imagination as the witches in *Macbeth*. His mother
was Sycorax, a 'foul witch', 'who with age and envy Was
grown into a hoop'. Before Prospero arrived, the island was
under the rule, not of beneficent Nature, but of this hag, who
imprisoned the delicate Ariel while letting the gross Caliban, her
offspring, roam unchecked. Prospero's advent was no doubt
unfortunate for Caliban, but it was a blessing for Ariel, who
gained from it a measure of freedom, with the promise of complete liberation in the end.

Caliban, whose name is a fairly obvious anagram of 'Cannibal',
has therefore a complex role in the action. On the one hand, he is
an indirect argument for Prospero's Art and against the policy of
leaving everything to Nature. On the other hand, he has the

pathos of the exploited peoples everywhere, poignantly expressed at the beginning of a three-hundred-year wave of European colonization; even the lowest savage wishes to be left alone
rather than 'educated' and made to work for someone else, and
there is an undeniable justice in his complaint:

> For I am all the subjects that you have,
> Which first was mine own king.

Prospero retorts with the inevitable answer of the colonist: Caliban has gained in knowledge and skill (though we recall that he
already knew how to build dams to catch fish, and also to dig
pig-nuts from the soil, as if this were the English countryside).
Before being employed by Prospero, Caliban had no language:

> thou didst not, savage,
> Know thine own meaning, but wouldst gabble like
> A thing most brutish.

However, this kindness has been rewarded with ingratitude;
Caliban, allowed to live in Prospero's cell, has made an attempt
to ravish Mirando; when sternly reminded of this, he im-
penitently says, with a kind of slavering guffaw,

> Oh ho! Oh ho! — would't had been done!
> Thou didst prevent me; I had peopl'd else
> This isle with Calibans.

Our own age, which is much given to using the horrible word
'miscegenation', ought to have no difficulty in understanding this
passage. Quite apart from an understandable wish not to have his
daughter ravished by anyone, Prospero could hardly maintain
his rule over an island whose inhabitants were partly Caliban's
offspring and partly his own. Small wonder that Caliban is
banished to a cell among the rocks, and put on to heavy labour.

All the Romances, as part of their general plan, afford us glimpses
of unregenerate humanity: the brothel in *Pericles*, Cloten and the
hangmen in *Cymbeline*, Autolycus in *The Winter's Tale*. This important role is well filled in *The Tempest*, which contains two
attempted murders, both foiled by Prospero's magic. The one

that concerns us at the moment is the plot made by Caliban in association with the two drunken seamen, Stephano and Trinculo. This episode (Act III, Scene ii, and Act IV, Scene i) is crucial because it shows the difference between wickedness produced by Nature and wickedness produced by Nurture. Caliban is vengeful and murderous, but he is not vulgar; when, on the way to Prospero's cell, the trio come upon some 'glistening apparel' and other baubles which Ariel has set to catch their attention, the sailors immediately forget their plan to murder Prospero, and fall to parcelling out the loot. In spite of Caliban's desperate plea 'what do you mean To dote thus on such luggage?' they cannot resist the lure. Their natures, unlike his, are corrupted by tawdriness and the cheap trash of urbanization. We should find exactly the same contrast between a modern suburbanite and a Dyak head-hunter who had never watched a TV commercial.

But the marvellous originality of Shakespeare's conception of Caliban is still not exhausted. His domain extends into the realm of psycho-analysis. He is the Id, the unregenerate lower nature, in the personality in which Ariel represents the imagination and Prospero the driving and organizing intellect. (I avoid using the formal classification of Id, Ego and Super-Ego, which does not, I think, quite fit the picture here.) Caliban is 'the inward animal', lustful and brutal, yet with the pathos of something struggling to evolve. In his terror at the vengeance that will be visited on him after the episode of the murder-plot, he says, 'we shall . . . all be turned to barnacles, or to apes With foreheads villainous low'. Sub-human he may be, but he knows the difference between himself and the anthropoids, and he does not want to be one of them. This fear is all the more touching inasmuch as the dividing-line between Caliban's nature and an animal's is necessarily thin. He is responsive to music, for instance, as animals generally are while remaining indifferent to the other human arts; no doubt the 'sounds and sweet airs' he so often hears are something to do with Prospero's magic, but for all that they seem to be the only thing in his life that brings him any happiness:

Sometimes a thousand twangling instruments
Will hum about mine ears; and sometime voices,
That, if I then had wak'd after long sleep,
Will make me sleep again: and then, in dreaming,
The clouds methought would open and show riches
Ready to drop upon me; that, when I wak'd
I cried to dream again.

A character who can talk in this strain is not wholly unsympathetic, however little we should like to meet him on a dark
night. 'A born devil,' Prospero calls him, 'on whose nature
Nurture will never stick'; but the Nature that rules Caliban's
being, and will brook no intervention from Nurture, is still a
divinity even though cruel.

In a less extreme way, the milder virtues of the pastoral world
also get their due in this play. Miranda is the product of Nurture,
since she not only comes of noble blood ('a gentler scion') but
has been elaborately educated by her father. Nevertheless, she is
pastoral in that she has never mixed in corrupting human society,
never been subjected to the tawdry city-life that makes vulgarians
of such as Trinculo and Stephano. Civilization has its heavy
penalties, as no one knows better than the representative of Art,
Prospero: when, in rapture, the girl cries out 'O brave new world
That hath such people in 't', he says drily, ' 'Tis new to thee'.

In the end, the characters leave the island and go back to
civilization, as they always do in Shakespeare; human work has
to be carried on, somebody has to govern, the dailiness of life
will start up again. The Forest of Arden and Prospero's island, the
'wood near Athens' or the Welsh mountains in *Cymbeline*, have
one thing in common: they are places where important lessons
are to be learnt. Once that is done, the characters go back to
their normal business. But it is right that some vision of an ideal
simplicity, of a life untrammelled by the hampering demands of
law and custom, should persist among them. In *The Tempest*, it
is noteworthy that the one character among the shipwrecked
party who really enjoys the idea of a golden-age simplicity is

Gonzalo, the good old courtier whose generosity to the doomed Prospero parallels that of Antigonus to the infant Perdita, when he fitted his boat out with necessities and even books. As Dr. Johnson pointed out, 'being the only good Man that appears with the King, he is the only Man that preserves his cheerfulness in the Wreck, and his Hope on the Island'. To the amusement of the two evil sophisticates, Sebastian and Antonio, he seeks to beguile the melancholy of King Alonso, mourning the supposed death of his son Ferdinand, by talking about the ideal commonwealth he would like to set up on such an island as this. His views turn out to be much the same as those of Montaigne — a sure sign that Shakespeare considered those views worthy of a courteous hearing.

> I' th' commonwealth I would by contraries
> Execute all things; for no kind of traffic
> Would I admit; no name of magistrate;
> Letters should not be known; riches, poverty,
> And use of service, none; contract, succession,
> Bourn, bound of land, tilth, vineyard, none;
> No use of metal, corn or wine, or oil;
> No occupation; all men idle, all;
> And women too, but innocent and pure;
> No sovereignty . . .
> All things in common nature should produce
> Without sweat or endeavour. Treason, felony,
> Sword, pike, knife, gun, or need of any engine,
> Would I not have; but nature should bring forth,
> Of its own kind, all foison, all abundance,
> To feed my innocent people.

It may be only a dream, but it is a healing and generous dream, fit to haunt the mind of a just man.

VI

The chief differences between *The Tempest* and the other Romances are two. It is tight in construction; the tragic events are told in a single long exposition by Prospero, and the action we see on the stage concerns only the working of Prospero's magic to draw his enemies into his power, and then the change of heart by which he forgives them. Secondly, it is political in flavour; the initial offence against Prospero was the usurping of his kingdom, whereas the jealousy of Leontes and the lack of faith of Posthumus are offences against love. Within that framework, the action follows very closely the accustomed pattern. The young people meet, fall in love, and intend to unite the opposed houses by means of that love. The quarrels and injuries of their elders do not concern them; they spend no time or energy on the past; from the moment they set eyes on each other, there is a fresh beginning. Alonso, King of Naples, lent his aid to Prospero's treacherous brother and supported the *coup* by which he came to power; but time has gone by, the children have grown up to marriageable age, and when Ferdinand has begotten children with Miranda, the old quarrels will be as if they had never been. But first there must be a patching-up among their elders. It is as if, at the end of his career, Shakespeare felt able at last to let Romeo and Juliet marry. But Montague must first shake hands with Capulet.

In *Cymbeline* and *The Winter's Tale*, the healing flow of forgiveness comes from the hearts of women; Imogen and Hermione forgive, and all their menfolk have to do is to feel sincere repentance. In *The Tempest*, it is an elderly man who must forgive injury; the heart in question is harder and drier. Hence the beautiful touch of making Prospero learn forgiveness from Ariel.

PROSPERO.   Say, my spirit,
How fares the King and 's followers?
ARIEL.   Confin'd together
In the same fashion as you gave in charge;
Just as you left them; all prisoners, sir,
In the lime-grove which weather-fends your cell;
They cannot budge till your release. The King,
His brother, and yours, abide all three distracted,
And the remainder mourning over them,
Brim full of sorrow and dismay; but chiefly
Him you term'd, sir, 'the good old lord, Gonzalo';

His tears run down his beard, like winter's drops
From eaves of reeds. Your charm so strongly works 'em
That if you now beheld them your affections
Would become tender.

PROSPERO.   Dost thou think so, spirit?
ARIEL.   Mine would, sir, were I human.
PROSPERO.   And mine shall.
Hast thou, which art but air, a touch, a feeling
Of their afflictions, and shall not myself,
One of their kind, that relish all as sharply,
Passion as they, be kindlier mov'd than thou art?
Though with their high wrongs I am struck to th' quick,
Yet with my nobler reason 'gainst my fury
Do I take part; the rarer action is
In virtue than in vengeance; they being penitent,
The sole drift of my purpose doth extend
Not a frown further.

It is his magic that has given Prospero this power over his
enemies, but it is Ariel who moves him to forgiveness; the
liberating imagination diverts to a higher purpose the hard,
driving intellect, till then intent only on the working of its will.
It is true that Prospero has already destined his daughter for
Alonso's son, but this need imply no forgiveness of Alonso, and
in any case his stern treatment of Ferdinand indicates a harsh
intention to test the young man by making him do the drudgery
of a Caliban, and thus subject him to the ordeals of the natural
man through which his nurture must shine forth. Prospero's forgiveness does not flow as spontaneously as that of Hermione
or Imogen; it is slowly won from him, in the teeth of his self-
regarding pride; in this respect the character he most resembles is
Isabella in *Measure for Measure*. And we are left with the impression that it was Ariel's mention of Gonzalo that finally tipped the
scale; an act of kindness and courage, many years before, opens
the rusted valves of forgiveness now.

As a matter of fact, the scene of general reconciliation in the
Fifth Act is a challenge to any stage-director. (And the fireside
reader, if he wishes to get the most out of any Shakespeare play,

will always mount a stage-production in the theatre of his mind; he will always be ready to say definitely what, at any given moment, he would instruct an actor or actress to *do*.) Prospero has a few words ready for each of the company. To Gonzalo, he expresses friendship and gratitude; to Sebastian, he hints at the possibility of exposing him as a traitor and regicide; to his brother, the chief offender against himself, his speech is harsh even though it pronounces forgiveness.

> For you, most wicked sir, whom to call brother
> Would even infect my mouth, I do forgive
> Thy rankest fault — all of them; and require
> My dukedom of thee, which, perforce, I know
> Thou must restore.

Alonso and Gonzalo are delighted and enter fully into the recognition. Sebastian and Antonio are silent. Are they included in the renewal of love and trust? Or do they merely go along with it, accepting an agreement they can do nothing to resist? Everything here will depend on a director's liberty of interpretation. If he thinks Antonio should share in the forgiveness (Sebastian hardly matters, being outside the main business of the play at this point), he can have him kneel and receive his brother's blessing in silence; or, as Nevill Coghill has suggested, Prospero's concluding words, 'Please you, draw near,' can be spoken to Antonio instead of merely used to herd the company offstage in the direction of the dinner-table. The others can go off to the feast; Antonio can hang back, alone on the far side of the stage, not daring to believe that the invitation includes him; and 'Please you, draw near' can bring the brothers together in a handclasp that completes the circle of reconciliation.

Far-fetched? I do not think so. There is, of course, no stage-direction that would warrant any such thing. But then stage-directions are notoriously casual in the early editions of Shakespeare. (There is, for instance, no stage-direction to indicate that Desdemona drops her handkerchief.) The dialogue is a stronger test; the fact that Prospero has nothing to say to Antonio, it has been argued, must indicate that he does not wish to carry his forgiveness any further. But in my view this does no more than link Prospero still more firmly with Isabella, who — it will be remembered — when confronted with her brother Claudio, alive and well after she has thought him treacherously murdered by Angelo, has nothing whatever to say to him. Clearly, a director would instruct the actress playing Isabella to cross the stage and embrace her brother in a silent rapture of tears, at some convenient point — unless he was trying to uphold some cynical interpretation of the play, which in my opinion would be quite mistaken. For that matter, in *King Lear*, Cordelia is ready with a rebuke when she is rejected by Burgundy after being shorn of her dowry, but when France accepts her she says nothing. These Shakespearean silences cannot be held to settle all questions of interpretation. If Prospero and his brother are given no dialogue of reconciliation, it is always open to the fireside director to make them join hands in silence.

The forgiveness of Caliban is a similar point. Prospero's language towards his 'slave' continues to be harsh and peremptory, but there is some significance in his remark, when the three malefactors are brought before the courtly company,

> two of these fellows you
> Must know and own; this thing of darkness I
> Acknowledge mine.

This may just possibly be a casual remark, but the scene is very sparing in casual remarks, and I myself believe that Prospero 'acknowledges' Caliban in the sense that he will not withdraw from him that sympathy and forgiveness he is giving to the others. Sending Caliban off to prepare his cell, Prospero adds 'as you look To have my pardon, trim it handsomely', and Caliban replies that he will 'be wise hereafter, And seek for grace'. The word 'grace' is one to whose overtones we have been especially alerted by *The Winter's Tale*, and there is no need to give it a theological meaning to believe that Caliban will end the play in a better state than he is in at the beginning.

I have seen a production of the play in which Caliban, at the words 'this thing of darkness I Acknowledge mine', knelt to Prospero and received something like a blessing. Certainly the temptation, in this play, to conduct important business non-verbally is very strong for any director, whether in the theatre or the armchair. The masque element is conspicuous throughout, and Shakespeare is evidently taking pleasure in contriving action which will sum up and symbolize important features of the play. Each of the two sub-plots (Alonso/Sebastian/Antonio and Caliban/Stephano/Trinculo) is brought to a climax and rounded off by an elaborate piece of stage business. In the first, a delicate banquet is spread before the 'men of sin', and they are just about to eat when 'Enter Ariel like a harpy; claps his wings upon the table; and, with a quaint device, the banquet vanishes'. In the second, the low-life assassins are hunted above the stage by 'divers Spirits, in shape of hounds'. And then there is the elaborate entertainment, specifically called 'A Masque', with which Prospero signifies his assent to the marriage of Ferdinand and Miranda. More important still is the exquisite piece of visual symbolism which comes after the reconciliation. Alonso, still thinking his son has been lost at sea, is led by Prospero to the door of his cell; 'The entrance of the Cell opens,' says the stage-direction, 'and discovers Ferdinand and Miranda playing at chess.' Mr. Kermode rightly calls this 'a symbol of aristocratic concord'. It is a visual equivalent of the dance in which Romeo and Juliet first link hands, and the sonnet in which they first speak to each other.

The older people are reconciled, Gonzalo's original generosity has borne fruit, Ariel is freed after one last service greater than any of his others, even Caliban is uplifted, and the business of the play is concluded. Except for one thing. Prospero must cease to be a magician and re-enter normal life. He has already said that when his last remaining tasks are done, he will abandon his art.

But this rough magic
I here abjure; and, when I have requir'd
Some heavenly music — which even now I do ——
To work mine end upon their senses that
This airy charm is for, I'll break my staff,
Bury it certain fathoms in the earth,
And deeper than did ever plummet sound
I'll drown my book.

This solemn renunciation of Prospero's art has been traditionally interpreted as Shakespeare's farewell to the stage. And if this meaning is indeed present, it is appropriate enough, coming towards the end of the last play written by Shakespeare alone. (The only later work, *Henry VIII*, is a collaboration.) But the lines have a deeper meaning, and one more apposite to the masterpiece in which they occur. Prospero's abjuring of his magic is the same thing as the descent of Hermione's statue in *The Winter's Tale*. It is the moment when Art, having done all that it can, hands over to Nature. What it signals is the conviction, very close to the heart of Shakespeare's work, that ordinary life must and will go on. Prospero's art has brought his enemies into his power, and en·bled him to forgive them; now he must go back to Milan and live with them. Hermione is restored to Leontes, Perdita has married Florizel and Miranda has married Ferdinand. Now they must live together. The art that went to their original mating is drowned in a sea 'deeper than did ever plummet sound'; the sea of time. And this, as always, is Shakespeare's final word. From 'art', even an art as great as his, we go back to the 'nature' of day-to-day living. The creative dream, the journey through the life-renewing region of the imagination, comes to an end, and we return, with new strength and new knowledge, to the lives we live and the scenes we know.

INDEX